# LADY
## OF THE
# PRESS

# LADY OF THE PRESS

## Radio's lost 1944 romantic-mystery serial

With an introduction by Larry Groebe
from the Generic Radio Workshop

BearManor Media
2015

Lady of the Press

© 2015 Larry Groebe

All rights reserved.

For information, address:

BearManor Media
P. O. Box 71426
Albany, GA 31708

bearmanormedia.com

Typesetting and layout by John Teehan

Published in the USA by BearManor Media

ISBN—1-59393-834-9
978-1-59393-834-5

Library of Congress Control Number: 2015908761
Bearmanor Media, Albany, GA

*To the patient folks at BearManor Media.*

*To the many radio fans across America and the world, who have visited genericradio.com and asked questions or expressed their appreciation. Your enthusiasm is what keeps it going.*

*And to my beautiful wife, Alexandra, who puts up with it.*

# INTRODUCTION

**On Monday, May 1, 1944,** the United States was in the third year of World War Two. This day—May Day—was intended to have been D-Day, but the increasing scale of the operation had pushed the start of the ground invasion of France back a month. Never mind. The Allies were busy bombing France from the air, attacking German positions, and striking out at Japan, as well. War news dominated the front page of every newspaper across the country.

A few other stories slipped onto the front page. "Siamese Twins, 'Cute Little Blonde Girls' born in Pennsylvania" (to a mother whose first reaction was evidently "Oh gosh") was splashed across many front pages that day.

In sports, the baseball season was underway, and big weekend crowds turned up at the ballparks. For entertainment, people could catch Mickey Rooney in another Andy Hardy movie, or Gene Kelly and Rita Hayworth in *Cover Girl*, or perhaps Alfred Hitchcock's war-themed *Lifeboat*. Or they could tune into the radio, which everybody did.

On the radio page of the *Los Angeles Times*, the broadcast listings for May 1, 1944 occupied three full columns of tiny type, an astounding list of over 600 programs. Here, as in so many other aspects of life in 1944, war was never far from people's minds. Easily 150 of the shows listed were news broadcasts, with many others simply marked "talk."

The broadcast day was also filled with classic radio fare. You could listen to soap operas, such as *The Romance of Helen Trent* and *Ma Perkins;* kid's adventures, such as *Jack Armstrong* and *Captain Midnight;* and primetime classics, such as *Cavalcade of America* and *Blondie*—shows that today's Old Time Radio fans still recognize and appreciate.

Not everything airing that Monday was later recognized as a classic. At the 4 p.m. slot on CBS station KNX, for example, sandwiched in between two war news broadcasts, there was a listing for *Lady of the Press*. It was a brand new CBS network soap opera having its debut broadcast, yet no fanfare marked the entry in the *Los Angeles Times,* and no notice marked its demise a year later. *Lady of the Press* aired every weekday for a year—well over 200 episodes—and then vanished from our collective memory.

That's how radio shows and movies went in popular culture. Their half-life was short. For every *Lifeboat* movie there was a *3 Russian Girls.* For every *Romance of Helen Trent* soap opera, there was a *Lady of the Press.* History records the victors, while the rest are swept up and tossed out like yesterday's script pages.

With Old Time Radio, it's often simply a matter of number questions, such as: How long did it run? How many people heard the original? How many recordings survived?

In the case of *Lady of the Press,* a single disc with one episode has survived, hardly enough to build a fan base on. Like so many of the era's shows, there was scarcely a need to commit it to disc. It wasn't a syndicated show but a network show of that low-class known as the "soap opera." And not just a lowly soap, it was also a West Coast-only radio program, airing on just eight Columbia Broadcasting System affiliates up and down the Pacific coast:

> KNX in Los Angeles
> KQW in San Francisco
> KARM in Fresno
> KGDM in Stockton
> KROY in Sacramento
> KFPY in Spokane, Washington
> KOIN in Portland, Oregon
> KIRO in Seattle, Washington

Today, the thought that there should be West Coast-only radio shows seems curious and quaint, but technology and time zones once made it necessary. Before the development of a simple, reusable recording medium of magnetic tape, shows had to be performed live, and time zones could wreak havoc with schedules. A soap opera that played out during lunchtime in New York City would be heard during breakfast in San Francisco. (Indeed, *Valiant Lady* was listed on that May 1, 1944 *Los Angeles Times* radio log at the awkward hour of 8:15 a.m.) Big network shows could afford to bring the cast back for a second performance for the West Coast four hours after the first show (or spend the money to record the show and play it back, which also left us a copy for posterity), but daily dramas were considered too ephemeral for such costly treatment.

So, out in California, the networks had some time to fill. *Young Widder Brown* was the last network soap opera of the day, playing its concluding theme song just before 2 p.m. What to do next? There were only so many news broadcasts, organ recitals, and children's adventures that local stations could fill the airwaves with while waiting for the evening shows. So, NBC and CBS programmed additional shows to their West Coast stations.

Sometimes it served as a good laboratory. With many talented, creative people clustered in San Francisco and Hollywood, some great shows emerged. A number of well-remembered radio shows either aired exclusively on the West Coast or got their start as regional broadcasts before moving to the full national networks, *Candy Matson, The Whistler, One Man's Family,* and *Pat Novak for Hire* among them.

For each of these successes there were failures or shows that reached no further than their original handful of coastal network affiliates. Titles such as *Eyes Aloft, Hollywood Mystery Time,* and *The Gallant Heart* are programs about which we now know very little.

You could put *Lady of The Press* in that latter group.

*Lady of the Press* probably originated, as so many vintage radio programs did, with a sponsor looking for an opportunity. Miles Laboratories was the maker of popular home remedies Alka-Seltzer and One-a-Day vitamins, the sort of consumer products that always got a boost from advertising. Miles Labs learned that lesson early in the twentieth century, handing out uncounted leaflets, calendars, almanacs and more. By 1933, Miles Labs had become an early believer in the power of radio when they sponsored the *Saturday Night Barn Dance* out of WLS Chicago. Radio worked for Miles Labs, and so by the start of World War Two, they spent between $4 million and $5 million yearly on advertising.

Miles Labs rarely sponsored the expensive shows and top stars, preferring to focus on small town and rural customers. Ads for Alka Seltzer were heard on *Lum & Abner, Quiz Kids,* and on news and commentary shows. In early 1944, Miles Labs tasked their long-time ad agency, Chicago-based Wade Advertising, to put together a radio program to boost sales of their recently-introduced One-A-Day Vitamins, as well as Alka-Seltzer across California, Oregon, and Washington. *Lady of The Press* was the result.

Most of the crew and cast were early in their careers, and would accrue more important credits later on. Versatile Gordon T. Hughes was selected as producer. Hardly a newcomer at the age of thirty-five, he had been a Vaudeville trouper as a young boy, and later moved through a variety of jobs into a role as radio producer and director. Hughes became the first radio director to receive NBC national on-air credit when directing Arch Obler's *Lights Out* in the late 1930s. Once in Hollywood, the versatile Hughes directed the radio soap opera *The Guiding Light;* comedies such as *Blondie* and *My Little Margie;* and dramas like *The Whistler, Broadway is My Beat,* and *Johnny Dollar.* Like everyone else, he followed the money into television in the 1950s, but also increased his writing output and ultimately came full circle to his performing roots by going on the lecture circuit with humorous talks about the inside world of broadcasting.

Writer Dwight Hauser was thirty-three when he penned *Lady of the Press*. In subsequent years, he wrote for radio shows *Destination Tomorrow*, *Mr. President*, and *Defense Attorney*. In the television era, he wrote for Walt Disney and episodes of *Lassie*. A short film he scripted, *Ama Girls*, won the Academy Award Oscar for Best Live Action Short Documentary in 1958.

Hauser's *Lady of the Press* story arc blended several genres into a daily 15-minute serial: soap operas, dramas, and adventure shows. By setting the story in a major metropolitan newspaper, fresh story lines were no further away than the headlines in real papers. His female protagonist was a noble young lady reporter, Sandra Martin. The lead male, Lieutenant "Hack" Taggart, was a police detective back on the force after a stint fighting overseas. What Hack had seen during the war deeply affected him and left him jaded. Hack and Sandra had been romantically involved before the war, but his cynical attitude upon his return prevented them from resuming the relationship. That opened the door for other men to enter Sandra's life, starting with the newspaper's over-eager staff photographer, Skip Williams.

It was a solid setup, with lots of plot possibilities. Actor auditions were made, and soon an audition record was cut for the sponsor. They must have heard what they liked because the agreed to sponsor the show, although they insisted on finding another actress to play Sandra Martin. Eventually, they decided upon a couple of promising young West Coast players for the two leads, both at the beginning of their careers. Janet Waldo was twenty-four but with a versatile voice that could play older or younger. Howard Culver was slightly older at twenty-six.

Waldo and Culver's chemistry and working relationship must have been good, as they had just spent much of the previous twelve months working together on another West Coast network soap opera, *The Gallant Heart*, "the story of a WAAC and the friends she meets in the world of war." *The Gallant Heart* premiered on March 29, 1943 in the 4 p.m. time slot on KFI and was fed to other NBC California stations. It later moved to 9 a.m. *The Gallant Heart* lacked one thing *Lady of the Press* had—a sponsor. Without the financial incentive of a Miles Laboratories, it ended its run in February 1944, several weeks shy of its intended 52-week commitment.

*Lady of the Press* would be a steady, five-day-a-week paycheck for a year, but both Waldo and Culver would go on to more important roles in their long and distinguished careers.

In the case of Janet Waldo, long is a serious understatement. As of this writing, Ms. Waldo is still actively performing at the age of ninety-four. At the time of *Lady of the Press,* hers was not yet a household name, but her credits already included *Lux Radio Theatre, One Man's Family, Cavalcade of America,* and *Doctor Christian.* Her first really big success was coming at just about this same time, when she inherited the role of the breathless teenage title character in *Corliss Archer.* She would play Corliss for years, and go on from there to many other roles, including the real-life role of wife to playwright Robert E. Lee. Later generations knew Janet Waldo's voice as Judy Jetson and Penelope Pitstop in TV cartoons that are still seen today.

Howard Culver was cast as the war-damaged, "terribly bitter" police detective Hack Taggart, and brought to it the kind of understated masculine authority that also served him well on future shows. In the late 1940s, he became familiar for his portrayal of the Comanche Indian, *Straight Arrow,* on the Mutual network radio show of the same title—another example of a West Coast show that became popular enough to go national. In the 1950s, he joined the cast of the TV version of *Gunsmoke,* portraying hotel clerk Howie Uzzell for twenty years.

The third important cast member was Eddie Marr, who portrayed wisecracking Skip Williams, a newspaper photographer, who distrusted Hack Taggart's motives but didn't always show the soundest judgment himself. A quarter-century older than Waldo and Culver, Marr also had a long, wide-ranging career. His known radio credits can be found as early as 1930. He appeared in motion pictures from the 1930s through the 1960s, and on TV he had multiple roles in everything from *Leave it to Beaver* to *Twilight Zone* to Bob Hope's early 1970s specials.

The important role of announcer was given to Dick Cutting. Announcers not only reintroduced the daily storyline but were required to convey enthusiastic and compelling readings of the sponsor's lengthy commercials for One-a-Day vitamins and Alka Seltzer. A decade later, Cutting could be heard as the announcer for *Yours Truly, Johnny Dollar.*

Organ music for the show, although never credited on air, was supplied by Mack Knight, who had been heard for at least a decade on various Los Angeles stations. He supplied a minor-key march for the show's theme, and various fills and underscores at key dramatic moments.

Cast, crew, story, and sponsor came together on May 1, 1944 at 4 p.m. for Episode #1 of *Lady of the Press* in the storyline titled "The Picture of Death." There was little fanfare. *Broadcasting* magazine did print a short blurb in their May 8, 1944 issue noting the show's premiere, but managed to confuse actors with their roles when it noted that the "cast also includes Hack Taggart, Eddie Marr, and Jay Novello." An even shorter note the following week observed that this was Miles Labs' first advertising on the CBS network in ten years. *Billboard* gave the show a mention the same week, as did the *New York Times.*

Radio shows (certainly not soap operas) were rarely reviewed in print, and public promotion was limited. Six weeks into the run, Howard Culver was heard briefly on another West Coast afternoon program called *CBS Open House,* chatting about the new program. Miles Labs bought a few newspaper ads here and there to try to capture new listeners. Another article in the December 11, 1944 issue of *Broadcasting* mentioned *Lady of the Press* as an example of how sponsors could reach smaller markets.

Early in 1945, the show switched time slots, moving to 2:15 p.m. and replacing a show called *Pot Luck Party.* In a few more months, its 52-week contract wound down and the show ended. *Lady of the Press* aired its last episode in the late spring of 1945. Everyone went on to other jobs. Scripts were bound up, one month's worth per book, and archived in the CBS Columbia Square studios in Hollywood.

*Lady of the Press* became just another forgotten show. Decades later, Old Time Radio reference books had little to go on, and their information was often inaccurate. For instance, there's no evidence that a weekly version of the show with a different cast ever existed, despite what's been written into some histories. There is also no evidence that the show was ever officially called "The Adventures of Sandra Martin," except for newspaper radio logs that appropriated the heroine's name for the title to save a little space.

Janet Waldo saved a few transcription discs; decades later a single episode was still playable and provides us our only audio evidence of how the show actually sounded.

Nearly seventy years later, the show's first month of twenty-three scripts that were still in their original Columbia binder were placed for sale on Ebay and from there into the archives of the Generic Radio Workshop. (Later scripts are reportedly archived with the Pacific Pioneer Broadcasters collection at the Thousand Oaks Library in California.)

Does an obscure 15-minute radio serial that only ran for a year on eight stations really matter? You can judge for yourself, but we think it does. For one, it's a rare opportunity to experience a show unfolding from the very start through four weeks of uninterrupted episodes. For another, there were major actors connected to the broadcast. Miles Laboratories was an important sponsor, whose daily commercial in their endless variations make amusing reading. ("If you mothers want to see some big smiles on the kiddy's faces when it's time for their so-called Cod Liver Oil vitamins, give them One-A-Day Brand Vitamin A and D Tablets. They taste like candy, you know!")

Finally, as a hybrid of adventure serial and soap opera, *Lady of the Press* expands the boundaries of those genres just a bit, and offers interesting evidence of how the war was handled on the airwaves. Sandra Martin is neither "John's Other Wife" nor kindly Ma Perkins. She's a working woman, a reporter, and not for the society pages either. She's out there uncovering corruption and important war-related issues. Her life is too busy—at least in the show's first month—to be overwhelmed by the improbable romantic entanglements that dominated so many soaps. Instead, *Lady of the Press* touches on war shortages, black market corruption, working women, and the difficulties faced by returning vets after they've faced a brutal fight—what we now think of as Post Traumatic Stress Disorder. Like any good serial, it's all done in ways that make you want to tune in tomorrow (or in this case, to turn the page).

In the end, *Lady of the Press* isn't a major discovery, but it is a small gem. It can still charm us, if for no other reason than the fact that its very obscurity makes it fresh and new to us now. After being hidden for seventy years, that's certainly good enough.

# A note about the scripts...

**DWIGHT HAUSER MAY HAVE BEEN** a fine writer, but he wasn't the best speller. His *Lady of the Press* scripts include numerous spelling errors and moments of quirky punctuation, but since the show was a low-budget project with only a few copies distributed, they were used with mistakes intact. We have left nearly all of these errors as they were, since that's what the cast and crew worked with.

During rehearsals, radio scripts inevitably underwent last-minute changes, tweaking a phrase to strengthen it, or cutting a scene in the interests of time. The archived *Lady of the Press* scripts include penciled-in cuts and additions throughout. We have reproduced these by striking through the portions that were cut, and notating the additions in brackets. So a line of dialog that appears in this book like this....

SANDRA: Gee, Dovey, it's nice to be home. ~~The let down in suspense is wonderful.~~ [To let your hair down.]

...was originally typed in like this...

SANDRA: Gee, Dovey...It's nice to be home... The let down in suspense is wonderful.

...but was then edited for broadcast like this...

SANDRA: Gee, Dovey...It's nice to be home...to let your hair down.

Even these marked-up scripts are not the final word. The surviving recording, which is of Episode #17, has several audible changes that don't appear in the script. Most of these were ad-libbed changes, a word or two here or there. (Eddie Marr in particular played around with his lines). Announcer Dick Cutting's introduction to the episode dropped several sentences and added one new detail. We've noted this in a footnote on that script.

– Larry Groebe
Generic Radio Workshop

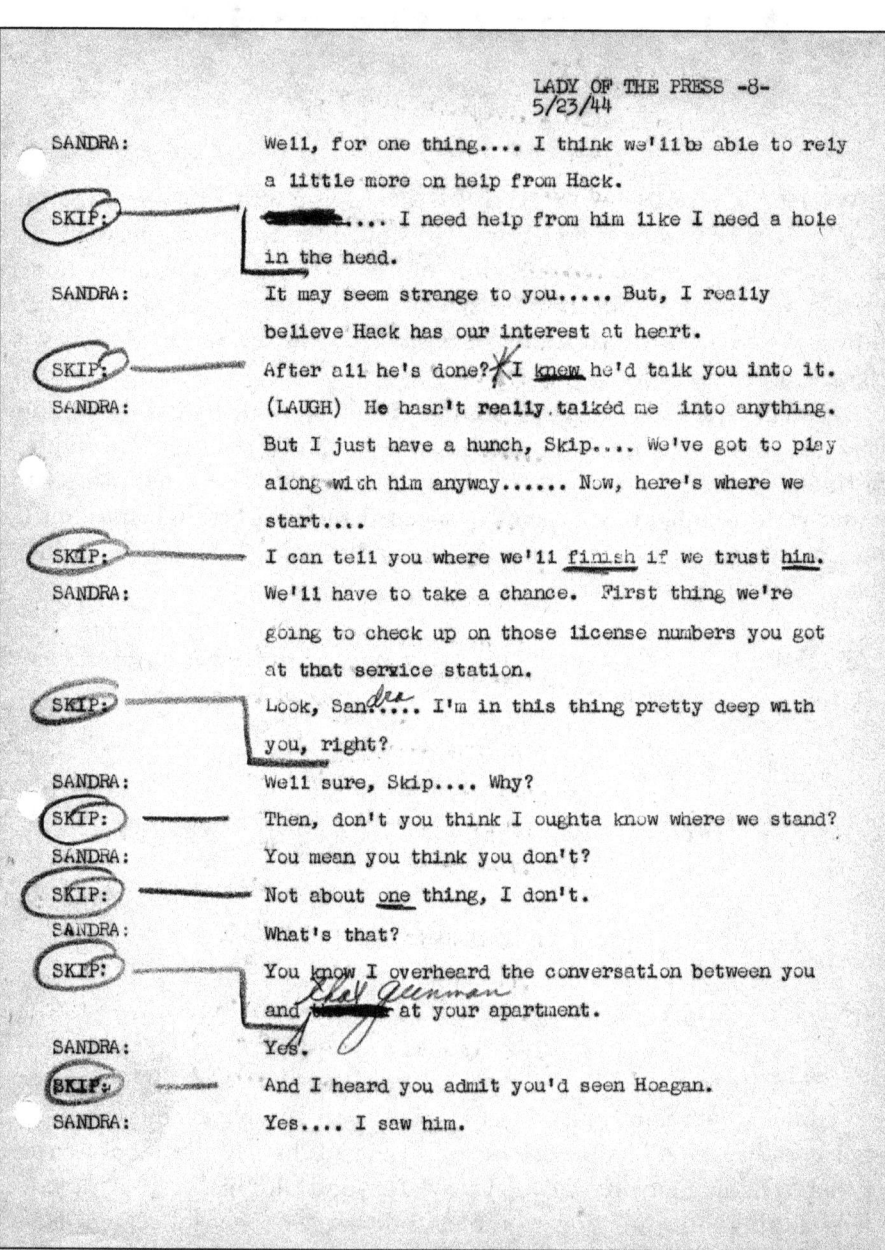

One of the original script pages from *Lady of the Press* with Eddie Marr's cues highlighted, along with a few last-minute additions and deletions pencilled in.

The original scripts for Lady of the press were bound in a thick folder onto which these streamlined CBS stickers were glued. Columbia Square housed the studios of station KNX.

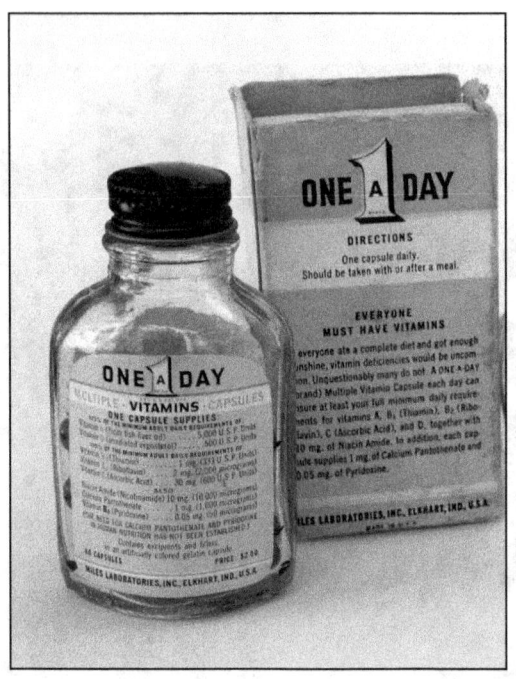

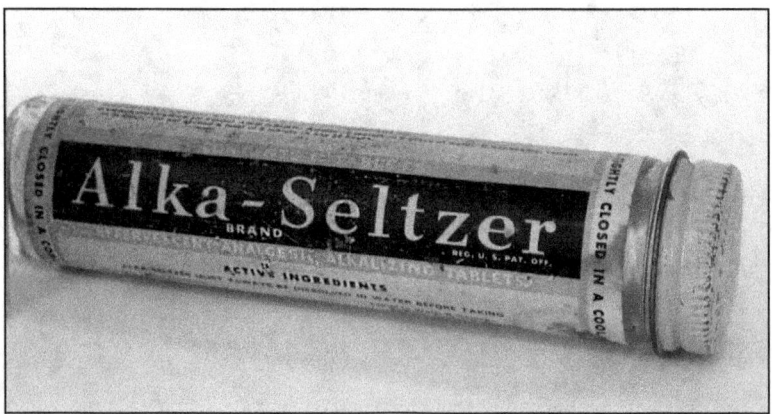

"Whenever you want FAST relief for a headache, a touch of acid indigestion, or the dull achy misery of a cold, ask your druggist for Alka-Seltzer. And whenever you need vitamins, ask for One-A-Day Brand Vitamins. You can pay more, but you can't get any better." 1940s versions of these still popular products from Miles Laboratories, who experimented with regional advertising by creating and sponsoring *Lady of the Press*.

**BLACK MARKET IDENTIFIED!**

SANDRA MARTIN identifies the Black Market leaders. Without the help or love of Hack or Bruce, can she alone get the convicting evidence before her murder trial?

LISTEN TODAY and everyday, Monday thru Friday, to radio's newest romantic-mystery, "LADY OF THE PRESS." Sponsored by the makers of Alka-Seltzer and One-A-Day Brand Vitamins.

**4 P. M., KARM, 1430**

**EVIDENCE AND BRUCE!**

SANDRA MARTIN, reporter, fights for evidence to clear herself of complicity in the Evers murder. Will Bruce's love fail her when she needs him most?

LISTEN TODAY and everyday, Monday thru Friday, to radio's newest romantic-mystery, "LADY OF THE PRESS." Sponsored by the makers of Alka-Seltzer and One-A-Day Brand Vitamins.

**4 P. M. KFPY 920**

Radio was considered competition to newspapers, but that didn't stop the papers from accepting advertisements for radio shows like *Lady of the Press*.

Janet Waldo ("Sandra Martin") and the the men in her life on *Lady of the Press*. Clockwise from upper right, Howard Culver ("Hack Taggart", photo from a 1953 fan magazine), Eddie Marr ("Skip Williams", undated photo), and producer/director Gordon Hughes (early 1950s photo)

# LADY
## OF THE
# PRESS

# EPISODE #1

# "PICTURE OF DEATH"

| | | |
|---|---|---|
| SPONSOR: | ALKA SELTZER | MAY 1, 1944 |
| AGENCY: | WADE 4:00–4:15 PM, PWT, PN | |

ANNCR: The makers of Alka Seltzer present—"LADY OF THE PRESS"

MUSIC: (STING) (QUICK PUNCTUATION)

ANNCR: The adventures of Sandra Martin, radio's newest romantic-mystery serial!

MUSIC: (THEME-ESTABLISH AND FADE OUT:)

(OPENING ANNOUNCEMENT)

CUTTING: Your friend, your druggist, and the makers of Alka-Seltzer and One-A-Day Brand Vitamins are mighty happy to bring you this new type of radio program—"Lady of the Press" and they sincerely hope that it becomes one of your favorites. They hope, too, that through these programs you will become acquainted with these famous products. We will never tire you with a lot of talk about Alka-Seltzer and One-A-Day Brand Vitamins because they are such fine products, we believe you'll accept them as such and as a result just naturally buy them whenever you are in need of their benefits. Remember then, whenever you want FAST relief for a headache, a touch of acid indigestion, or the dull achy misery of a cold, ask your druggist for Alka-Seltzer. And whenever you need vitamins, ask for One-A-Day Brand Vitamins. You can pay more, but you can't get any better.

MUSIC: (THEME UP AND UNDER)

ANNCR: And now "Lady of The Press, and episode one, in "A Picture of Death."

MUSIC: (THEME UP AND DOWN UNDER:)

ANNCR: Whenever there's a really hot news break, the editor of the "Courier" assigns his star reporter, Sandra Martin, and the staff's best photographer, Skip Williams to cover the story. Today, they've taken over a little idea of their own. The Young Womans' League For Progressive Government has uncovered incriminating evidence against an organized Black Market Ring and Sandra has asked Frances Evers, the League's Chairman, to pose for some pictures to accompany the story. Skip is at work in the Photographic department with Miss Evers as Sandra enters the office.

MUSIC: (STING AND OUT FAST)

SOUND: NEWSPAPER OFFICE

SANDRA: 'Morning everybody!

CAST: (AD LIBS) Hi San. Morning. (ETC. ETC.)

SANDRA: Skip come in, Pete?

PETE: (DOUBLE) Yes, he's in the studio with some girl.

SANDRA: That would be Miss Evers. Thanks, Pete.

SOUND: FOOTSTEPS—DOOR OPEN—CLOSE. OFFICE NOISE OUT

*FOOTSTEPS ALONG CORRIDOR—STOP—DOOR OPEN*

SANDRA: Hello, Skip.

SKIP: Morning, San.

SANDRA: I see we're getting some shots. Good morning, Miss Evers.

EVERS: Hello.

SANDRA: How many have you, Skip?

SKIP: Twelve.

SANDRA: That should be enough.

SKIP: Yeah. I just want one more profile. Would you turn your head a bit, Miss Evers?

EVERS: Certainly I want to thank you, Miss Martin, for taking such an interest. This publicity will certainly help us accomplish our purpose.

SKIP: Not if you don't hold still. The pictures I'm getting' will scare people.

SANDRA: Why, Skip . . . how rude.

SKIP: Well, can the chatter then, till I get a decent shot.

SANDRA: Okay. We'll be quiet. Shoot.

SKIP: Okay. Quiet. Still. A little more smile please. That's it hold it. Hold it.

SOUND: *FLASH BULB*

SKIP: Okay. That's a good one.

SANDRA: Fine. All right. I think that will do. We have several shots? (PAUSE)

I say, that will do, Miss Evers. You may relax now.
(PAUSE)
Miss Evers.

SOUND: *TWO FOOTSTEPS*

SANDRA: Miss Evers. Skip. Come here, quickly.

SOUND: *FOOTSTEPS*

SKIP: What's the matter?

SANDRA: The heat of the lights I guess. Miss Evers has fainted.

SKIP: Aw, these society dames can't take it. Here, I'll—Hey! Hey, wait a minute!

SANDRA: What's wrong?

SKIP: This dame, didn't faint . . . she's dead!!!

SANDRA: Look out. Grab her. She's falling.

SOUND: *BODY FALL*

SKIP: Sorry. Couldn't get to her. She just crumpled up and fell off the chair.

SANDRA: Well, do something. Pick her up and put her on that cot.

SKIP: I don't think we better touch her. It's obvious we can't do anything for her. Look at that bullet hole—straight to her heart.

SANDRA: How on earth—

SKIP: I can't understand it. She was sittin' there smilin'. I know she was alive ten seconds before I shot the picture.

SANDRA: Skip, that's it! Don't you see? Just as you shot the picture, someone else fired a gun.

SKIP: Hey! I thought that flash bulb made more noise than usual. But, I figured it broke.

SANDRA: Skip, how long would it take you to develop that picture?

SKIP: I could get a negative right away.

SANDRA: Then do it. And Skip, see if that bullet mark shows on the print.

SKIP: And what do you intend doing after you find that out?

SANDRA: I don't know. But, I want as many details as I can get before calling Hack.

SKIP: Taggart? You gotta get that flat foot in on it?

SANDRA: Now, wait a minute, Skip. Things have been pretty strained between Hack and me lately, but I still have to admit he's the best man on the homicide squad. Now, get on with that developing, will you?

SKIP: Okay, but I sure could do without that copper.

SANDRA: Personal matters shouldn't enter into this sort of thing. I assure you if I had any choice, I'd stay as far away from Hack Taggart as possible.

SKIP: I think you believe that all right, but, I don't.

SANDRA: Go develop the pictures.

SKIP: Okay.

SOUND: *FOOTSTEPS OFF DOOR OPEN AND CLOSE...DIALING OF PHONE*

SANDRA: Hello? Homicide Squad? Lieutenant Taggart, please. What? Well, when do you expect him? I see. Well, if he calls in will you tell him to come right over to the Courier office? That's right. Yes, there's been a murder in the photographic department.

ORGAN: (BRIDGE)

HACK: And that's all you know about it, huh?

SANDRA: That's it, Hack.

HACK: Just taking pictures of a beautiful woman and all at once she's shot. No apparent motive. No identification of the killer. No sound of a shot.

SANDRA: I know it sounds impossible, but it's the truth.

HACK: As far as we know it. However, I imagine we'll find out more as we follow out the routine.

SANDRA: Routine? Hack, are you out of your mind? Francis Evers, an important person in the community is killed and you call it routine.

HACK: Well, what do you call it?

SANDRA: Murder; cold blooded, calculated murder. A young life has been taken and you act as though it was nothing more than picking up a bookie. Hack, how can you be so cold and hard?

HACK: Look, where I've been I've seen plenty of dead girls. Butchered ones. Some of 'em even with kids in their arms. You don't expect me to break into tears over one dead woman, do you?

SANDRA: I realized being discharged from the army made you terribly bitter, Hack, but I didn't suppose anything could have ever made you so completely heartless. How could you possibly have changed so?

HACK: Because I was in a big show. And I was doing something in it. Just because I got a little shrapnel scattered around the frame, I get sent back here to fool around with inconsequential stuff like this, and in a world that's like a keg of dynamite. How do you think I should feel about that?

| | |
|---|---|
| SANDRA: | I don't expect you to be happy about it. But, I should think you'd be man enough to realize that it's all part of the war. You did your best while you were over there. You shouldn't do less now that you're back. |
| HACK: | Isn't it my business if the same things aren't important to me anymore? Nothing back here means the same once you've been across. |
| SANDRA: | Yes. I'm the outstanding example of that. |
| SOUND: | *DOOR OPEN FOOTSTEPS FADE IN FAST* |
| SKIP: | *(EXCITED)* I got the negative, San. It's *(TRANSITION)* Oh. John Law is with us I see. |
| HACK: | And anxious to ask you some questions. |
| SKIP: | And don't think I haven't got some answers . . . for you. |
| HACK: | Okay. First, just exactly what were you doing when this woman was shot? |
| SKIP: | Takin' her picture. |
| HACK: | You find that interesting work, taking pictures of murder victims? |
| SKIP: | How did I know she was about to be a murder victim? |
| HACK: | How do I know you didn't shoot her? With a gun instead of a camera? |
| SKIP: | I don't suppose you do, but, a smart detective could easily figure that out. |
| HACK: | Suppose you tell me . . . just for the record. |
| SKIP: | Okay. San will tell you I was behind the camera. Miss Evers was facing that door at right angles to my camera, and, if you'll take a look you'll see the bullet struck her in the chest. |

HACK: So it was someone standing in that doorway. Someone who had a gun with a silencer on it. Now who could have had a motive for killing Frances Evers?

SANDRA: Say, we were getting those pictures to feature with a story regarding an expose of a Black Market Ring. Miss Evers had the evidence!

HACK: Right now I'm more interested in the identity of the murderer than the motive.

SKIP: Well, why didn't you say so.

HACK: You have an idea who the murderer might be?

SKIP: An idea? Naw. I don't fool around with that guess work. I've got a picture of him.

HACK: What?

SKIP: Sure, I just developed it.

SANDRA: But I thought you were developing the last shot of Miss Evers.

SKIP: Sure, but, I look here. You remember, we were shooting her using that large window as a background?

SANDRA: Yes?

SKIP: Well, I didn't notice it in my set up at the time. But, it seems I had the lights placed in such a way that the left wall of the room was reflected in that window behind her. Look.

SANDRA: Well, I'll be.

HACK: Here, lemme see that.

SKIP: Be careful. It's still wet.

SANDRA: Look, you can see the figure of a man in the doorway.

| | | |
|---|---|---|
| SKIP: | And the puff of smoke from the gun he's holding. Meaning that he fired at the same time we flashed the picture. | |
| HACK: | The impression isn't clear enough to see the guys face. | |
| SKIP: | Not now, but, I think it will be as soon as we can get a dry proof. | |
| HACK: | Then all we'll have to do is pick him up. | |
| SANDRA: | Hack! Doesn't it make any difference to you why he did it? | |
| HACK: | Not especially. Except that we'll be able to hang a heavier rap on him if we establish a motive. Why don't you try and figure it out for me, darling? | |
| SANDRA: | Don't think I won't. There has to be pretty important reason for a man committing murder. To me that's as important as the act itself. I'm going to find out why Frances Evers was murdered. Either with—or without your help. | |
| HACK: | Okay, Detective. Let me know when you have the case on ice. | |
| *MUSIC:* | *(BRIDGE)* | |
| *SOUND:* | *FOOTSTEPS DOOR OPEN CLOSE MORE FOOTSTEPS* | |
| SKIP: | Mornin' San. | |
| SANDRA: | Hello, Skip. | |
| SKIP: | Anything new? | |
| SANDRA: | No. | |
| SKIP: | No news from out misguided detective friend? | |
| SANDRA: | He's misguided all right, but he's no friend of mine at this point. | |

SKIP: If I thought that would last I'd be greatly encouraged. But, I fear it's the impulse of the moment. You'll forgive him.

SANDRA: Not unless he changes his attitude. It's positively sickening to see a man like Hack let himself down so completely.

SKIP: To say nothing of letting his friends down.

SOUND: PHONE RING A FEW STEPS RECEIVER OFF HOOK

SANDRA: Hello.

HACK: *(FILTER)* Hello. San?

SANDRA: Oh, Hack. Yes. What do you want?

HACK: Just checking up on how you're doing with our little case.

SANDRA: I've made some progress, and I've no doubt that's more than you've done.

HACK: Oh, I wouldn't say that. We've identified the murderer!

HACK: Ever hear of Elbert Hoagan?

SANDRA: The Fashion editor here on the Courier?

HACK: Right, his latest fashion seems to be murder.

SANDRA: But, he's a meek little guy. It's unbelievable. He's a mouse.

HACK: Nevertheless, that's his picture standing there in that door with the gun in his hand. Furthermore, he hasn't been to his home all night . . . and he hasn't showed up for work this morning. We're dragging the city for him. Let you know if anything develops.

SOUND: CLICK OF RECEIVER ON FILTER

SANDRA: Wait. Hack. Hello?

| | |
|---|---|
| SOUND: | JIGGLING RECEIVER |
| SANDRA: | Hello. Hello. Oh, darn. |
| SOUND: | *RECEIVER ON HOOK* |
| SKIP: | Hang up on you? |
| SANDRA: | Yes, the big dope. He's the most inconsiderate— |
| SKIP: | Go on. Those words are music to my ears. |
| SANDRA: | Never mind that now. Right now, I want to find Hoagan before those cops get hold of him. I might find out his motive. |
| SKIP: | You mean our "Debutantes Pride" isn't so lily white as we thought? |
| SANDRA: | Lily white? Say, if Hack is right that Lily has blood on his petals. |
| ORGAN: | *(BRIDGE)* |
| SOUND: | *TYPEWRITER* |
| SKIP: | What are you up to now, San? |
| SANDRA: | I think it's time the people of this community were made aware of the indigence of some members of the Homicide Squad. |
| SKIP: | Meaning, most especially Lieutenant Hack Taggart? |
| SANDRA: | Exactly. |
| SKIP: | You better lay off. You've already put yourself in a spot. |
| SANDRA: | In what way? |
| SKIP: | This. |

SOUND:      RATTLING NEWSPAPER

SANDRA:     The story I wrote on the murder? Well, I meant every word of it. I'm going to get to the bottom of it.

SKIP:       I wish you'd take it easy, after all, you and I were the only people in the room when Miss Evers was shot. Certainly, Hoagan realizes that.

SOUND:      PHONE RINGS RECEIVER OFF HOOK

SANDRA:     Yes.

VOICE:      Miss Martin?

SANDRA:     Yes.

VOICE:      This is the Desk Sergeant at the Homicide Squad. I'm calling for Lieutenant Taggart. He had to leave in a hurry. He asked me to call and tell you they'd located Hoagan.

SANDRA:     Oh? Where?

VOICE:      He said to give you this address . . . 8419 Semple Street. He wants you to meet him there just as soon as you can.

SANDRA:     Okay. I'll go right out there. Thanks. Goodbye.

SOUND:      RECEIVER ON HOOK

SANDRA:     Gotta run, Skip. Hack's got Hoagan, down on Semple St. Keep the presses hot for me!!!

MUSIC:      (BRIDGE)

SOUND:      DOOR OPEN

SKIP:       Well, what brings you down here?

HACK:       Where's Sandra?

| | |
|---|---|
| SKIP: | She went to meet you right after she got your phone call. |
| HACK: | Just what are you talking about? |
| SKIP: | She got your call saying you had Hoagan cornered at some address on "Semple St. She busted out of here in a flurry an' I haven't seen her since. |
| HACK: | How long ago was that? |
| SKIP: | About a half an hour. Why? |
| HACK: | Nothing, except that I haven't had any trace of Hoagan and I didn't make any phone call. |
| SKIP: | What? You . . . hey! You think— |
| HACK: | Figure it out for yourself. Hoagan has killed one woman in the last twenty four hours. Sandra was in the room when he did it and she didn't make any bones about the fact that she intended breaking the case. She gets a phony message to meet me on Semple St. Naturally I won't be there. But, Hoagan will be. |
| SKIP: | Well, what are we waitin' for? She may be killed. Let's get down there now. |
| HACK: | There's just one flaw in that idea. |
| SKIP: | Never mind the correspondence school detective theories, let's go! |
| HACK: | Where? Semple St. is about eleven miles long, and I take it you didn't bother to take down the address. |
| MUSIC: | *(TO TAG)* |
| | *(CLOSING ANNOUNCEMENT)* |
| CUTTING: | How about it, ladies, has this been a pretty hectic day for you? If it has, and as a result your headaches and your |

|          |                                                              |
|----------|--------------------------------------------------------------|
|          | stomach's a bit upset, why don't you let Alka-Seltzer be your friend in need? Remember, when you take Alka-Seltzer for headaches and minor acid stomach upsets, you can feel better FAST. Try it all druggists have Alka-Seltzer Tablets by the sixty and thirty cent size package. |
| MUSIC:   | THEME—ESTABLISH AND FADE UNDER                               |
| ANNCR:   | If Hoagan was the man who made that phone call, Sandra Martin at this moment could be in the hands of a man who has just committed one murder and will not hesitate to commit another. Be sure to listen again tomorrow when Hack and Skip forget their rivalry long enough to join in the search for our "LADY OF THE PRESS" in episode two of "THE PICTURE OF DEATH" |
| MUSIC:   | THEME UP AND UNDER                                           |
| ANNCR:   | "LADY OF THE PRESS" is written by Dwight Hauser, and produced by Gordon T. Hughes and is brought to you every day, Monday through Friday at this same time by the makers of Alka Seltzer. |
| MUSIC:   | THEME UP TO FILL                                             |
| ANNCR:   | This is CBS. The COLUMBIA BROADCASTING SYSTEM.               |

# EPISODE #2

# "PICTURE OF DEATH"

| | | |
|---|---|---|
| SPONSOR: | ALKA SELTZER | MAY 2, 1944 |
| AGENCY: | WADE  4:00—4:15 PM, PWT | |

---

ANNCR: The makers of Alka Seltzer present—"LADY OF THE PRESS"

MUSIC: *(STING) (QUICK PUNCTUATION)*

ANNCR: The adventures of Sandra Martin, radio's newest romantic-mystery serial!

MUSIC: *(THEME-ESTABLISH AND FADE)*

*OPENING ANNOUNCEMENT*

CUTTING: Say mother, you wouldn't even think of forgetting to give your baby his cod liver oil, would you? But what about yourself? And dad and the older kiddies? Well, those same vitamins A and D which make cod liver oil important to baby, are also mighty important to the rest of the family too. You see, Vitamin A helps keep up normal resistance to colds . . . also aids in preventing night blindness. And Vitamin D helps in maintaining sound teeth and bones. Now since it's mighty hard to be sure that you get enough of these vitamins from natural sources, it will pay you to give each member of your family a single pleasant tasting

One-A-Day Brand Vitamin A and D Tablet every day. That single One-A-Day Brand Vitamin A and D Tablet is as rich in these two vitamins as a teaspoon and a half of USP minimum cod liver oil—an amount which is twenty-five percent more than a person's basic daily requirements. And because one tablet does the job, that makes them mighty economical—just slightly more than a penny a day, when you buy the large family size package. Why not ask your druggist for One-A-Day Brand Vitamin A and D Tablets right away and give each member of your family their protective benefits. Look for the big "One" and the name Miles Laboratories on the Yellow package. That's the "One" to buy.

ANNCR: And now "Lady Of The Press" and episode two in, "The Picture of Death!"

MUSIC: (QUICK FIGURATION AND UNDER FOR)

ANNCR: Following the murder of Frances Evers, in the presence of Sandra and Skip, Elbert Hoagan, The Courier's Society Editor has disappeared. This fact, together with a photograph which shows his reflection in a window of the murder room fastens the guilt unquestionably upon him. However, in order to clear themselves it is necessary for Sandra and Skip to produce Hoagan in court. To this end Lieutenant Hack Taggart of the Homicide Squad has been called and given the facts. Later, Sandra received a phone call instructing her to meet Hack at an address on Semple Street. But, we know that Hack did not make that call. Try as he will, Hack is unable to cover up his romantic interest in Sandra as he realizes that she has been tricked into a position of extreme danger.

MUSIC: (PUNCTUATE AND FADE INTO)

SOUND: RUNNING CAR SNEAK IN AND HOLD UNDER

HACK: Of all the—why didn't you ask her for the address before she left?

| | |
|---|---|
| SKIP: | Well, how was I to know the message was a phony? You've called her before, you know. |
| HACK: | But with a murder as hot as this on our hands, you should have been more careful. |
| SKIP: | She's not in the habit of keeping me informed as to her whereabouts, especially when you're included. |
| HACK: | Well, I'm satisfied of one thing . . . if we can't find her and stop her before she gets to that address . . . she'll be at the mercy of this maniac Hoagan. |
| SKIP: | How can you be so sure of that? |
| HACK: | I told you before. You and Sandra were the only two present at the time of the murder. Hoagan doesn't know about the photo. So, as far as he is concerned you are the only ones with any evidence. |
| SKIP: | So? |
| HACK: | The first thing any criminal does is to start destroying evidence, and Hoagan is starting with Sandra, but give him time. He'll get around to you. |
| SKIP: | Thanks. |
| HACK: | That's our best bet right at present. |
| SKIP: | *(A TAKE)* Huh? |
| HACK: | Sure—use'n you for bait! More criminals are caught trying to cover up crimes than in committing them! |
| SKIP: | That's swell, just so long as I don't get covered up first. |
| HACK: | You want to help her, don't you? |
| SKIP: | Of course. But, I'd like to begin by finding her. |

| | |
|---|---|
| HACK: | Don't you think that's what I want? Don't you think I'll do everything in my power to get her out of this safely? |
| SKIP: | Yeah, but, I got a feelin' you could use a lot more power than you've got. |
| HACK: | Look, it's pretty obvious how both of us feel about Sandra. I've never had much time for you, and I know you haven't for me. |
| SKIP: | You can say that again. |
| HACK: | Okay, so we don't like each other. But right now we have the same objective in common . . . that's to find Sandra and keep her from danger. Right? |
| SKIP: | Right. |
| HACK: | Then, it might be a good idea to drop the animosity long enough to work together in the matter. |
| SKIP: | I'm willing. But, don't get the idea that you're the whole show! |
| HACK: | Don't worry about that. |
| SKIP: | Yeah, well knowin' you, I do worry about that. I have some interest in this myself! |
| HACK: | Why don't you give up? Don't you know by now that a mere flash bulb popper, doesn't stand a chance with Sandra? |
| SKIP: | Now, listen, here, Flat foot, I'll have you know that my job's an art. It's . . . . |
| HACK: | I thought we were going to skip the feud? |
| SKIP: | Okay, but, don't be makin' any more derogatory remarks about my photography. I've capped some of the hottest picture in the business. |

| | |
|---|---|
| HACK: | All right, artist. Forget it. |
| SKIP: | And just what makes you think a gal like Sandra is going into the home stretch with a dumb cop? |
| HACK: | I haven't asked her to, yet. |
| SKIP: | Well, lemme give you a tip. Save your feelins by keepin' it that way. |
| HACK: | Here's a Service station. Think I'll pull in and call the desk. |
| SOUND: | *CAR SLOWING AND TO STOP* |
| HACK: | I won't be but a minute. Keep your eye on the street for any sign of her. |
| SKIP: | Look, I don't see any percentage in playin' cop and robber with you. We're wastin' our time. |
| HACK: | Do you have any better ideas? |
| SKIP: | Plenty! I'm going back to the Courier and tell the chief. He'll get out an extra! And bud, when the Courier gets out an extra, things get done. |
| HACK: | You idiot! Don't you realize that publicity on this thing would simply put Sandra in more danger than ever? |
| SKIP: | You and your correspondence courses. Got everything figured out in advance, haven't you? |
| HACK: | I just happen to know criminals. |
| SKIP: | Yeah. But, you don't know where Sandra is. You take your criminal psychology and I'll take the circulation of the Courier. We'll see who finds her first. |
| HACK: | Now wait a minute . . . I know what I'm talking about. If you give two whoops about Sandra's safety you better listen to me. |

| | |
|---|---|
| SOUND: | *CAR DOOR OPENS* |
| SKIP: | Can't see it, copper. I got some ideas right up here in my own little beezer, and this time I think they'll make yours look pretty rudimentary. So long, Boy Scout. I'm takin' some action. |
| SOUND: | *CAR DOOR SLAM SHUT* |
| MUSIC: | *BRIDGE* |
| SOUND: | *OFFICE NOISES HURRIED FOOTSTEPS FADE IN UNDER* |
| SKIP: | Hey, hey, boy! Get some plates in my camera and meet me in front in twenty minutes. And you baby, get the chief on the phone. Switch it to the rewrite office. I'll take it in there. And hurry it up, will you? |
| SOUND: | *FOOTSTEPS HURRY TO DOOR. DOOR OPEN. CLOSE. OFFICE SOUND OUT* |
| SKIP: | *(TO HIMSELF)* Now, we'll see who gets action and who doesn't. |
| SOUND: | *PHONE RINGS. A FEW STEPS. RECEIVER OFF HOOK* |
| SKIP: | Hello? Oh, hello Chief. This is Skip Williams. Look Chief we got a get out an extra. Huh? Williams. Skip Williams. You know, you're ace photographer. What? Well, I been workin' here for three years. Yeah. Hey look. We gotta get out an extra. We. Yeah, Chief. Yeah, I know, but—but, Chief—all right. I'm just a dumb photographer. Sure. You run the paper and I'll take the pictures. But look! SANDRA MARTIN HAS DISAPPEARED! That's what I said—disappeared. *(SMUGLY)* Yeah, I sorta thought you'd want to do something about that. That's what I thought. If anything can be done. A Courier extra will do it. |
| SOUND: | *DOOR OPEN—WOMANS FOOTSTEPS* |

| | |
|---|---|
| SKIP: | That's right. When a paper's leading reporter gets into a jam, the paper ought to do something . . . especially when that reporter happens to be San. |
| SANDRA: | Hi Skip. |
| SKIP: | *(NOT RECOGNIZING HER)* Hi' San. *(TAKE)* SANDRA! *(SWALLOWING)* What—Well—Where—Where did you come from? |
| SANDRA: | From a little wild goose chase. |
| SKIP: | But—but—*(IN PHONE)* Chief—look, something has come up. I—I guess you better kill the whole idea. Yeah, Chief. That's right. Kill it. |
| SOUND: | RECEIVER ON HOOK |
| SKIP: | How in the—look, Hack and I have been all over this town huntin' you. Where you been? |
| SANDRA: | I got a phone call, remember? |
| SKIP: | That's just it. When Hack showed up here, we compared notes and knew it was a phony. We've been half nuts figurin' you were in the hands of that Guy Hoagan. |
| SANDRA: | That's good figuring. I might well have been. |
| SKIP: | But, you did go to that address? |
| SANDRA: | Yes, but, I'm not such a dope, as whoever made that call seems to think. |
| SKIP: | What do you mean? If you went there you ought to know who it was. |
| SANDRA: | I have a pretty good idea. I think it was Hoagan, too, but I wasn't fool enough to go in. |
| SKIP: | Then, what did you do? |

SANDRA: Went to the address I was given. It was a large old apartment house. Pretty run down. But, who ever called said Hack would be there. I took a quick walk around the place and when I saw no sign of Hack's car or any other police car, I knew something was up, so I didn't go in.

SKIP: Then where did you go? We been combin' that street for you.

SANDRA: Over to the department looking for Hack. But, they didn't know where he was, so I came back here.

SKIP: Well, I might say just in passing, that I was never any happier to see you. We figured you'd be in plenty of trouble by now.

SANDRA: We're both in plenty of trouble. Unless Hoagan is caught we'll both be held as accomplices in this crime.

HACK: But, the picture proves Hoagan's guilt.

SANDRA: Yes, but you and I were responsible for having her in that room at the time. Unless we find Hoagan, the Grand Jury is going to want a pretty good explanation of that.

SKIP: Well, what are we waitin' for? Let's go back to that house and get him.

SANDRA: No. This is a job for Hack.

SKIP: Aw, look—just this once can't we get the credit for this without lettin' him in on it?

SANDRA: 'Fraid not, Skip. This fellow is dangerous. I don't want to take any chances. Where'd you leave Hack?

SKIP: At a service station down on Semple Street. He's still down there lookin' for you. Boy! Will he be burned up when he finds out I found you.

SANDRA: You didn't find me; I just walked in.

SKIP: Yeah. But, I was here when you did, and he wasn't. He's cruisin' around down there lookin' for somebody that isn't lost. *(LAUGHS)*

SANDRA: Never mind the vindictive humor, Skip. Hoagan won't stay there forever. Get the Homicide Squad and tell them to contact Hack immediately.

SKIP: Okay. If that's the way you want it. But, I've got a hunch we'd do better without him.

SOUND: *RECEIVER OFF HOOK-DIALING*

SKIP: I don't know why it is, but, every time there is a set up for you and me to do somethin' together, that lug has to have his nose in it some—*(IN PHONE)* Hello? Yeah, this Boy Scout headquarters? All right, all right! So it's the Homicide Squad. Look, get in touch with troop leader Taggart and tell him that Mister Skip Williams and Miss Sandra Martin would appreciate his presence in the latter's office for a tea party. Anytime this P.M. Oh, don't worry, we'll make it weak tea. Yeah. Bye.

SOUND: *RECEIVER ON HOOK*

SANDRA: You certainly do go out of your way to needle the police department, don't you, Skip?

SKIP: Well, why shouldn't I? Did they ever do anything for me?

SANDRA: Well, you're out of jail, aren't you?

SKIP: Sure, but that's not Hack Taggart's fault; that's because I keep my nose clean. If that guy had his way nothing would suit him better than putting a few bars between you and me.

SANDRA: What makes you think he'd do a thing like that?

SKIP: He's jealous. (QUICKLY) I know he hasn't any reason to be. Worse luck for me, but he is anyway.

| | |
|---|---|
| SANDRA: | Don't be silly. It's pretty obvious that Hack isn't interested in much of anything since he got back. Least of all me. |
| SKIP: | Oh yeah? Then why's he in such a dither over findin' you? |
| SANDRA: | Part of his job, I suppose. |
| SKIP: | Well all I can say is that anybody that stupid has no business on the police force. Why if you cared half as much for me as you do for him—I'd do somethin' about it. |
| SANDRA: | (SADLY) Please, Skip, I—I'd rather not talk about it, if you don't mind. |
| SKIP: | Okay, but, I still think he's a dope. And we'd do much better in this whole deal without him. |
| SANDRA: | No. We can't do this alone. I'm certain Hoagan is waiting for me in that house on Semple Street. If Hack would only get here we could go down and pick him up. |
| SKIP: | If he doesn't pick one of us off on the way in. |
| SANDRA: | He's not that dumb. He had plenty of chance to take a shot at me when I was down there if he'd wanted to do it that way. |
| SKIP: | Then, what do we do? |
| SANDRA: | I'm not sure. All that I am sure of is that having such definite proof on a murderer doesn't exactly place one in a position of safety. Until Hoagan is behind bars. That little morsel of information is going to give us a lot of trouble. |
| MUSIC: | (TO TAG) |
| ANNCR: | (COMMERCIAL) |
| | CLOSING ANNOUNCEMENT |
| CUTTING: | You know, friends, some folks think that just because colds aren't as prevalent during the Summertime as they are in |

the Winter months, they can afford to neglect keeping up their year-round resistance to this miserable ailment. Well, don't YOU make this mistake because now it's so easy and economical to be SURE at least of your vitamin A guard. Simply bolster up your meals with a single One-A-Day Brand Vitamin A and D Tablet each day. That single pleasant-tasting One-A-Day Brand Vitamin A and D Tablet gives you your normal daily requirements of these two vitamins—vitamin A to help in maintaining normal resistance to colds—vitamin D to help maintain strong bone structure. So we say, start EVERY day with One-A-Day. Ask your druggist for One-A-Day Brand Vitamin A and D Tablets without delay. Tell him you want the kind with the big "One" and the name Miles Laboratories on the Yellow package.

MUSIC: *THEME ESTABLISH AND FADE UNDER FOR*

ANNCR: Will the jeopardy in which her life has been placed help to bring Sandra and Hack together? Or, will the danger of holding evidence which can condemn a man to death prevent her from aiding in the capture of Hoagan? Be sure to tune in again tomorrow as Sandra, Hack and Skip continue their search for Elbert Hoagan in Episode three of "THE PICTURE OF DEATH"

MUSIC: *UP AND UNDER*

ANNCR: "Lady Of The Press" is written by Dwight Hauser, and produced by Gordon T. Hughes and is brought to you each day, Monday through Friday at this same time by the makers of Alka Seltzer.

MUSIC: *TO FILL*

ANNCR: This is CBS. The COLUMBIA BROADCASTING SYSTEM.

# EPISODE #3

# "PICTURE OF DEATH"

| | | |
|---|---|---|
| SPONSOR: | ALKA SELTZER | MAY 3, 1944 |
| AGENCY: | WADE 4:00—4:15 PM, PWT | |

ANNCR: The makers of Alka Seltzer present—"LADY OF THE PRESS"

MUSIC: *(STING) (QUICK PUNCTUATION)*

ANNCR: The adventures of Sandra Martin, radio's newest romantic-mystery serial!

MUSIC: *(THEME-ESTABLISH AND FADE OUT)*

*OPENING ANNOUNCEMENT:*

CUTTING: Tell me, friends, are YOU among the millions of modern people who are enjoying healthier, more active lives because you get sufficient vitamins? Well, if you aren't, why don't you start taking One-A-Day Brand Multiple Vitamin Capsules. This newest product of the Miles Laboratories—makers of Alka-Seltzer—is "tops" for all-around vitamin protection. "Tops" because just one capsule each day is all you take—because this one capsule supplies your full basic daily requirements of all the vitamins whose requirements are known—because One-A-Day Brand Multiple Vitamin Capsules are the very highest quality vitamins that can be made. And of course they are economical. Since one capsule each day does the job that makes One-A-Day Brand Multiple Vitamins cost you less than other kinds which require you to take three or four capsules daily. Why say, a full sixty day supply of sixty capsules only costs two dollars. So for general, all around vitamin protection ask your druggist for One-A-Day Brand Multiple Vitamin Capsules—in the new BLUE package with the big "One".

MUSIC: (THEME- ESTABLISH AND FADE)

ANNCR: And now, "Lady Of The Press" and episode three in, "The Picture Of Death."

MUSIC: (QUICK FIGURATION AND FADE UNDER FOR)

ANNCR: Arriving at the address on Semple Street, given her over the telephone, Sandra Martin discovered no sign of a car from the Homicide Squad. Realizing that, the information she has, regarding the murder of Frances Evers, has placed her in extreme danger. Sandra refused to fall into the trap and returned to the Courier Office without going into the house. Now Skip Williams has informed the Homicide Squad of Sandra's return and they in turn, have told Lieutenant Taggart. Fully aware of the danger which awaits them in this old house on Semple Street, Hack Taggart, Sandra, and Skip have gone back. We find them now walking cautiously up the steps to the front door.

SOUND: SNEAK FOOTSTEPS IN UNDER ABOVE-UP AND STOP

SKIP: Shall I ring?

HACK: No. I'd want to take him by surprise. Try the door.

SOUND: RATTLE DOOR KNOB

SKIP: (SOTTO VOCE) Yeah. It's unlocked.

HACK: Push it open.

| | |
|---|---|
| SKIP: | Okay. |
| SOUND: | *DOOR SQUEAKS OPEN* |
| HACK: | Stand away from the door, Sandra. |
| SKIP: | Well, doesn't look like any welcoming committee was here to meet us. |
| HACK: | Come on. |
| SOUND: | *A FEW STEPS* |
| SKIP: | No sign of life here! |
| SANDRA: | The place seems to be deserted. Gives me the creeps! |
| HACK: | See if the lights work, Skip. |
| SKIP: | Okay. |
| SOUND: | *A FEW STEPS—FADE OFF* |
| HACK: | Nobody's lived here for sometime, that's certain. |
| SOUND: | *CLICKING ON AND OFF OF SWITCH* |
| SKIP: | Didn't pay their light bill, I guess. The juice is off. |
| HACK: | All right. Here's a flash. Come on. |
| SANDRA: | Where—where are you going? |
| HACK: | That door probably leads to the rear of the house. Lets have a look. Coming Skip? |
| SOUND: | *A FEW STEPS* |
| SKIP: | Yeah, I'm coming. Hold the light back this— |
| SOUND: | *CRASH OF TABLE FALLING* |

SANDRA: What's that?

HACK: Don't move! You're covered—

SKIP: Owwwww! Oooooh! Put down your pistol, boy scout. I just broke my shin on a table!

HACK: Well, that settles any secrecy which might have surrounded our presence. If there's anyone here, you've certainly announced us!

SKIP: Well, it's impolite for guests to walk in on folks, unexpected.

HACK: All right. You two stay behind. But, follow me. Come on.

SOUND: *FOOTSTEPS*

HACK: You stay between us, Sandra. Then we'll know where you are.

SANDRA: All right. But, I can think of more comfortable places to be.

SKIP: Oh, I think it's cozy.

HACK: Cut it, will you?

SOUND: *DOOR OPEN*

SKIP: Gee, the housing project should hear about this place. Nothin' but vacancies.

HACK: The whole place is deserted all right.

SANDRA: Wait. There's something.

HACK: What? Where?

SANDRA: There . . . on that table. Looks like an envelope.

SOUND: *FOOTSTEPS*

| | |
|---|---|
| HACK: | Yes, it is. |
| SANDRA: | Anything on it? What's it say? Maybe it's a message. |
| HACK: | Yes it is a message. It has your name on it. |
| MUSIC: | *(STING AND INTO BRIDGE)* |
| SOUND: | *NEWSPAPER OFFICE—BACKGROUND* |
| HACK: | Well, we muffed that chance all right. If it was Hoagan who left that note in that house he certainly didn't wait around for it to be picked up. |
| SANDRA: | Maybe he never intended meeting me there. Maybe he just left it and then phoned me. |
| HACK: | Whatever he figured, he's succeeded in throwing us completely off his trail again. |
| SANDRA: | Let me see the note again, will you Hack? |
| HACK: | Sure. Here you are. |
| SOUND: | *RATTLE OF PAPER* |
| SANDRA: | *(READING)* Sandra Martin. This message comes to you from a man condemned. Surely you realize that one who commits murder will not hesitate repeating the act to escape capture. If you saw me that day, you'll know who writes this, and I suggest you keep that information strickly confidential. If you did not see me, this will not disclose my identity. You will be safe as long as you cooperate. If you do not, I suggest you check on your future by going down to the morgue for another look at the body of Frances Evers. You will get no further warning. Signed . . . Desperate. |
| SKIP: | Sounds like a letter to the lonely hearts column. |
| SANDRA: | What do you make of it, Hack? |

| | |
|---|---|
| HACK: | Nothing more than I've figured right along. It's from Hoagan. He thinks you and Skip are the only source of evidence. Skip will get a warning also, but, when it happens don't either of you try to contact him alone. We'd have had him this time if you'd called me first. |
| SKIP: | Oh, sure. All we have to do is take a picture of the murderer. Then make an appointment with him and you can catch him. |
| HACK: | Now look, stupid, I've had about enough from you. One more— |
| SANDRA: | Oh, for heavens sake! Can't you too keep your fights to yourselves long enough for us to make some plans? |
| HACK: | My plans are all made. Whoever wrote you that note will try and contact Skip. And when he does, I want to know it before either of you try anything, and, that's an order . . . unless both of you would like to go down and explain your presence in the room at the time of the murder. |
| SANDRA: | Hack . . . you don't think—? |
| HACK: | I don't think anything yet. But, I know you're being present at the murder, will be mighty hard to explain if it gets out. Until we get Hoagan, that situation is going to remain the same. So, if you're smart, you'll both play ball with me. If not, well—you can face the consequences by yourselves. That's all I've got to say. Lemme know if anything turns up. |
| SOUND: | *FOOTSTEPS TO DOOR-DOOR OPEN-CLOSE* |
| SKIP: | I never saw a guy that could get spiffed off so easy. |
| SANDRA: | I—Skip—I'll be right back. |
| SOUND: | *FOOTSTEPS* |
| SKIP: | Hey, wait a minute. I'm supposed to keep any eye on you. Where you goin'? |

| | |
|---|---|
| SOUND: | *DOOR OPENS—OFFICE NOISES UP* |
| SANDRA: | I—I want to catch Hack before he gets away. |
| SKIP: | Yeah, I know, but, I got a hunch you better change your bait. |
| SOUND: | *DOOR SLAMS—RUNNING FOOTSTEPS* |
| SANDRA: | *(CALLING)* Hack! Hack! Oh, darn! |
| SOUND: | *DOOR OPENS—CLOSE—OFFICE SOUND OUT* |
| SANDRA: | Hack! Hack, wait a minute, will you? |
| HACK: | *(OFF)* Yeah? What's up? |
| SOUND: | *FOOTSTEPS* |
| SANDRA: | I—I wanted to see you alone a minute, before you left. |
| HACK: | Yeah? Something on your mind? |
| SANDRA: | Well, yes, that is— |
| HACK: | Well, out with it. If there's anything I can do, you know— |
| SANDRA: | There is something you can do, Hack, something terribly important. |
| HACK: | What? |
| SANDRA: | Hack, what are you doing, tonight? |
| HACK: | Working, why? |
| SANDRA: | Well, I thought . . . I thought maybe we could sort of pick up where we left off before you want away. I mean, why can't we have dinner together? |
| HACK: | Sure. Come over to Murphy's around seven. I'll have about an hour then. |

SANDRA: No, Hack, that's not what I mean. Forget your work for tonight. Let's go out to dinner . . . and then maybe to a show, the way we used to.

HACK: Sorry, San. Haven't time.

SANDRA: You haven't time for much of anything anymore, have you, Hack?

HACK: Look San, I've explained things to you the best I know how. Maybe it's hard to understand, but, that's the way things are.

SANDRA: Then, you won't go out with me tonight?

HACK: I just can't see myself getting' all steamed up watchin' a lot of grease painted four-F's playin' soldier for the flickers.

SANDRA: Well, we don't have to go to a war picture. We don't even have to go to a movie. We can go see a floor show or something. Or just—just be together, anyplace.

HACK: Can't see it.

SANDRA: I can't believe that you're the same person, Hack.

HACK: Maybe I'm not.

SANDRA: No, there's nothing about you now that resembles the man I was in love with.

HACK: That's a break for you.

SANDRA: No, it isn't. I want to find that man again—that boy who held me in his arms at the station two years ago and promised he'd come back—to me.

HACK: Yeah, well, the same guy didn't come back. It is my fault that a cock-eyed world blasted a lot of silly dreams out of my head? Is it my fault that for the rest of my life I'll have blood and battle and butchering murder on my mind?

| | |
|---|---|
| SANDRA: | (FLARING UP) Yes! Yes, it is your fault, because you won't do anything to forget it. Thousands of men are going through the same thing. And if they all come back like you. Then, what they fought for, will die along with your dreams. Wars have come and gone for centuries, Hack, but, the decent things like love and devotion have managed to outlive all wars. But, it's not people like you who save the decent things; it's those who can put aside the horror, once it over—and—and try to pick things up on an even keel again. But, I guess you wouldn't understand that. All you've come back with is a stupid idea in a hard head full of bitterness. |
| HACK: | That's a pretty childish display of emotion, Sandra. |
| SANDRA: | Maybe a little childish emotion is what the world needs. |
| HACK: | Getting this world straightened out is no job for kids. |
| SANDRA: | (NEAR TEARS) All right. Go and straighten it out your way. But, when you have it all straightened out, and you find that you don't fit, you just don't belong. Remember this . . . while you've been building this—this wall of bitterness around you, you will have hurt yourself a great deal. But you will have hurt someone else, too, someone who used to love you very very much. Remember that, Hack! |
| HACK: | I'll remember. As a matter of fact, of all the past, I'm finding that the hardest to forget. |
| SOUND: | *FOOTSTEPS FADE OFF-DOOR OPEN AND CLOSE OFF* |
| SANDRA: | (SOBS) |
| SOUND: | *SOFT FOOTSTEPS FADE IN* |
| SKIP: | What's the matter, baby? |
| SANDRA: | Oh, Skip . . . Skip . . . . |
| SKIP: | The big lug let you down? |

SANDRA: It's awful. What's happened to him?

SKIP: Like I've told you, he's a dope!

SANDRA: He—he used to be so different.

SKIP: I—I don't suppose this is any time to bring it up, but I don't know what else to say except that if I could step into his place, you know there's nothing I'd rather do.

SANDRA: You're sweet, Skip.

SKIP: That's as far as it goes, huh?

SANDRA: Please, Skip, I—

SKIP: Never mind, baby. I'm just a common lug. I should have known better than to bring it up. I—I heard somewhere, about catchin' people on the rebound. But, I guess that was just in a story.

SANDRA: Sorry, Skip. Maybe I just didn't bounce high enough.

SKIP: Then, I guess you never will. At any rate, I don't want to be around if you ever get tossed hard enough to make you bounce any higher.

SANDRA: Skip—I—*(BURSTS INTO TEARS)*

SKIP: *(CONFUSED)* Well, gosh! I mean, Gee San, cut it out will ya? Holly cats, I didn't mean to say anything that'd make it worse. I—

SANDRA: *(CHOKING BACK TEARS)* It's all right, Skip. Just lost control for a minute. Nervous tension I guess. I'll be all right now.

SKIP: Sure. You'll be all right. I've never seen the person yet that could get you down.

SANDRA: That's right. And I don't intend to start with him. The best thing we can do about Hack is to forget that he's anything

|          |                                                                 |
|----------|-----------------------------------------------------------------|
|          | but a good cop and let it go at that. Come on, Skip, we've got a paper to put to bed. |
| MUSIC:   | (TO TAG)                                                        |
|          | CLOSING ANNOUNCEMENT:                                           |
| CUTTING: | Ladies, do the three square meals that you serve your family each day supply them with all the vitamins they need for general good health? That's a hard question to answer, even if you try your best to serve balanced meals. But there won't be any doubt at all about their guaranteed intake of EIGHT different vitamins, IF you give each member of your family a single One-A-Day Brand Multiple Vitamin Capsule each day. Laboratory tested for purity, potency-guaranteed—each small economical One-A-Day Brand Multiple Vitamin Capsule is so vitamin rich that a single capsule supplies a person's full basic daily requirements of all the vitamins whose requirements are known. Why then run the risk of such conditions as nervous fatigue, or lowered resistance to colds, or a general run-down condition resulting from a lack of sufficient vitamins? Just ask your druggist for One-A-Day Brand Multiple Vitamin Capsules, by Miles Laboratories. Remember, the brand with the big "One" on the blue package is the "One" to buy. At all drug stores. |
| MUSIC:   | (THEME—ESTABLISH AND FADE UNDER)                                |
| ANNCR:   | Can Sandra gain peace of mind in her work alone, or has her love for Hack been so firmly established that she will find it impossible to look upon him purely as a business associate? Be sure to tune in tomorrow when our, "LADY OF THE PRESS" starts carrying her burden alone in episode four of "A PICTURE OF DEATH." |
| MUSIC:   | (THEME UP AND UNDER)                                            |
| ANNCR:   | "Lady Of The Press" is written by Dwight Hauser, and produced by Gordon T. Hughes, and is brought to you each day, Monday through Friday at this same time, by the makers of Alka Seltzer. |

MUSIC: *(THEME TO FILL)*

ANNCR: This is CBS. THE COLUMBIA BROADCASTING SYSTEM.

# EPISODE #4

# "PICTURE OF DEATH"

| | | |
|---|---|---|
| SPONSOR: | ALKA SELTZER | MAY 4, 1944 |
| AGENCY: | WADE  4:00—4:15 PM, PWT,P | |

---

ANNCR: The makers of Alka Seltzer present—"LADY OF THE PRESS"

MUSIC: (STING) (QUICK PUNCTUATION)

ANNCR: The adventures of Sandra Martin, radio's newest romantic-mystery serial!

MUSIC: (THEME-ESTABLISH AND FADE OUT:)

OPENING ANNOUNCEMENT:

CUTTING: If you listeners can spare fifty seconds right about now, I have something that'll be mighty interesting to those of you who might be called "fifty percenters." Here's what I mean. Maybe you find that you have only about fifty percent of your usual energy—you tire more easily than usual. Maybe you get kinda cross and irritable—get less enjoyment out of life than you should because you're oh, just "below par." Well, if this is your case, it might be that your diet isn't supplying you with sufficient B-vitamins. And if that's true, you're just the one who ought to get acquainted with One-A-Day Brand Vitamin B Complex Tablets. Try the One-

A-Day way. If you're low in B Complex vitamins, they'll make a difference. And remember you don't have to take them three or four times a day. Just one tablet each day and the job is done. That single tablet makes for economy too. Actually, One-A-Day B-Complex Vitamins cost you only two and one-half cents a day, when you buy the large $2.25 size package. Ask your druggist for them right away. Look for the big one and the name Miles Laboratories on the GRAY package—One-A-Day Brand Vitamin B Complex Tablets. At all drug stores.

MUSIC: (THEME UP AND UNDER)

ANNCR: And now, "Lady Of The Press" and episode four of "The Picture Of Death."

MUSIC: (QUICK FIGURATION AND UNDER FOR)

ANNCR: Hurt and disillusioned by her failure to rekindle any part of the previous feeling between herself and Hack, Sandra decides to try and forget that he was the man who once had all her love. Were it possible to stop seeing Hack, her task would be much easier, but, Sandra has been caught inadvertently in a situation which may implicate her in the murder of Frances Evers. And in order to clear herself, it is necessary that she work with the police in trying to apprehend the real murderer, Elbert Hoagan. Hack's position, as ace criminologist on the Homicide Squad, throws them together on the case much more often than Sandra would choose. However she realizes the importance of case and is doing her best to work with Hack to solve it.

SOUND: TYPEWRITER

SKIP: Workin' on somethin' hot, San?

SANDRA: As hot as I care for.

SKIP: What is it?

SANDRA: Some copy on Hoagan. It's for my files. I'll want to use it as soon as Hack will let us break the story.

SKIP: What do we always have to wait for him for? I still have the negative of that shot showin' the reflection of Hoagan with the gun in his hand. Why don't you write a story and we'll run the picture right alongside? With the circulation we've got, somebody's sure to recognize him from that picture.

SANDRA: ~~Hack~~ [Lt. Taggart] doesn't want Hoagan to be tipped off about that picture. He says as long as Hoagan thinks ~~we have the only clues~~ [we're the only source of evidence against him], he'll try to contact us.

SKIP: Lt. Taggart—~~is~~ [He's] nuts!

SANDRA: He's been right so far. Hoagan contacted me. Now, all we have to do is wait for him to try you. But, if we print that story and picture, he'll lay low and be that much harder to catch.

SKIP: You know somethin'? I'm glad I'm not a cop. All I have to do, to finish a job, is set up a tripod, focus a lens, flash a bulb, and presto! I got it . . . all the dope, accurate and finished. But, a cop, all he can do is try and out-guess another guy, usually a guy with more brains than he's got.

PAUSE

SANDRA: Why, Skip . . . you sound like a philosopher.

SKIP: Oh, I <u>am</u>, baby. Didn't you <u>know</u>?

SANDRA: <u>That</u> is a quality of your personality which, up to now, you have kept successfully hidden from me.

SKIP: Now you know I never hid anything from <u>you</u> in my life.

SANDRA: No?

SKIP: Of course not.

SANDRA: Then what about that phone call you got this morning?

SKIP: Phone call? What are you talking about?

SANDRA: Don't play dumb. Skip. I know you got a call. Betty told me about it when I came in this morning.

SKIP: Leave it to that blabby [telephone] operator to broadcast everybody's business.

SANDRA: Then you <u>admit</u> you did <u>get</u> a call?

SKIP: Yeah. Some guy called. Wanted a picture made for some story.

SANDRA: He didn't leave his name by any chance?

SKIP: No. No, he didn't.

SANDRA: Then how are you going to meet him?

SKIP: I didn't say I was.

SANDRA: Oh, come off it, Skip. I know what's on your mind. You think it was from Hoagan, and you're planning to meet him alone.

SKIP: Why Sandra, your attitude hurts me—deeply.

SANDRA: Yes. I'll bet it does. Nevertheless, that's what's on your mind, isn't it?

SKIP: Well, maybe so. But, I don't see any reason for draggin' the whole staff of the Courier, along with our very inefficient police force down there with me. I think I can handle it pretty well all by myself.

SANDRA: Stop playing detective. You're a top photographer and I wouldn't want anything to happen to you. Hack will handle the law enforcement, and you and I will just go along for the story.

SKIP: Leave it to a couple of babes to bust up a guy's party. Someday, I'm gonna—

| | |
|---|---|
| SOUND: | *KNOCK. DOOR OPENS QUICKLY* |
| SKIP: | Don't shoot, officer! I'll put the bananas back on the stand. |
| HACK: | Oh, you here. I was hoping I'd be spared your brilliant repartee this morning. |
| SKIP: | The best way to avoid that is stay away from the Courier. |
| SANDRA: | All right, boys, lay your swords down. |
| HACK: | Well, he burns me. |
| SKIP: | And I suppose you think you positively <u>delight</u> me? |
| HACK: | I'll <u>destroy</u> you! |
| SANDRA: | *(ANGRY)* Did you hear me? Honestly, you two act like a couple of school kids. |
| HACK: | Sorry. |
| SANDRA: | Well that's better. What's on your mind? |
| HACK: | Just dropped in to see what the latest developments are. |
| SANDRA: | I'm not sure. But, we <u>may</u> have something. Skip got a phone call. Some fellow wants his picture taken. |
| HACK: | Lots of people want their picture taken. |
| SANDRA: | Yes, but this looks a little phony. Usually, the procedure is to call the paper. Then a reporter is assigned to the story if it's worth anything. But, this guy called Skip direct. |
| HACK: | That ever happen to you before? |
| SKIP: | Naw. |
| HACK: | That makes it look a little different. Think it was Hoagan? |

SANDRA: It's a thought.

HACK: You talked to him, Skip?

SKIP: U-huh.

HACK: Sound like Hoagan?

SKIP: How, should I know?

HACK: You knew Hoagan, didn't you?

SKIP: Sure.

HACK: If I'm not mistaken he had a very distinctive style of speech. That right, Sandra?

SANDRA: Yes. If Skip talked to him he'd have recognized his voice. I'm sure of that. Well, Skip, what about it? ~~Going to come along with us on the deal, or not~~?

SKIP: Okay. Big Hearted Skip, they call me. Once in a lifetime an opportunity for a photographer to break a story comes along [and Bang!] Boy! I have to toss it right into the laps of the cops. ~~Okay~~ [Alright] So it was Hoagan. I knew it when I was talkin' to him, but I didn't let on to him that I did.

HACK: Great. When are you to meet him?

SKIP: Four o'clock tomorrow afternoon. Room 643 in the Alto Hotel.

HACK: Now, we're getting someplace. Well, maybe we can fix up a little surprise for Hoagan tomorrow. Maybe we can arrange to take a lot of pictures of him.

SANDRA: Wonderful! But it seems to me we have a lot of work cut out for us between now and four o'clock tomorrow afternoon.

HACK: What?

SANDRA: Well, as far as I'm concerned there's a great deal more at stake in this case than the mere capture of Frances Evers' murderer.

HACK: Maybe so. But, most of the other elements in the case depend on his capture.

SANDRA: That's where I don't agree with you. There's a lot we could do between now and then.

HACK: Such as?

SANDRA: Such as trying to find out what connection Elbert Hoagan had with the people Frances Evers was about to expose. True we know Hoagan fired the shot which killed her, but, do we know what was behind it?

HACK: Do you?

SANDRA: Not now. But, I intend to find out.

HACK: Okay. I can't keep you from snooping in the case if you want to. But, if you'll take my advice, you'll let it lie as quietly as possible until we have Hoagan.

SANDRA: Well, I didn't exactly have in mind publishing all our suspicions.

HACK: And I don't intend having any, especially groundless suspicions. I'll take up the track after I've talked to Hoagan.

SANDRA: Okay. But, don't blame me if a really important case turns out to be just another murder because you refuse to recognize the implications.

HACK: I'm not in the habit of blaming things on to you . . . or anyone else.

SANDRA: Get out your camera Skip.

SKIP: Yeah? What for?

SANDRA: Thought you might like a picture of a self-sufficient man.

HACK: Cut it. Save the mental exercises for tomorrow afternoon. Now, here's what I want: you go to the Alto tomorrow just as you've planned. Take your camera along and go right up to 643. I'll have a couple of the boys stationed there. Sandra and I will be watching. As soon as we see you go in, we'll follow and make the arrest. That clear?

SKIP: Perfectly.

HACK: All right. Keep quiet and both of you meet me here at three o'clock tomorrow afternoon.

SKIP: Right.

SANDRA: We'll be here.

HACK: Okay. And I hope your scoop complex doesn't get the better of your judgment in the meantime.

SOUND: FOOTSTEPS—DOOR OPEN AND CLOSE

SKIP: Just a big dumb cop. That's all he is.

SANDRA: Scoop complex. I'll show that big—that—!

SKIP: Yes, I'm waiting for the words I love to hear. Go ahead baby. Say it. What were you going to call him?

SANDRA: At the moment I can't think of an adequate adjective.

SKIP: Maybe I can help. I've thought of a lot of words for him.

SANDRA: Yours wouldn't express my feelings for him.

SKIP: Okay. Suppose we forget the whole thing. Suppose we do it while takin' on a steak at Smitty's and then a show?

| | |
|---|---|
| SANDRA: | Sorry, Skip. Won't have time. |
| SKIP: | Why is it that you always manage to be busy when I want to go out with you? |
| SANDRA: | You _are_ going out with me, Skip. |
| SKIP: | Huh? What we going to do? |
| SANDRA: | We're going to try and dig up the evidence Frances Evers had on the Black Market Operators. If we find it, I think by the time Hoagan is arrested, we'll know _why_ she was murdered, as well as _who_ did it. |
| MUSIC: | (BRIDGE) |
| SOUND: | RATTLING OF DRAWERS—SHUFFLING PAPERS |
| SKIP: | I don't know. I don't think I like this business. Going through the possessions of a dead girl. |
| SANDRA: | Well, where else would you start looking for the evidence? |
| SKIP: | If I had my choice I wouldn't. |
| SANDRA: | She must have kept some records someplace. Surely she wouldn't have relied completely on memory for all the dope. |
| SKIP: | Maybe she didn't keep it in her own home though. |
| SANDRA: | Maybe not. But, until we've looked we can't be sure. |
| SOUND: | FOOTSTEPS APPROACHING FROM OUTSIDE THE ROOM |
| SANDRA: | Listen. One of the servants' coming. Pretend to be busy with your camera. |
| SKIP: | (SOFT VOICE) Yeah. I'm all set. |

SANDRA: If they come in, don't forget we came here to take pictures. For heavens sake don't let on as though we're doing anything else. (PAUSE)

SOUND: FOOTSTEPS UP-CONTINUE ON DOWN HALL. FADE OFF

SKIP: (WHISTLES) Why couldn't I have been a powder monkey or a fireman or something less exciting on the nerves?

SANDRA: Nevermind the philosophy. We have to hurry. After all, the servants know it wouldn't take all night to get a few shots of her room.

SOUND: RATTLING OF DRAWERS AND PAPERS

SANDRA: Find anything in that dresser drawer?

SKIP: Naw. Just a bunch of letters . . . all tied up in pink ribbons.

SANDRA: Probably a good story there. Unrequited love or something.

SKIP: What do you mean <u>unrequited</u> love?

SANDRA: Oh, it means when you love somebody and that love isn't returned. You wouldn't understand that.

SKIP: Oh. No. I guess you're right. I wouldn't.

SANDRA: Hey Skip, come here.

SOUND: A FEW STEPS

SKIP: Yeah? What is it?

SANDRA: I think we've found what we're looking for. Look. A folder marked . . . B.M.R.

SKIP: Well, open it.

SANDRA: I am. (READS) Records of investigation of Black Market Ring, as carried on by the Young Women's league For Progressive Government. Skip, this is it! This is—

MAN: *(MUG)* I'll take that, Sister.

SANDRA: *(STARTS)* What—who—who are you? How'd you get in here?

MAN: Through the door. I opened it nice and quiet-like, while you was rifling Miss Evers' personal papers. All right. Hand over them papers.

SANDRA: Why—I'll do nothing of the sort. How do I know who you are?

MAN: You don't… ~~But~~ [Maybe] this may help you to understand that I mean business.

SKIP: Better give it to him, San. That gun has a very persuasive look.

*MUSIC:* *(TO TAG)*

CLOSING ANNOUNCEMENT

CUTTING: Friends, do you have what is known as "hidden hunger?" Sure you probably put away enough food every day to satisfy your appetite—but does that food supply enough of the B Complex vitamins you need for normal energy, steady nerves, good digestion? Too many of us don't get enough of these vitamins from natural sources. So be sure of YOUR B Complex vitamins by taking a single, easy to remember One-A-Day Brand Vitamin B Complex Tablet daily. That single tablet is so rich in these vitamins that it supplies your full basic daily requirements of all the B vitamins whose requirements are known. And the cost is much lower than you'd expect to pay for other brands requiring three or four tablets a day. But remember, there are now three kinds of high-quality, potency-guaranteed One-A-Day Brand Vitamins at your druggists. When you want the B Complex Vitamins, ask for the gray package with the big "One" and the name Miles Laboratories. You may pay more but you can't buy any better.

| | |
|---|---|
| MUSIC: | (THEME. ESTABLISH AND FADE UNDER) |
| ANNCR: | Having finally gotten possession of the evidence file on the Black Market, Sandra now finds that this is the very thing which puts her life in more danger than ever. Be sure to tune in tomorrow when our "Lady of the Press" decides whether to give up the file or try and make a break for it in episode five of "The Picture Of Death." |
| MUSIC: | (THEME UP AND UNDER) |
| ANNCR: | Lady Of The Press is written by Dwight Hauser, and produced by Gordon T. Hughes and is brought to you each day, Monday through Friday at this same time by the makers of Alka Seltzer. |
| MUSIC: | (THEME TO FILL) |
| ANNCR: | This is CBS. THE COLUMBIA BROADCASTING SYSTEM. |

# EPISODE #5

# "PICTURE OF DEATH"

| | | |
|---|---|---|
| SPONSOR: | ALKA SELTZER | FRIDAY, MAY 5, 1944 |
| AGENCY: | WADE  4:00—4:15 PM, PWT, PN | |

---

ANNCR: The makers of Alka Seltzer present—"LADY OF THE PRESS"

MUSIC: *(STING) (QUICK PUNCTUATION)*

ANNCR: ~~The~~ Adventures of ~~Sandra Martin,~~ radio's newest romantic mystery serial!

MUSIC: *(THEME-ESTABLISH AND FADE OUT:)*

OPENING ANNOUNCEMENT

CUTTING: I wonder how many of you folks are letting a vitamin deficiency keep you from being your normal smiling self, with the vitality and steady nerves Nature intended you to have? That's a really personal question, I know, but I have a good reason for asking it. You see, now that Miles Laboratories' newest product, One-A-Day Brand Multiple Vitamin Capsules, are available at all drug-stores it's so easy and inexpensive to be sure you get your full basic daily requirements of all the vitamins whose requirements have been established—all in one capsule. Think of that for convenience—just one capsule, once each day. Not only does that make One-A-Day Brand Multiple Vitamin Capsules easy to remember to take, but also mighty inexpensive, in spite of the fact they are the very highest quality in vitamins that money can buy. So why run the risk of a vitamin deficiency and its consequences? Instead, ask your druggist for One-A-Day Brand Multiple Vitamin Capsules right away and give each member of your family their protective benefits. Look for the brand with the big "One" and the name Miles Laboratories on the new blue package.

MUSIC: (THEME-ESTABLISH AND FADE UNDER FOR)

ANNCR: And now, "Lady Of The Press" and episode five in "The Picture Of Death."

MUSIC: (STING AND QUICK FIGURATION ... FADE OUT UNDER)

ANNCR: Sandra Martin, star reporter for the Courier, went with Skip Williams, photographer, to the home of Frances Evers in search of evidence against the Black Market operators. She finds the papers which she believes will involve this ring in Frances Evers murder. Due to the quarrel between them, Sandra has not told Hack her plans. We know now that it would have been better if he were with her. Because before Sandra and Skip could leave the murdered girls room with the evidence a strange man stepped silently into the room ... with gun drawn, and said—

MAN: All right, sister. Cut the stalling and hand over that file.

SANDRA: Well, I suppose if you say so.

MAN: I do say so.

SANDRA: All right. Here you are.

| | |
|---|---|
| MAN: | Now, just so there won't be any slips, you two are going to take me out of here with you. |
| SANDRA: | But we don't belong here. We just came to get a story and—and some pictures. |
| MAN: | I know why you came. The servants won't suspect anything when we leave. That is unless you tip them off. And sister, if you make one false move, you're a dead pigeon. I'll have my hand on this gun until we're outside. And you better act like I'm supposed to be with you. All right, let's go. |
| SKIP: | Well, gee. [Wait a minute longer.] I mean, I better take my stuff. It would look kinda funny if I left it here. |
| MAN: | Okay. Get it together and come on. And no funny business. |
| SKIP: | Oh, don't worry about that. I'm a very serious-minded young man. Nothin' funny about me, especially when I'm facing the muzzle of a gun. |
| MAN: | And don't forget. It's a loaded gun. I'll have it in my pocket as we leave this house. It's up to you whether you leave walkin' or layin' down. |
| SANDRA: | You make yourself extremely clear. Well, ready Skip? |
| SKIP: | Yeah. Just as soon as I get this stuff picked up. |
| MAN: | Well, hurry up. |
| SKIP: | Okay. |
| SOUND: | *RATTLING OF PHOTOGRAPHIC EQUIPMENT* |
| MAN: | Come on—Come on. |
| SKIP: | All right, I'm ready. |
| MAN: | Walk in front of me and one on each side. I ain't warnin' you again. No funny stuff. All right, out into the hall. |

MUSIC: (BRIDGE)

SOUND: FOOTSTEPS ON PAVEMENT

MAN: So far, so good. Just keep on followin' instructions and you'll keep out of trouble.

SANDRA: What do you call this?

MAN: Why, this is a picnic compared to what may happen to you. All right, that's my car in front. Just walk out and get in like nothing was wrong.

SKIP: You must think you've captured a couple of actors.

MAN: Yeah, and you better be good ones.

SANDRA: We're doing our best.

MAN: Very smart. Just keep it up.

SOUND: CAR DOOR OPEN

MAN: In the back seat. Okay, get in.

SKIP: Coming.

SOUND: CLIMBING IN. CAR DOOR CLOSE

MAN: Okay, Joe, let's go for that little ride we were talkin' about.

VOICE: (DOUBLE) Okay, boss.

SOUND: CAR START. DRIVE AWAY. CONTINUE RUNNING. .UNDER

SANDRA: Look here, just where do you think you're taking us?

MAN: Just for a little ride. ~~Couldn't very well talk back there in that house... and I gotta few things to say to you.~~

SANDRA: ~~Well, why don't you say them.~~

MAN: ~~Okay... Lady... I just don't like to press business.~~

SANDRA: ~~Business?~~

MAN: ~~Yeah, business..... Somebody else's business that you been pushin' your nose in.~~

SANDRA: ~~My business is reporting for the Courier. If I happen to see a story in the murder of Frances Evers.... Then it certainly becomes my business.~~

MAN: ~~Sure... Only it happens that the way you're doin' it, makes it the business of some people who are a little shy of publicity.~~

SANDRA: ~~Yes, Black Marketing is one case where it doesn't pay to advertise. And of course you are referring to those chiselers.~~

SKIP: You have lost your marbles.

MAN: What d'ya' mean?

SKIP: You're ~~nuts~~ [crazy]! If you think you can get away with bumpin' off the Courier's star reporter and best photographer you're plain nutty.

MAN: I know my business.

SANDRA: But, he's right. Why, our paper knows where we went, and if anything happens to us, they'll comb the town to find the guilty party.

MAN: What's the matter with you two? In these days, I'd think you'd enjoy a nice ride.

SKIP: Yeah, but not the kind you got figured out!

MAN: You're takin' a lot for granted aren't you?

SANDRA: What do you mean?

MAN: I just want to have a little talk with you. Couldn't very well talk back there in that house, so, I thought I'd take you for a little ride. I got a few things to say to you.

SANDRA: Well then, say them and get it over with.

MAN: Okay, Lady. Only I just don't like to press business. Especially when you got such charmin' customers.

SANDRA: Business?

MAN: Yeah. Somebody else's business that you been pushin' your nose in.

SANDRA: My business is reporting for the Courier. If I happen to see a story in the murder of Frances Evers, then it's certainly my business.

MAN: Sure. Only it happens that the way you're doin' it, makes it the business to some people who are a little shy of publicity.

SANDRA: Yes, Black Marketing is one case where it doesn't pay to advertise. And, of course, you are referring to those chiselers.

MAN: I'm not saying. I'm only here to tell this much. You're barking up the wrong tree. The people you're trying to pin that murder on had nothing to do with it.

SANDRA: Then why are you so interested in keeping me from writing a story on it.

MAN: Because, you might stumble onto some things we wouldn't like you to know. You haven't got any evidence now. [Leave it right here] and you're much better off that way. Oh, all right. Joe. You can pull up now.

JOE: ~~Okay~~ [Right], boss.

| | |
|---|---|
| SOUND: | CAR SLOWS TO STOP |
| MAN: | Think it over sister. Whatever you pick up on the wrong trail of that murder can't be worth your career . . . or your life. |
| SANDRA: | I'll do the job my way if you don't mind. |
| MAN: | But we do mind. And if you keep on trying to do it the way you've started, well, then I'll just have to stop you from doin' it at all. Okay, Bud. Pile out. |
| SKIP: | Who me? You mean you're letting us go? We're free? |
| MAN: | Yes. Your company bores me. While on the other hand, the young ladies, well, I sorta hate to break off so sudden. |
| SKIP: | Now, look, you big lug. If you think I'm getting out of this car and leave her with you, you're nuts. |
| MAN: | Shut up! ~~Don't forget I got a gun!~~ [Unless you want a couple slugs in your belly] All right. Get out, both of you. |
| SOUND: | CAR DOOR OPEN. TRAFFIC SOUNDS UP. |
| MAN: | And there's really no use going on with your idea, especially now that I got all the evidence. *(SLIGHT LAUGH)* All right, Joe. Go ahead. |
| SOUND: | CAR PULLS AWAY |
| SANDRA: | Skip! Get the license. Get the— |
| SKIP: | I'm tryin' to see it. It's too muddy. Could you see it? |
| SANDRA: | No. Oh, darn! I'd give my right eye for that license number. |
| SKIP: | What makes you want that so bad? |
| SANDRA: | Don't you realize that that man has some connection with the Black Market Ring Miss Evers was going to expose? And don't you realize discovering the identity of the |

|          |                                                                                                                                      |
|----------|--------------------------------------------------------------------------------------------------------------------------------------|
|          | operators would establish the criminal guilt of the people behind the murder?                                                        |
| SKIP:    | Yeah. I understand all that?                                                                                                         |
| SANDRA:  | Then [certainly] you can see how important it was to find out who he was.                                                            |
| SKIP:    | Sure. But, I know an easier way than checkin' a license number.                                                                      |
| SANDRA:  | Oh you do?                                                                                                                           |
| SKIP:    | Yeah.                                                                                                                                |
| SANDRA:  | Well suppose you explain in simple terms that I can understand. Just how you'd go about establishing his identity.                   |
| SKIP:    | I'd take a picture of him.                                                                                                           |
| SANDRA:  | By remote control, I suppose?                                                                                                        |
| SKIP:    | No. As a matter of fact, I have a little item here, which, if you're at all interested in, I—                                        |
| SANDRA:  | Don't tell me you've got a picture of him, too?                                                                                      |
| SKIP:    | [Oh,] That I have, Lady. That I have.                                                                                                |
| SANDRA:  | Well, why do we fool around with a homicide squad when we have you to take pictures of all the criminals?                            |
| SKIP:    | That's a point about which I have often wondered. However, the important thing is that I do have a picture. Only this time, it wasn't any accident. |
| SANDRA:  | I don't see—                                                                                                                         |
| SKIP:    | Well, when he pulled that gun, it reminded me of the picture we got of Hoagan's reflection in that window.                           |

SANDRA: It reminded me of the same thing. And I don't mind telling you that I was afraid it was going to end the same way... with somebody killed.

SKIP: That's what I thought. So, I figured if there was going to be another murder, I might as well have another picture. Remember, I had my camera set up to fool the servants, so when the guy told me to get my stuff together, I swung the camera around so that he was in focus and presto, we got a negative of the guy.

SANDRA: Well, come on! What are we waiting for? Let's go develop it.

SKIP: Okay. But we better plan on some rest sometime tonight. We're facing quite a task [in that appointment with Hoagan] at four o'clock tomorrow afternoon.

MUSIC: (BRIDGE)

SOUND: FOOTSTEPS ON CORRIDOR

SANDRA: What time is it, Hack?

HACK: Three minutes to four.

SANDRA: This Alto Hotel isn't very classy.

SKIP: We better split up. Remember, I didn't make arrangements with Hoagan to bring company.

HACK: 641. His will be the next room down on the right. You go ahead. We'll give you five minutes alone, in case he may drop some evidence, then we'll be in.

SKIP: Okay.

HACK: And don't let anything slip. Don't forget the grand jury sits next week. And if we don't have Hoagan, both you and Sandra may have some tall explaining to do.

SKIP: I'm aware of that. You just hold up your end and I'll take care of Hoagan...

SANDRA: Be careful, Skip. Remember, he's killed one person. He'll not hesitate to kill another.

SKIP: Don't worry about me.

HACK: You still have that gun, I gave you?

SKIP: Yeah. It's right here.

HACK: Don't use it unless you have to.

SKIP: Don't worry. I never was very fond of loaded guns.

HACK: You may be glad there are bullets in it before you're through. All right, it's four o'clock. We'll stay back here out of sight. Get going.

MUSIC: (BRIDGE)

SANDRA: How long has he been in there?

HACK: Five minutes. come on.

SOUND: FOOTSTEPS

HACK: You stand back when I open the door. There may be shooting.

SANDRA: Oh, I hope not.

HACK: So do I. Bringing him in dead won't help clear you and Skip. That little matter is going to depend on mister Hoagan alive.

SOUND: FOOTSTEPS UP AND STOP

SANDRA: You don't have to tell me how important it is.

HACK: Okay. Stand back. Here goes.

SOUND: DOOR FLUNG OPEN

| | |
|---|---|
| HACK: | All right, Hoagan. Put up your—Skip, Sandra, come here. |
| SANDRA: | What? Skip, what's happened?. |
| HACK: | He's knocked cold. Quick, over there at the basin. Run some cold water on a towel. |
| SOUND: | *HURRIED FOOTSTEPS* |
| HACK: | He's pretty badly hurt. Nasty blow on the back of his head. |
| SOUND: | *RUNNING WATER* |
| SANDRA: | Then, Hoagan did frame him! |
| HACK: | That's what it looks like. |
| SOUND: | *FOOTSTEPS* |
| SANDRA: | Here's the wet towel. |
| HACK: | Thanks. Rub his wrists while I bathe his face. *(GRUNTS AS THOUGH LIFTING BODY)* Here, boy. Come on. Skip Snap out of it, boy! |
| ~~SKIP:~~ | ~~*(GROANS)*~~ |
| ~~HACK:~~ | ~~He's coming around…. Skip… Skip… Can you hear me?~~ |
| ~~SKIP:~~ | ~~Hoagan…… The man who took the file, Sandra… He had Hoagan bound and gagged…. Over by that door…. He was waiting for me. Had a gun…. Didn't dare call you…. He…. hit me…. *(GROAN)*~~ |
| ~~HACK:~~ | ~~Did you hear that, Sandra.~~ |
| ~~SANDRA:~~ | ~~Yes… It seems that our friends not only have the file of evidence but now they've kidnapped the one person that could clear Skip and me..~~ |
| SANDRA: | Is he seriously injured? |

HACK: Can't tell yet. Looks like he'd been hit with some heavy object.

SANDRA: Probably a gun. That Hoagan is a little guy. He couldn't stand up to Skip physically.

HACK: Well, somebody certainly did. Look at this bump.

SANDRA: It's close to the base of his skull, too. Dangerous spot for conclusion.

HACK: Turn the towel over.

SANDRA: All right.

HACK: Come on boy. Snap out of it.

SANDRA: Oh, we should never have let him come in here by himself.

HACK: That was the only chance of getting Hoagan to show his hand.

SANDRA: Well, he's certainly done a good job of showing it now.

HACK: Skip. Skip, boy. Try and snap out of it.

SKIP: *(GROANS)*

HACK: Oh! He's coming around. Skip. Skip. Can you hear me?

SANDRA: Oh, thank heaven.

HACK: Can you understand me Skip? It's Hack.

SKIP: Hoagan . . . the man who took the file, Sandra.

SANDRA: Yes—yes?

SKIP: He had Hoagan bound and gagged. Over by that door. He was waiting for me. He had a gun. Didn't dare call you. He—he slugged me. *(GROAN)*

HACK: Did you hear that, Sandra?

SANDRA: Yes. It seems that our friends not only have the file of evidence—but now they've kidnapped the one person that could clear Skip and me.

HACK: That's right. And they know that as long as they hold him, you'll face the grand jury on the charge of murder.

MUSIC: (TO TAG)

CLOSING ANNOUNCEMENT:

CUTTING: Friends, here is something worth knowing about One-A-Day Brand Multiple Vitamin Capsules… Did you know they can be the means of helping you enjoy a more active, healthy, happy life? Strong words, but true. You see in order to feel your best, you must get—among other things—plenty of vitamins—because vitamin deficiencies can lead to such conditions as nervous irritability, undue fatigue, lowered vitality and lowered resistance to colds. Now since all to many of us don't get enough vitamins from natural sources, it will pay you to start taking a single One-A-Day Multiple Vitamin Capsule each day. Just one easy-to-take, easy-to-remember, vitamin rich One-A-Day Capsule each day and you get your full basic daily requirements of all the vitamins whose requirements are known. So for all around protection against vitamin deficiencies, ask your druggist for One-A-Day Brand Multiple Vitamin Capsules. They come in the BLUE package with the big "One" and the name Miles Laboratories.

# EPISODE #6

# "PICTURE OF DEATH"

| | | |
|---|---|---|
| SPONSOR: | ALKA SELTZER | MAY 8, 1944 |
| AGENCY: | WADE 4:00—4:15 PM, PWT, PN | |

---

| | |
|---|---|
| ANNCR: | The makers of Alka Seltzer present—"LADY OF THE PRESS" |
| MUSIC: | *(STING) (QUICK PUNCTUATION)* |
| ANNCR: | The adventures of Sandra Martin, radio's newest romantic-mystery serial! |
| MUSIC: | *(THEME-ESTABLISH AND FADE OUT:)* |
| CUTTING: | I wonder how many of you folks are like a friend of mine. He tried to tell me that he didn't need any One-A-Day Brand Vitamin B-Complex Tablets because, as he put it, "he wasn't sick." Well, actually, you don't have to be sick to need B-Complex vitamins. But if your food doesn't supply you with enough of these vitamins, the deficiency can cause you to be nervous and irritable, to tire easily, and to have certain digestive upsets. Thus, particularly these days when many vitamin-rich foods are hard to get, it will pay you to bolster up your diet with a single One-A-Day |

Brand Vitamin B-Complex Tablet each day. That way you can be sure of getting your full basic daily requirements of all the B-vitamins whose requirements are known. And they cost so little—because it stands to reason that a single One-A-Day Brand B-Complex Tablet would cost you less than lower potency kinds that require you to take three or four tablets daily. So for the vitamins that can help you avoid jumpy nerves, that "always tired feeling," and certain digestive upsets, ask your druggist for One-A-Day Brand Vitamin B-Complex Tablets.

MUSIC: *(THEME ESTABLISH AND FADE OUT UNDER)*

ANNCR: And now, Lady Of The Press" and episode six, "The Picture Of Death"

MUSIC: *(STING AND QUICK FIGURATION FADES DOWN UNDER)*

ANNCR: Following the murder of Frances Evers, in their presence, Sandra Martin and Skip Williams have set out to track down the guilty parties in order to prove their own innocence. Hack Taggart, whose romantic interest in Sandra seems to have been cooled by bitterness, has been called to assist, and the three have gone to the Alto Hotel for Skip has gone into the appointed room, with Sandra and Hack waiting outside. Five minutes have passed, time enough for Skip to trap Hoagan. Now, Sandra and Hack enter the room to arrest the murderer. To their surprise they find the room unoccupied except for the prostrate form of Skip lying unconscious on the floor. Bringing him to, they learn that entering the room, he came face to face with a gun in the hands of the strange man who took the evidence file. And, that Hoagan had been sitting, bound, and gagged in a chair next to another door leading out of the room.

HACK: That was a nasty blow you took Skip.

SKIP: Yeah. My noggin feels like a block buster had gone off inside of it.

SANDRA: You're lucky to get off with your life, if you ask me.

SKIP: What I'm worried about is what happened to Hoagan.

HACK: That door . . . it leads to the next room, and the door out of it leads to the far corridor. Whoever that man, is, he wanted Hoagan. Obviously he's taken him out that way.

SKIP: Well what are you doin' here? Why don't you go after him?

HACK: No use. If he had Hoagan bound and gagged as you say, then it's obvious that he had laid his plans carefully. He's made his get away by now.

SKIP: You and your correspondence school. Don't you ever think of relying on facts instead of theories?

HACK: Just what facts would you have relied on?

SKIP: I'd have tried to overtake him when there was still time.

HACK: That's easy to figure out now. But, none of us had any idea of the turn things would take. We were exercising precaution against the possibility of Hoagan killing you. We weren't expecting him to be kidnapped.

SKIP: You think Hoagan was kidnapped?

HACK: Obviously.

SANDRA: But, why?

HACK: You don't realize it, I know, but, you're the victim of a recurrence of an old ailment.

SANDRA: What?

HACK: Nose trouble. You're always sticking your nose into things that get you in a jam.

SANDRA: That's not so. That's part of my job, and I try to do it well.

HACK: You've done it very well up to now. So well that you've given the Black Market operators three strikes against you already.

SANDRA: Just what are you driving at?

HACK: Just this. You've stirred up so much trouble for them, they're out to get you. Oh, they won't attempt to kill you. But, they've got Hoagan, and until we get him, you're faced with explaining your presence in the room which Frances Evers was murdered. They figure that will keep you busy enough to stop your efforts against them.

SANDRA: Well, they're going to be badly fooled. I'll crack that ring, if it's the last thing I do.

HACK: Then, you better get started. I have a feeling your time isn't going to be entirely you own much longer.

SANDRA: You mean that you'd—

SKIP: He means that he's just the kind of hard hearted flat foot that would lock up his own mother.

HACK: Somebody's going to have to face the Grand Jury. There's been a murder. You and Sandra are the nearest things to suspects that we have.

SKIP: But, you can't hold Sandra on a murder charge.

HACK: Nobody intends to. If she's charged with anything it will only be as an accomplice to the crime.

SANDRA: Oh, thanks.

HACK: That's all right. I know what both of you are thinking about me, but, don't forget you got yourselves into this. You can't rely on the police department for protection from everything.

SANDRA: No. I'm beginning to learn just how much to rely on the police department. You know as well as I that we had nothing to do with that murder.

| | |
|---|---|
| HACK: | Look Sandra, I'm only an officer. Judgment is up to the courts. My job is placing all the evidence before them. You and Skip are part of that evidence. What sort of verdict they reach is none of my business. |
| SANDRA: | You know something? Someday, something is going to crack shell of yours. When your heart breaks, it's going to make an awful blast. I just hope I'm around to see it happen. As a matter of fact, I wish I could be the one to do it. |
| *MUSIC:* | *(BRIDGE)* |
| HACK: | Got a few minutes, Mac? |
| MCDANISH: | Something on your mind, Taggart? |
| HACK: | Plenty. |
| MCDANISH: | Official . . . or private? |
| HACK: | It's official. But, there's a special way I'd like to handle it, and the reason for that is private. |
| MCDANISH: | Well, what's it all about? |
| HACK: | I know who Frances Evers murderer is! |
| MCDANISH: | You what? Then why in blazes ~~aren't you out trailing him~~ [haven't you brought him in]? |
| HACK: | Because . . . I don't want him picked up just yet. |
| MCDANISH: | Oh you don't? Now see here, Taggart, I'm the Chief Inspector of this bureau and we'll do things my way. If you know the identity of that criminal, it's your duty to apprehend him as quickly as possible. |
| HACK: | Well, all I know is who he is. I don't know where he is. And, all I wanted was to make my report to you without stirring up too much publicity. |

MCDANISH: Well, that's different. Naturally, any information will remain confidential as long as it suits the public good.

HACK: But, I couldn't very well make my report to you withholding what I know. And, now that you know it, I hope you'll have patience if it seems that ~~this criminal's apprehension~~ [the case] isn't progressing as rapidly as you think it should.

MCDANISH: I can't agree to out and out stalling in taking him into custody. What's your reason for this, Taggart?

HACK: I think we might catch a lot bigger fish, if we use this one for bait.

MCDANISH: Well, that's about as illusive an answer as I ever heard. However, you've always been a good man, Taggart. Your methods aren't very conventional, but I must admit you usually produce results. Take your time ~~as long as you~~ [but] don't slip up.

HACK: Thanks Mac. And don't worry. I won't slip.

~~MUSIC: (BRIDGE)~~

~~SOUND: NEWSPAPER OFFICE~~

MCDANIELS: This is one case on which we can't afford to slip, Taggart.

HACK: How does this one differ from any other? It's a murder, isn't it?

MCDANIELS: Sure. But, the circumstance of a murder being committed in the offices of the Courier put an entirely different complexion on this one.

HACK: I don't get the connection.

MCDANIELS: Well, for one thing, the Mirror hasn't raised enough of a howl to suit me. They're layin' for something. And, unless I miss my guess they're holding their fire until they can take a pot shot at us ~~along with~~ [as well as] the Courier.

HACK: That's typical of their type of journalism.

MCDANIELS: Whether you like it or not, you've got to agree that they'll do anything in their power to discredit ~~the Courier~~ [a rival paper]. Unfortunately, this time, any discredit will reflect on this department just as much as it does the Courier.

HACK: Well, don't worry about it much [Mack]. If things work out the way I plan, the Mirror will have a plenty hot story. And I will see to it personally that they scoop the Courier.

MUSIC: *(BRIDGE)*

SOUND: *NEWSPAPER OFFICE*

SKIP: H'ya Betty. San, here?

OPERATOR: She's in re-write. Shall I ring her?

SKIP: Naw. I'll just bust in on her. Maybe I can catch her up to something.

OPERATOR: It'll take a faster cookie than you to catch San Martin . . . at anything.

SKIP: Oh, yeah. Say listen, Baby, you better be pretty good to me. How do you know I haven't got a picture of you and the copy boy in a compromising pose?

OPERATOR: Will you get out of here and leave me alone?

SOUND: *SEVERAL BUZZES ON SWITCHBOARD*

SKIP: Sure, sure, Baby. But, you better pay closer attention to your work. You're lights are showin'.

SOUND: *FOOTSTEPS*

OPERATOR: You—you—get outa here. *(TRANS)* Good Afternoon—"Courier". *(FADING OUT)* Classified? One moment please. I'll ring it for you. Good afternoon—Courier. What is it please?

| | |
|---|---|
| SOUND: | FOOTSTEPS CONTINUE TO DOOR-DOOR OPEN CLOSE. OFFICE SOUND OUT |
| SKIP: | Hi San. What's up? |
| SANDRA: | Plenty, only I don't know where to begin. |
| SKIP: | Can I help you any? |
| SANDRA: | Maybe. I'm certainly going to need some help, now that Hack's deserted us. |
| SKIP: | I could have told you which way he'd go when the time came. |
| SANDRA: | I just can't believe it. I know he's changed a lot, but I did think the past would have meant more to him. |
| SKIP: | Nothin' means anything to him except just being a big shot. |
| SANDRA: | Well, worrying about him won't help us out of the spot we're in. We've got to dig up some evidence and dig it up fast. |
| SKIP: | What good does it do us to dig it up? As fast as we do, those mugs from the Black Market Ring snitch it. Look, they've got the file of evidence . . . and Hoagan. |
| SANDRA: | I know. But there's bound to be some way of getting more evidence against them. From all that Frances Evers said about it, I'm certain their activities are very widespread. |
| SKIP: | Probably too wide spread. |
| SANDRA: | Frances Evers and The Womens League For Progressive Government got it, didn't they? |
| SKIP: | Yes. I guess so. |
| SANDRA: | Then why can't we get it? |

SKIP: ~~Look San.... Frances Evers and a lot of unknown woman could get evidence in a thousand places that would be closed to you.~~

SANDRA: ~~Why so?~~

SKIP: ~~Because you're too well known in this town.... Why every operator in town would know you were after a story. You think they'd take a chance on exposing themselves to you?~~

SANDRA: ~~I don't expect them to hand me the evidence.~~

SKIP: ~~Then just how do you plan on getting it?~~

SANDRA: ~~Well... Miss Evers got it by each one of that group of women getting one small bit.~~

SKIP: ~~Sure.~~ That's a great idea . . . except for one thing.

SANDRA: What's that?

SKIP: Time baby. It takes time. Why, a person might have to go to a Black Market a dozen times, before getting concrete evidence.

SANDRA: I know that.

SKIP: And you also know that the grand jury sits one week from yesterday. If you had the dope on the Black Market ring by then, you could probably force the release of Hoagan. But, without it, you can be certain they'll use his absence to pin part of that murder guilt on us.

SANDRA: Oh, I know Skip. I know. It looks as though we'd run up against a blank wall.

SKIP: Yeah.

SANDRA: If we try to crack down on them, they'll hold Hoagan. If we don't, a Black Market Ring is going to continue sapping unity and strength of the home front.

SKIP: That's better than facing a murder rap!

SANDRA: Even so, I don't see how we can avoid going before the Grand Jury.

SKIP: It's not so much going before them that I'm worried about. It's going before them without Hoagan.

SANDRA: Well, there doesn't seem to be much we can do about that now. But after the hearing, if that gang of thieves see we've let up on them, maybe they'll release him.

SKIP: I can tell you a better way . . . if you're interested.

SANDRA: What's that?

SKIP: All you have to do is write a story . . . giving all the facts about the murder. Don't publish what you know about Evers Story; just make it look as though Hoagan had no one back of him. Write it in such a way that the Black Market Operators will know you've pulled in your horns ~~on them~~.

SANDRA: But . . . that would tip Hoagan on the evidence we have against him.

SKIP: Right, and get both of us out of the spot we're in.

SANDRA: But, it might also mean that Hoagan makes a get away.

SKIP: Take your choice. The real criminal escaping or the wrong people paying for the crime. Since we are those people, it shouldn't take too much figuring.

SANDRA: I guess you're right, Skip. It's stupid to keep fighting a losing battle. There doesn't seem to be any ~~other~~ way out except to write the story!

MUSIC: (TO TAG)

CUTTING: Have you ever had this experience, friends? Hundreds do every day. You decide that since you're working so hard nowadays, you want to be absolutely sure you get enough of the B-vitamins each day to maintain your normal energy, nerves and digestion. So, you go to your druggist to buy some B-Complex vitamins—but when you get there, you find he has so many different kinds, you don't know which one to buy. Well, here's a mighty easy, sure way to get all the guesswork out of buying vitamins. Just ask your druggist for the "number one" brand—One-A-Day Brand Vitamin B-Complex Tablets (in the gray package) because unit for unit, penny for penny, you can't buy a better

B-vitamin product. Nor, can you find another that can beat its single tablet convenience, pleasant taste and economy. Remember then, for the vitamins that help you maintain normal energy, nerves and digestion, ask your druggist for One-A-Day Brand Vitamin B-Complex Tablets. They come in the gray package and are made by Miles Laboratories. Look for the big "1" on the gray package.

MUSIC: (THEME ESTABLISH AND FADE UNDER)
ANNCR: Will Sandra sacrifice the secrecy necessary for the capture of Hoagan in order to clear herself of an implication in the murder? Can she keep up a fight against such strong opposition from the man she once loved? Listen again tomorrow as "Our Lady Of The Press" fights this battle of her conscience in episode seven of "The Picture Of Death"
MUSIC: (UP AND UNDER)
ANNCR: "Lady Of The Press" is written by Dwight Hauser, and produced by Gordon T. Hughes and is brought to you each day, Monday through Friday at this same time by the makers of ALKA SELTZER
MUSIC: (UP TO FILL)
ANNCR: This is CBS. THE COLUMBIA BROADCASTING SYSTEM.

# EPISODE #7

# "PICTURE OF DEATH"

| | | |
|---|---|---|
| SPONSOR: | ALKA SELTZER | MAY 9, 1944 |
| AGENCY: | WADE 4:00—4:15 P.M. PWT | |

---

ANNCR: The makers of Alka Seltzer present—"LADY OF THE PRESS"

MUSIC: (STING) (QUICK PUNCTUATION)

ANNCR: ~~The~~ [Thrills and] adventures ~~of Sandra Martin,~~ [with] radio's newest romantic-mystery serial!

MUSIC: (THEME - ESTABLISH AND FADE OUT:)

(OPENING COMMERCIAL MISSING FROM THIS EPISODE)

MUSIC: (THEME—ESTABLISH. AND FADE FOR)

ANNCR: And now, "Lady Of The Press", and episode seven in, "The Picture Of Death."

MUSIC: (STING AND QUICK FIGURATION FADING OUT UNDER)

ANNCR: Realizing that all her efforts to connect the black market ring with the murder of Frances Evers, and that as long as Elbert Hoagan, the guilty person, remains at large, she herself will be charged with complicity in the crime,. Sandra Martin has weighed her position carefully and reached a decision. It was not an easy decision to make, for, on the one hand, was her duty as a reporter and a patriotic citizen; and on the other, her personal position, untainted by suspicion of guilt. The other course, that of exposing the Black Market, seeming hopeless, Sandra has decided upon the course that will save her! Against Lieutenant Hack Taggart's wishes, she has determined to publish what she knows about the circumstances surrounding the murder. We find her now with Skip Williams . . . as she finishes the story.

SOUND:      TYPEWRITER. STOP. PAPER PULLED OUT

SKIP:      Finished?

SANDRA:      There it is.

SKIP:      Lemme see it, will ya?

SANDRA:      Sure. Sandra Martin's white paper. Girl reporter sells out public to absolve self from suspicion of Crime. Here you are, Skip.

SOUND:      RATTLE OF PAPER

SKIP:      *(READING)* The cold-blooded murder of Frances Evers has conclusively been solved! The evidence at hand has been in the possession of the writer for several days, but has been withheld in compliance with requests from the police. However, the time has come when the unquestionable guilt of Miss Evers Assailant must be brought to the attention of the public. By the indisputable evidence of a photograph of Elbert Hoagan, Society Editor of the Courier, holding the murder weapon in his hand, his unquestionable guilt is established. Although there has been much talk to the contrary it is believed by this source that Elbert Hoagan committed this act without accomplices . . . and without pressure from any group or other person . . . *(ELATED)* Hey! This is swell, San! This will do the trick in a breeze.

| | |
|---|---|
| SANDRA: | That is the dirtiest piece of journalism I've ever heard. It didn't seem so bad writing it, but hearing it read back I—I can't do it, Skip. I just can't do it. |
| SKIP: | Whata you mean you can't do it? It's done. |
| SANDRA: | Oh, no. It isn't. It's not turned in to the copy desk yet. And it's not going to be! Here, give it to me. |
| SOUND: | *RATTLE OF PAPER. TEARING OF PAPER* |
| SKIP: | Hey! Have you lost your marbles? Do you realize that that's your freedom you're tearing up and throwing in the waste basket? |
| SANDRA: | Maybe it is. But, that's exactly what I've done. |
| SKIP: | And just what do you think you'll do now? |
| SANDRA: | Now . . . I'm going to do what I knew I should have done in the first place. |
| SKIP: | And what's that? |
| SANDRA: | I'm going to stand my ground. I'm going to Hack Taggart and try to reason with him. Maybe I can get him to postpone our arrest long enough so that we can get that evidence. And if I can't, then we're going to stand up and <u>face</u> that Grand Jury. And we're going to keep on facing them until we crack this thing. And as for the story, you write it yourself. Headline it . . . TO THE BLACK MARKET . . . and tell them that Sandra Martin is out to get them. |
| MUSIC: | *(TO TAG)* |
| SANDRA: | You must realize that coming to you after what you said is not easy for me, Hack. |
| HACK: | I don't see why simply carrying out my duty should make any difference. |

SANDRA: No. I don't suppose you do. But has it occurred to you that carrying out your duty may deprive us of an opportunity to expose this vicious Black Market Ring.

HACK: That's pure guess work, Sandra. A belief that the Black Market operators had any part in Frances Evers murder is based purely on circumstantial evidence.

SANDRA: Do that rule it our necessarily?

HACK: No. Not entirely.

SANDRA: Then, why won't you let us continue?

HACK: I didn't say you couldn't continue.

SANDRA: But, you've threatened to take us into custody to face the Grand Jury.

HACK: Yes, but, that has nothing to do with the Black Market operations. You'll have to face the Grand Jury simply by virtue of the fact that you and Skip were in the room when Frances Evers was murdered.

SANDRA: But without Hoagan and proof of his motive, we won't stand a chance.

HACK: That's entirely up to the Grand Jury. If they feel the facts point strongly enough toward you and Hack as accomplices, then you'll be held for trial. On the other hand, you may be held only as material witnesses. Then again you may be completely exonerated.

SANDRA: And in the meantime, the Black Markets continue to do a flourishing business.

HACK: Until we have concrete evidence rather than suspicion, I'm afraid that's true.

SANDRA: (ANGRY) Just what do you call concrete evidence? Frances Evers was murdered just as she was preparing to expose them. When we tried to get the evidence, the file was stolen

|          | from us. Then the same man comes along and kidnaps Hoagan. What do you want? |
|----------|---|
| HACK:    | None of those things proves a positive connection between the Black Market Operators and the actual murder. And the case coming before the Grand Jury has to do only with the murder. |
| SANDRA:  | All right. So, let's say that legally, and as far as your duty goes, you're perfectly right. But—Hack—doesn't your duty as a citizen mean anything to you? |
| HACK:    | What has that to do with the issue. |
| SANDRA:  | You're in a responsible position, Hack. The people depend upon you to enforce our laws. |
| HACK:    | That's what I'm doing. |
| SANDRA:  | You're trying to enforce a law at the sacrifice of a much more important thing. Don't you realize how important this Black Market thing is? |
| HACK:    | It's not as important as murder. |
| SANDRA:  | Oh, isn't it? Did it ever occur to you that in some respects the Black Market isn't far removed from murder? |
| HACK:    | How did you figure that one out? |
| SANDRA:  | We have rationing so that our boys, fighting on the battlefields will have the stuff they need to protect themselves. If a lot of profit-mad chiselers here deny them that stuff, it may result in their deaths. And if that isn't murder, what is? |
| HACK:    | I don't know anything about that. I have a job to do. The course of duty is plain. All I can do is follow it. |
| SANDRA:  | But doesn't you personal interest in the welfare of the country mean anything to you? Don't you see what it could mean to you personally if you help crack this vicious thing? |

HACK: Look, San, personal matters don't count in this thing. If they did, do you think I could go through with it? Do you think I could remember—that last night before I left—and then place this on a personal basis?

SANDRA: We loved each other then, Hack. You meant the things you said on that night! You were a human being then!

HACK: Maybe I am different now. But don't think I don't remember.

SANDRA: I remember, too. We drove way up to Circle Pass. I remember you said you wanted to get as far from the earth as possible. It was foggy down in the city, but when we got there, the fog was beneath us.

HACK: *(SLIGHTLY SOFTER)* Yes. It was beautiful.

TECHNICIAN: *(BOARD FADE)*

SANDRA: Remember, you were holding me in your arms, looking down at me. I could see the sky and the stars off up beyond. *(AS SHE WAS THEN)* Hack . . . look at the stars. They're so bright . . . so shining . . . .

HACK: *(ROMANTICALLY)* So are your eyes, my darling. Big, beautiful eyes, looking up at me with all the wonderful devotion in the world.

SANDRA: Nothing can ever deny us this—this love tonight. Nothing! Can it, Hack?

HACK: Sandra, you really feel that way, don't you? I mean you're not scared of anything happening to me, are you?

SANDRA: Of course not, darling. Why I wouldn't love you so much if I thought a silly old Nazi or a Facist could ever hurt you.

HACK: That's my girl. All the bullets they're putting my name on have one of the "G's" left out.

SANDRA: In that case, you're a cinch. They certainly can't put your name on any bullets if they can't spell Taggart.

HACK: That's right.

*(BOTH CHUCKLE)*

HACK: Seriously though, San, when I do get back, well, you know I love you.

SANDRA: That's what you have led me to believe.

HACK: And . . . you know that I want to marry you?

SANDRA: *(SERIOUS)* Hack! Oh, Hack my darling, I—I thought you were never going to say it! I have been counting the days, afraid you'd put it off too long.

HACK: I've been thinking about it all the time, but—I—well, I couldn't seem to do it until now. But we only have a few hours. I couldn't go over without knowing. You'd be waiting for me when I got back.

SANDRA: Oh! I will be, darling. No matter how long, I'll be waiting.

HACK: And the day I get back—no, the very hour—we'll march down that aisle together.

SANDRA: *(STUNNED)* The day you get back?

HACK: Right. As soon as I get off the boat.

SANDRA: But Hack, why should we wait until you get back? Why can't we do it now . . . before you go?

HACK: Don't you suppose I want to?

SANDRA: Then, why not right now?

HACK: I couldn't bring myself to do that, Sandra.

SANDRA: But why?

HACK: Listen to me, darling. Maybe I won't come back as we expect. And, if I don't . . . I couldn't have you facing an obligation to go through with anything that might mean a handicap.

SANDRA: Hack, darling, how can you say such a thing? How can you even think it? There's nothing—absolutely nothing that could make me feel differently that I feel right this minute.

HACK: War has played some mighty queer tricks on people, darling.

SANDRA: Oh Hack, maybe your reasoning is sound and your arguments are logical. I don't know. But, I do know one thing . . . we're faced with something that all the reasoning and logic in the world won't overcome. I love you, Hack, and you love me.

HACK: Sandra darling. Don't you see how I feel? It's only because I love you so much that I can't let you in for what might be heartbreak and sorrow.

SANDRA: Don't you think my heart will break every day? Do you think the hurt will be any less because I know that you're out there alone instead of having marriage as a token of our love.

HACK: It's not that, Sandra. I want you . . . more than anything I've ever wanted in my life. But I want you when I come back, too. And I want you to want me then because we're the same to people we are now, not because you'll have an obligation to stick no matter what.

SANDRA: But can we risk the ties of our hearts between the two people we are now by taking a chance on what we'll be then?

HACK: We must, Sandra. But I promise you this: if it's possible under heaven for me to come back the same, I will. And I'll come back to you because you'll be the thing I'm fighting for. You and our love. And nothing will ever change that.

SANDRA: Oh, Hack, Hack, darling! I love you so.

HACK: Sandra!

(PAUSE)

HACK: No matter what happens, Sandra darling, nothing on earth will ever be as beautiful—as sacred. Nothing will ever take the place of my love for you.

TECHNICIAN: (BOARD FADE)

SANDRA: Can you remember that, Hack?

HACK: (FIGHTING EMOTION) Do you think I could ever forget it?

SANDRA: And remembering it, can you really say nothing's changed?

HACK: (SOFT) I—I don't know, Sandra. Right now, I truly don't know.

SANDRA: Is your bitterness capable of shutting out all that love we knew, Hack?

HACK: No. I've never shut out the memory, San.

SANDRA: But you can't live on memories alone, Hack. There's the present to think of. Right now. The present and future of us both is pretty much in your hands. What are you going to do about it?

MUSIC: (TO TAG)

(CLOSING COMMERCIAL MISSING FROM THIS EPISODE)

MUSIC: (THEME ESTABLISH. AND FADE UNDER)

ANNCR: Will the nostalgic memory of the love they have just recalled serve to break the recent between Hack and Sandra? Can Hack go through with what he considers

|  |  |
|---|---|
|  | hard, straight duty, against this girl whom he loves? Listen tomorrow when our "Lady of The Press" hears his answer in episode eight of "The Picture of Death." |
| MUSIC: | *(UP AND UNDER)* |
| ANNCR: | Lady of the Press is written by Dwight Hauser, and produced by Gordon T. Hughes and is brought to you each day, Monday through, Friday at this same time by the makers of ALKA SELTZER. |
| MUSIC: | (UP TO FILL) |
| ANNCR: | This is CBS. THE COLUMBIA BROADCASTING SYSTEM. |

# EPISODE #8

# "PICTURE OF DEATH"

| | | |
|---|---|---|
| SPONSOR: | ALKA SELTZER | MAY 10, 1944 |
| AGENCY: | WADE 4:00—4:15 PM, PWT PN | |

---

ANNCR: The makers of Alka Seltzer present—"LADY OF THE PRESS"

MUSIC: *(STING) (QUICK PUNCTUATION)*

ANNCR: The adventures of Sandra Martin, radio's newest romantic-mystery serial!

MUSIC: *(THEME-ESTABLISH AND FADE OUT:)*

*(OPENING ANNOUNCEMENT)*

CUTTING: You know, friends, a lot of folks have been surprised to learn in recent years just how important a part vitamins play in their everyday lives. For example, we have known for many years that doctors prescribed cod liver oil for babies and growing children—and now we are told that we grownups also need the protective benefits of these two important vitamins. But the trouble is that it's mighty hard to be sure we get enough vitamins A and D each day from food and sunlight to meet our needs. That's why we urge each and every one of you—children and adults alike—to bolster up your diet by taking a single One-A-Day Brand

Vitamin A and D Tablet every day. You see, each pleasant-tasting little One-A-Day A and D Tablet is so rich in these so-called cod liver oil vitamins that it supplies your full basic daily requirements. And because you take but a single easy-to-remember tablet each day, that brings the cost way down-actually, they cost just slightly more than a penny a day when you buy the large family size package. But be sure you get the genuine One-A-Day Brand Vitamin A and D Tablets. They come in the bright <u>yellow</u> package with the big "One" and the name Miles Laboratories. At all drug stores.

MUSIC: *(THEME ESTABLISH AND FADE DOWN UNDER)*

ANNCR: And now, "Lady Of The Press" and episode eight in, "The Picture Of Death."

MUSIC: *(STING AND QUICK FIGURATION FADES OUT UNDER)*

ANNCR: Going to Hack in desperation over the turn of circumstances regarding her involvement in the murder, Sandra Martin has turned in desperation to her former sweetheart, Hack Taggart. This seems to have re-awakened memories of their past love in Hack's mind. However unintentional on her part was the reason behind this, the results bid well for Sandra and Skip. Hack had previously told them determinedly that he intended bringing them both before the grand jury. As Sandra left him a few minutes ago, she felt certain that this re-awakened feeling would have a definite bearing on Hack's future attitude. It is a different Sandra who returns to the editorial rooms of the Courier a few minutes later to be greeted by . . . .

SOUND: NEWSPAPER OFFICE-SNEAK UNDER ABOVE

SKIP: *(CALLS OUT)* Hey, Sandra! San—

SANDRA: Oh, hello, Skip.

SKIP: San, can I see you a minute?

| | |
|---|---|
| SANDRA: | Sure. What's wrong, Skip? |
| SKIP: | *(FADING IN)* Nothing wrong especially, but, I just want to talk to you a minute. |
| SANDRA: | Well, go ahead, I'm listening. |
| SKIP: | Not out here. Come on in the re-write room a second. |
| SANDRA: | Okay. |
| SOUND: | *FOOTSTEPS* |
| SKIP: | There's nothin' so nosy as a bunch of news hounds. |
| SANDRA: | Naturally. That's their business. |
| SKIP: | Tell me one thing that they think isn't. |
| SOUND: | *DOOR OPEN—CLOSE—OFFICE SOUND OUT* |
| SKIP: | There. That's better. I wanted to know how you made out with our boy detective, only I didn't want to say anything out there. |
| SANDRA: | I think part of our worries are over, Skip. |
| SKIP: | Meaning? |
| SANDRA: | I think Hack's beginning to see the light. |
| SKIP: | "Our worries are over?" See the light?" Talk sense, will you? What did he say? |
| SANDRA: | He said he did remember. |
| SKIP: | Remember what? |
| SANDRA: | That he and I used to love each other very much. |
| SKIP: | *(DOWN)* Oh . . . I see. |

SANDRA: I don't think he'll go ahead with the Grand Jury business. I think he's going to give us the time necessary to get the evidence so we can expose the Black Market operators.

SKIP: Yeah. Well, gee, that's swell!

SANDRA: Yes, Skip. I think Hack's started back on the road to becoming the same wonderful guy that he used to be.

SKIP: Well, looks like this was where I came in.

SANDRA: I'm so happy, Skip! *(PAUSE)* Oh Skip, you know, I think that you're just about the best friend a girl ever had. I can always rely on you to understand and stand by me.

SKIP: Now, don't tell me I'm like a brother to you. I'm not interested in brotherly love. If I can't have the real kind, I'll do without.

SANDRA: I'm sorry, Skip. If there wasn't any Hack, well, maybe . . . .

SKIP: But, there is a Hack. A situation which has an entirely different effect on various people. Well, I don't suppose there's much sense in me sticking around any longer.

SANDRA: What are you talking about? You're not implying you'd desert at this point?

SKIP: You have to be signed up before you can desert, Sandra. Looks like I signed on the wrong line.

SANDRA: Stop it, Skip! You know how I feel about you. I wouldn't hurt you for anything in the world. That's why I've told you the truth. Because I know that the truth now won't hurt half as much as lies would later.

SKIP: Oh, you've been fair, San. It's not that. It's just that, well, I sorta got all the wind out of my sails.

SANDRA: Look, Skip, we're in the newspaper business. On top of that, we're in a spot. We're in it together, and we've got to see it through together. We need each other.

SKIP: Yeah. I know.

SANDRA: Okay then, let's dig into it, and forget that everything else isn't just the way one of us might like it.

SKIP: Sure, sure, I know. That's the way it has to be.

SANDRA: That's more like it. Now, suppose we check up on where we stand?

SKIP: That's already been done for us.

SANDRA: Been done for us? What are you talking about?

SKIP: Here.

SOUND: *RATTLE OF PAPER*

SKIP: Take a look.

SANDRA: The Mirror?

SKIP: Yep. Our competition scooped us.

SANDRA: *(INCREDULOUSLY)* What?

SKIP: Read it. Page one, column one.

SANDRA: *(READING)* In the matter of the murder of Frances Evers, these are the known facts: Frances Evers was shot while being photographed by Skip Williams, in the Offices of this city's "Other"—paper. Present was Sandra Martin, self-styled star reporter of this associated member of the fourth estate. [Hmm, neat little dig.] Up to and including the present time, that is the entire story. Nothing, so far as can be learned by the Mirror, has been done in the matter of questioning the two logical suspect . . . or in the matter of trying to identify the murderer. Police headquarters are as mum as our competitor on the matter. In the meantime, the citizens of this community impatiently await some gesture [on the part of the Police] that will at least indicate an interest in solving this vicious murder. *(WHISTLES)* Well, they didn't pull any punches, did they?

SKIP: Nope. They're sore. After all, we got a murder. What have they got?

SANDRA: A beef.

SKIP: And what is Lieutenant Hack Taggart going to have?

SANDRA: A beef from the chief.

SKIP: You ain't just kiddin'! When the chief sees this, he's going to hit the roof.

SANDRA: Darn! This would have to break just when I had Hack coming along.

SKIP: Well, you can rely on one thing: now, that the Mirror has started, they'll go to the bottom of the bag for dirt.

SANDRA: The worst of it is that there's plenty of them to go on if they ever find out just how deeply involved we are.

SKIP: And, if the Grand Jury ever gets hold of all the evidence against us, we're sure to be stuck.

SANDRA: That's true.

SKIP: Except for one thing . . . .

SANDRA: What's that?

SKIP: The photograph of Hoagan holding the gun. That would clear us.

SANDRA: Only of the actual murder. They might still hold us as accomplices. Besides, Hack doesn't want the picture brought out yet.

SKIP: Hack doesn't want it brought out? What's he think? That we'll go to trial in order to let him play around with his

|         | correspondence school detective theories? |
|---|---|
| SANDRA: | I don't see that the picture makes much difference to us anyway. What we've got to prove is that we got Frances Evers in the studio to make pictures of her and not to place her at the disposal of Hoagan. |
| SKIP: | And just how are we going to do that? |
| SANDRA: | Without Hoagan, I don't know. |
| SKIP: | Look, Taggart only has the print of that picture. I still have the negative. |
| SANDRA: | But, don't you see that that won't absolve us completely? |
| SKIP: | No. I guess your right. But, I'd a lot rather be suspected as an accomplice . . . than the actual murderer. |
| SANDRA: | Even if our innocence can be proved, we may still be held as material witnesses. |
| ~~SKIP:~~ | ~~Well…If you're so sure of Taggart's attitude….What are you worrying about?~~ |
| ~~SANDRA:~~ | ~~Just this…Hack doesn't know any more about the case than we do…… The question is not so much holding back evidence that we already possess…Rather, it's finding some way to prove that we weren't implicated…If we haven't any solid evidence to that effect…How do you expect Hack to have it?~~ |
| ~~SKIP:~~ | ~~I don't…But, just in passing….And speaking of implication, if the Mirror ever finds out we have that photograph and are keeping it a secret…we're cooked.~~ |
| ~~SANDRA:~~ | ~~What makes you think that?~~ |
| SKIP: | ~~Well~~ Yes. It's already hard to explain what we had to do with Evers, being in that room at the time of the murder. Now, we've got a picture of the murderer, which we refuse to publish, and, even though we didn't assist him in the murder, we're certainly helping him to avoid arrest. |

SANDRA: That's where I disagree with you. Withholding that picture is the one thing upon which Hack basis his hopes for Hoagan's arrest.

SKIP: Well, just in case that doesn't happen before the grand Jury sits, keep your eye open for a nice corner where I can set up a snap shot shop.

~~MUSIC: (BRIDGE)~~

~~SANDRA: The worst of it is that there's a plenty for them to go on if they ever find out we're holding out on that photograph.~~

~~SKIP: Yeah….Well, if that happens, and you hear of a good corner, for a snap-shot shop….lemme know.~~

MUSIC: (BRIDGE)

CHIEF: Well, Taggart what have you to say to this?

HACK: It's a shot in the dark. The Mirror simply printed that story in order to smear the Courier.

CHIEF: It seems to me that the Homicide Squad comes in for more of a smear than the paper.

HACK: Well, you know the Mirror. They represent all that's rotten in journalism. Give them any opportunity what-so-ever and they'll start taking pot shots at somebody.

CHIEF: That's all right with me as long as their pot shots are aimed at another newspaper. But when this bureau gets involved, it's time to act.

HACK: Just what do you suggest?

CHIEF: Action. Investigations. The arrest of some suspects. At least make it appear that we're trying to solve the crime.

HACK: Stirring up a lot of publicity won't help; it will only hinder us in our attempt to crack the case.

CHIEF: But, we have the public to think of, Taggart. A few more write-ups like this and I'll hear from the Mayor! The whole town will be on our necks. We've got to make some sort of a showing in this thing.

HACK: But if we do anything now, we'll simply be showing our hand to the criminal.

CHIEF: This is no time for philosophical theories, Taggart. This is time for action. Put out a round-up call for all the regular characters. Get 'em down here and do some questioning. Then, release a story to the press about the progress we're making.

HACK: It seems to me that the important thing is the apprehension of the criminal rather than the immediate impression we make on the public or the press.

CHIEF: Listen, Taggart, the public keeps us in our jobs, and the public opinion is largely formulated by the press. If we lose the support of the one, we lose the other.

HACK: And if we put everything we know in the papers, we lose our quarry.

CHIEF: Are you trying to say you refuse to follow the policies of this bureau?

HACK: No. I'm merely saying that results shouldn't be sacrificed regardless of Public Opinion.

CHIEF: That smacks very much of insubordination, Taggart.

HACK: Sorry. I didn't mean it that way. Naturally, if you insist on arrests, regardless of whether the evidence will substantiate them, well, we can make them.

CHIEF: I don't say arrests are necessary at present. But, certainly investigations are. And I intend to see that they're made. As long as you're in charge of the case, you'll follow that policy. If you don't, well, you might find yourself no longer in charge.

| | |
|---|---|
| HACK: | Okay. I'll do it your way. |
| CHIEF: | That's better. Now, let's see how things stack up. Know anything about the weapon? Caliber, make, and so on? |
| HACK: | No. The bullet has never been found. |
| CHIEF: | Make a complete penetration? |
| HACK: | Yes. |
| CHIEF: | Then, it must have lodged somewhere in the room. |
| HACK: | That sounds reasonable, but, there's no sign of it or of a bullet mark. |
| CHIEF: | You've been over the room thoroughly? |
| HACK: | ~~Certainly.~~ |
| CHIEF: | ~~But, you say the bullet did not lodge in the body.~~ |
| HACK: | ~~That's right.~~ |
| CHIEF: | ~~I don't understand what's happened to you Taggart. You used to be our best man before you went overseas…Now…Well, you don't seem to have hit your stride since you got back.~~ |
| HACK: | ~~Why do you say that?~~ |
| CHIEF: | ~~It's obvious to any detective…That bullet either lodged in the body…Or, it's somewhere in that room…..Lodged in a wall….or…..or someplace…...It's got to be….Seems to me you should know that.~~ |
| HACK: | ~~Logically….You're right….But, logic or not…It isn't there…I tell you.~~ I've been over every inch of that room. |
| CHIEF: | Well, go back and go over every quarter inch. All we know is that Frances Evers was shot. Now, the first thing to try and found out is . . . the identity of the gun she was shot with. |

| | |
|---|---|
| HACK: | Sure. I know that . . . if it can be done. |
| CHIEF: | It can, and you know it . . . if you'd just rely on the principles you once learned instead of a lot of silly ideas about catching a criminal through some mysterious withholding of evidence. |
| HACK: | Well, if you want to try and solve this case by the process of elimination, why not start by checking up on silencers? |
| CHIEF: | You think the murderer used a silencer? |
| HACK: | Nobody heard a shot fired. And there were at least a hundred people on the same floor. What do you think? |
| CHIEF: | Well, that's a start at least. Why do I have to go over these things with you as if you were a boy scout? |
| HACK: | Maybe I am enough of a boy scout to want to do my good deed for the day. |
| CHIEF: | Find Frances Evers' Murderer and you'll have done it. |
| SOUND: | *CLICK OF INTER-COM SWITCH* |
| CHIEF: | Inspector Brinson? |
| VOICE: | *(FILTER)* Yes? |
| CHIEF: | I want a report on every silencer in the city. Get me names and records of anyone with any connection with one. |
| VOICE: | *(FILTER)* Yes, sir. |
| CHIEF: | And hurry it up! It's on a murder case. |
| SOUND: | (CLICK OF SWITCH) |
| CHIEF: | Now, as soon as we get that, we can eliminate all except those who might logically have access to the Courier Office. In the meantime, you come with me. We're going over to the murder room and I'll show you how to track down a spent bullet. |

MUSIC:        (TO TAG)

MUSIC:        (THEME ESTABLISH FADE DOWN UNDER)

ANNCR:        If the bullet can be found and identified with the gun used by Hoagan, the Chief of the Homicide Bureau will also have the evidence against Hoagan. But, why does Hack insist on withholding what he knows? And, why does he insist that Sandra keep the story out of the papers? Listen tomorrow when our "Lady Of The Press" hits upon a new scheme in trying to round up the Black Market Ring, in Episode Nine of "The Picture of Death."

MUSIC:        (UP AND UNDER)

ANNCR:        "Lady of the Press" is written by Dwight Hauser, and produced by Gordon T. Hughes and is brought to you each day, Monday through Friday at this same time, by the makers of Alka Seltzer.

MUSIC:        (UP TO FILL)

ANNCR:        Dick Cutting speaking—

This is CBS. The COLUMBIA BROADCASTING SYSTEM.

# EPISODE #9

# "PICTURE OF DEATH"

| | | |
|---|---|---|
| SPONSOR: | ALKA SELTZER | MAY 11, 1944 |
| AGENCY: | WADE | 4:00 -- 4:15 PM PWT |

---

ANNCR: The makers of Alka Seltzer present -- "LADY OF THE PRESS"

MUSIC: (STING) (QUICK PUNCTUATION)

ANNCR: The adventures of Sandra Martin, radio's newest romantic-mystery serial!

MUSIC: (THEME-ESTABLISH AND FADE OUT:)

(OPENING ANNOUNCEMENT)

CUTTING: You know, folks, Nature never intended you to go through life feeling fagged out, nervous, irritable, troubled with poor digestion and colds because of a vitamin deficiency. Nature intended you to feel GOOD -- and today, countless thousands of people know how important it is to get, among other vital substances, plenty of vitamins to insure ~~them~~ against a vitamin deficiency and its consequences. That's why we're sure you'll want to join the swing to the new One-A-Day-Brand eight-in-one Multiple Vitamin Capsules. Think of it, friends. By taking a single -- remember, a single One-A-Day-Brand Multiple

Vitamin Capsule each day, you are sure of getting your full, basic, daily requirements of all the vitamins whose requirements are known. What's more, One-A-Day-Brand Multiple Vitamin Capsules are scientifically standardized for full potency, and are laboratory tested. Yet, the cost is amazingly low -- the sixty day size package of sixty capsules only costs two dollars. So for general all around vitamin protection, be sure to ask your druggist for the new One-A-Day-Brand Multiple Vitamin Capsules. They come in the blue package and are offered by Miles Laboratories. Look for the big "One" on the blue package.

MUSIC: (THEME ESTABLISH AND FADE UNDER)

ANNCR: And now, "Lady Of The Press" and episode nine in "The Picture of Death".

MUSIC: (STING AND QUICK FIGURATION FADING OUT UNDER)

ANNCR: Sandra Martin has not heard from Lieutenant Hack Taggart since early yesterday, when she left him believing he had [had] a change of heart and that he would do all he could to save her from facing the Grand Jury. In the meantime, Hack, because of his seeming negligence in duty, has been called on the carpet by his Superior, Chief Inspector McDaniels. McDaniels has made known his intention of exposing every conceivable clue connected with the case. He does not know, however, as we do, that Sandra, Skip, and Hack are in possession of a picture of Elbert Hoagan as he fired [showing him in the act of firing] the gun which killed Frances Evers. Believing she has things fixed with Hack, Sandra takes up once more the gathering of evidence for an [Sandra is now ready to take up once more her] expose of the Black Market.

SOUND: [BELL] MOTOR RUNNING

SKIP: What I don't get is why that Taggart won't let us bring out the evidence on Hoagan.

| | |
|---|---|
| ~~SANDRA:~~ | ~~Well....I don't know either. But, as long as Hack plays ball with us...I'm willing to play ball with him.~~ |
| ~~SKIP:~~ | ~~Just be careful he doesn't fan you.~~ |
| ~~SANDRA:~~ | ~~He won't. He's got a reason all right.~~ |
| ~~SKIP:~~ | ~~But, what....??~~ |
| ~~SANDRA:~~ | ~~Well, I think it's simply that he doesn't want to tip Hoagan or the Black Market operators on how much we know about either of them.~~ |
| SOUND: | DOOR BELL |
| SKIP: | *(WHISTLING)* |
| SOUND: | DOOR BELL RING AGAIN |
| SKIP: | *(TO HIMSELF)* Come on, San. What's the idea? Gonna sleep all day? |
| SOUND: | DOOR BELL RING. DOOR OPEN |
| SKIP: | Hi, San. |
| SANDRA: | Why, Skip, what on earth are you doing here so early in the morning? |
| SKIP: | Oh, I'm drivin' to work this morning. Just thought I'd drop by an' see if you wanted to ride. |
| SANDRA: | Well, that's sweet of you, Skip. I'll enjoy forgoing that bus ride, this morning. Come in, while I finish getting ready. |
| SKIP: | Thanks. |
| SOUND: | DOOR CLOSE |
| SKIP: | What's on the fire for us today, San? Anything hot? |

SANDRA: I wasn't aware that our last mix-up had cooled off any yet.

SKIP: No, I guess not.

SANDRA: From now on, we're both going to be pretty busy roundin' up evidence against those chiselers.

SKIP: Where do we start that?

SANDRA: I'm not sure yet. But, I am sure of one thing: now that we can count on Hack, it's going to be a lot easier.

SKIP: I wouldn't build any hope chest based on his support, if I were you.

SANDRA: Don't worry. If I know Hack, he'll be a lot different from now on.

SKIP: Yeah. If you know him. But, I got a hunch nobody knows him anymore, not even himself. I doubt if even he knows how he's going to act.

SANDRA: You misjudge him. After all, he's been through a lot. It's not easy for a man who's seen a war front to come back and settle down to the relative quiet of the home front.

SKIP: Quiet? Have you lost your marbles? I suppose nothing is so peaceful and quiet to you as facing a murder rap.

SANDRA: We're not facing a murder rap, Skip. We're not facing it because, with Hacks help, we're going to produce the evidence that will clear us, and in doing so, we'll have the evidence that will bottle up the Black Market Operators.

SKIP: Sounds good. Now all we have to do is make the little fairy tale come true. Where do you plan on starting to wave your magic wand?

SANDRA: Right under the noses of the Black Market Ring.

SKIP: That is providing you can find out who they are.

| | |
|---|---|
| SANDRA: | There's only one way, and that's to do it the way Frances Evers did it . . . get a lot of people digging up evidence. |
| SKIP: | Okay. If that's what we're facing, we better get going on account of that is going to take some time. |
| SANDRA: | All right. I'm ready. Let's go. |
| *MUSIC:* | (BRIDGE) |
| *SOUND:* | *MOTOR RUNNING* |
| SKIP: | What I don't get is why that Taggart won't let us bring out the evidence on Hoagan. |
| SANDRA: | Well, I don't know either. But, as long as Hack plays ball with us, I'm willing to play ball with him. |
| SKIP: | Just be careful he doesn't fan you. |
| SANDRA: | He won't. He's got a reason all right. |
| SKIP: | But, what? |
| SANDRA: | Well, I think it's simply that he doesn't want to tip Hoagan or the Black Market operators on how much we know about either of them. |
| SKIP: | That's all very fine. But, I'd rather have them tipped than to get indicted by the Grand Jury. |
| SANDRA: | Making public that evidence wouldn't affect that one way or the other. We know Hoagan is guilty. But we can't prove him solely guilty until he's caught. |
| SKIP: | Hey! I better get some gas. Look at that gauge. |
| SANDRA: | I'd rather not. Gas gauges discourage me, nowadays. |
| SKIP: | Here's a station. I'll get three gallons. |

SANDRA: You're supposed to use the same brand of gas all the time. This is one of those freak brands.

SKIP: I know, but, I can't help it. Any brand is better than running out.

SOUND: CAR PULLS TO STOP

SKIP: Hi? How's the gas situation today?

ATTENDANT: *(MUG TYPE)* How much you want??

SKIP: *(LAUGHINGLY)* Oh, just fill her up. I'm going for a drive in the country over the week-end.

ATTENDANT: Got a card?

SKIP: You mean a book?

ATTENDANT: I mean a card. Lemme see yer card. I ain't fillin' no tanks without a card.

SKIP: What d'ya mean, a card? I got a B book. What more do you—

SANDRA: Oh, what he means is we-we forgot our card. But, we can come back later for the rest. Why don't you just take three for now, dear? We can go back and get the card and then get the tank filled.

SKIP: Have you lost your marbles? I ain't—

SOUND: THUD OF SHOE LANDING ON SHIN

SKIP: *(IN PAIN)* Ooooo! Hey! Oh, oh, yeah. Yaah, I guess that would be better. Just gimme three for now. We'll come back later. Won't we, dear?

SANDRA: So silly of us to forget.

ATTENDANT: Okay. *(FADES OFF)* Only don't come around without it any more.

SKIP: Hey, what's the idea? You just about busted my leg.

SANDRA: *(SOTTO VOCE)* Be quiet, you idiot. Don't you realize where we are?

SKIP: Certainly. Fifty-two and York. Drive it every morning

SANDRA: No, I mean the place. Don't you get it? Don't you realize what this place is?

SKIP: Certainly. It's a service station.

SANDRA: It's a Black Market, you dope.

SKIP: Hey, maybe. Aw, I don't know. Maybe the guy just usually sells to regular customers.

SANDRA: I don't think so. If this isn't a Black Market, that guy's attitude is a very dark shade of grey.

ATTENDANT: *(FADING IN)* Okay. Anything else?

SKIP: No. That'll be all, unless you'd like to wipe off my windshield.

ATTENDANT: Are you kiddin'?

SKIP: No. It's got some water spots on it.

ATTENDANT: *(LAUGHS)* Hey, Mike! Get a load of this. This guy wants me to clean his windshield! *(LAUGHS UPROAROUSLY)*

SKIP: Well, what's so funny about that?

ATTENDANT: Look, bud, we don't wash no windows here. That ain't exactly your business. Now, gimmie the ticket and the dough and go wash your own windows.

SKIP: Well, okay, only, don't expect any more business from me.

ATTENDANT: (LAUGHS AGAIN)

| | |
|---|---|
| SKIP: | All right. Here. Fifty-four cents and one ticket. And, I don't like your attitude. |
| SOUND: | STARTER-MOTOR START |
| SKIP: | What kind of a business— |
| SANDRA: | Be quiet. Come on. Let's get out of here without attracting any more attention. |
| SKIP: | Well, if it's a Black Market, I thought that's what you were after. |
| SANDRA: | Certainly, but, you have to have proof. Come on. Pull away. |
| SKIP: | Okay. |
| SOUND: | CAR STARTS-GEARS SHIFT |
| SKIP: | I don't see why— |
| SANDRA: | Never mind about trying to understand things now. Take me down to the corner and let me out. |
| SKIP: | But, I thought you wanted to ride to work with me? |
| SANDRA: | I changed my mind. I'm taking a street car. |
| SKIP: | Well, gee, San. You don't need to get sore. As long as I'm going to the Courier anyway, you might as well ride. |
| SANDRA: | I'm not sore. And you're not going the Courier. I want you to pull up at this stop sign and park. Then keep an eye out for the cars that pull out of that station. When they come to this stop, you'll have a chance to get their license numbers. |
| SKIP: | What do you want of a lot of license numbers? |
| SANDRA: | I'd like to talk to their owners about a certain kind of card. |
| SOUND: | CAR STOPS |

| | |
|---|---|
| SANDRA: | Stick around until you get a dozen or fifteen. Then come on down to the office. |
| SOUND: | *CAR DOOR OPEN* |
| SKIP: | But—I— |
| SANDRA: | Never mind the objections. This is important. I'd stay myself except that I have an appointment at the paper. See you there later. |
| SOUND: | *CAR DOOR SLAMS SHUT* |
| MUSIC: | *(BRIDGE)* |
| SOUND: | *OFFICE SOUNDS OFF* |
| EDITOR: | This is the photographic studio boys. You have my permission to do anything necessary. I'm as interested in getting this thing cleared up as you are. |
| CHIEF: | Thanks, Wilson. Appreciate your cooperation. We want to have a look at a few things. |
| EDITOR: | Go right ahead. If there's anything I can do to help, feel free to call me. I'll be in my office. |
| CHIEF: | Thanks. |
| SOUND: | *DOOR CLOSE OFFICE SOUND OUT* |
| CHIEF: | Well, not much in the place. This is the way it was when you were called? |
| HACK: | Except for Skip Williams' camera and tripod. |
| CHIEF: | One chair. Dressing table. And a sofa. Did you go over all those for bullet marks? |
| HACK: | Everything. |

CHIEF: How about that window? Was it open?

HACK: It's built in. Doesn't open.

CHIEF: Then, what do they do for air?

HACK: Air conditioning. Here's the vent right over—wait a minute.

CHIEF: Yes. Just what I was thinking. Maybe that's where our bullet went.

HACK: Could be.

CHIEF: Okay. Get the janitor and have him take that mask off.

HACK: Sure.

SOUND: *A FEW STEPS RECEIVER OFF HOOK*

HACK: Get me maintenance, will you?

CHIEF: I'm surprised at you, Taggart. Any patrolmen should have caught that.

HACK: I—I guess I was thinking about something else at the time.

CHIEF: Apparently, but that's not the way to catch a murderer.

HACK: Hello? Maintenance? Bring a screw driver and come up to the photographic studio will you?.
Lieutenant Taggart of the Homicide Squad. Yes, right away.

SOUND: *RECEIVER ON HOOK*

HACK: He'll be right up.

CHIEF: Let's see, according to the report the girl was seated just about the middle of the floor, right?

HACK: That's right.

| | |
|---|---|
| CHIEF: | And you say the gun must have been fired from that doorway? |
| HACK: | I didn't say that. In my report, I quoted statements by Sandra Martin and Skip Williams to that effect. |
| CHIEF: | They were the ones who were with her at the time? |
| HACK: | Yes. |
| CHIEF: | Have you questioned them further? |
| HACK: | As much as I thought was necessary. |
| CHIEF: | Well, have them picked up and brought down to the bureau. I'd like to talk to them myself. |
| HACK: | Okay. If you say so. |
| SOUND: | *DOOR OPEN. OFFICE NOISE UP* |
| HACK: | Oh, good. You the janitor? |
| VOICE: | Yep. |
| HACK: | Take the mask off that vent. |
| VOICE: | Okay. |
| SOUND: | *A FEW STEPS* |
| CHIEF: | Now, to get back to this girl . . . Sandra Martin. |
| SANDRA: | *(OFF)* Did I hear my name mentioned? Oh—*(FADING IN)* Hello, Hack. |
| HACK: | Hello, Sandra. You know the chief. |
| SANDRA: | Oh, yes. Hello, Inspector McDaniels. |
| CHIEF: | I'm glad you're here, Miss Martin. Saves us the trouble of having you picked up. |

SANDRA: Me? Picked up? What for?

CHIEF: I wanted to ask you some questions.

SANDRA: Well, go right ahead. I'm certain there's nothing I know that Lieutenant Taggart hasn't told you.

CHIEF: That is . . . if you told him.

~~SANDRA: Look here…Are you insinuating that I --~~

~~CHIEF: I'm insinuating nothing…It's simply that I want all the facts at my disposal….You were here at the time of the murder… consequently, it seems to me that you should know more about it than anyone else.~~

~~SANDRA: All I know is what I've told the Lieutenant.~~

HACK: ~~I believe that, chief~~ I questioned her immediately following the murder, and I'm certain she withheld nothing.

CHIEF: I'm not accusing her of withholding anything. It's just that I'd like to hear what she has to say myself. It might mean something to me.

JANITOR: There you are, Lieutenant.

HACK: Oh. All right, thanks. That's all.

SANDRA: Look, I don't know much about it. But, I've written a copy of what I do know. I have it hear in my purse.

SOUND: *RATTLE OF PAPER*

SANDRA: I had an idea there'd be—

SOUND: *THUD OF PIECE OF METAL FALLING TO FLOOR*

CHIEF: Well, what's this?

SANDRA: I don't know. I guess I dropped something out of my purse.

| | |
|---|---|
| CHIEF: | Yes, I guess you did. Where did you get this? |
| SANDRA: | What is it? |
| CHIEF: | It's a bullet . . . a bullet that has been fired and mushroomed against some object. |
| SANDRA: | Why, I never saw it before in my life! |
| CHIEF: | Just a minute, Miss Martin. I must warn you that from now on anything you say may be used against you. Oh, and you can keep that report of yours. There won't be any more questions. At least not until you've arranged for representation. |
| SANDRA: | Representation? |
| CHIEF: | Yes. Legal. You're going to need it. |
| *MUSIC:* | *(TO TAG)* |
| | *(CLOSING ANNOUNCEMENT)* |
| CUTTING: | Friends, are you getting enough of ALL the vitamins, for general good health? Well, that's a mighty hard question to answer if you are depending on your food alone to supply them. But, there won't be any doubt at all about your basic vitamin intake IF you take a single One-A-Day-Brand Multiple Vitamin Capsule each day. They're the newest of Miles Laboratories' vitamin preparations, you know -- the ones which give you eight vitamins, all in each single capsule. And just one capsule each day is all you take to do the job. So, why run the risk of such conditions as nervous fatigue, or lowered resistance to colds, or a general run-down condition, resulting from a lack of sufficient vitamins. Ask you druggist for the new One-A-Day-Brand Multiple Vitamin Capsules right away and give each member of your family their protective benefits. Look for the brand with the big "One" and the name Miles [Laboratories] on the blue package. At all drug stores. |

MUSIC: (THEME. ESTABLISH. AND FADE UNDER)

ANNCR: How can Sandra explain the presence of a spent bullet in her purse? And will it prove to be the bullet which killed Frances Evers? If so, even the expose of Elbert Hoagan as the man in the photograph may not be enough to clear Sandra Martin of guilt. Listen tomorrow as events cast more suspicion on our "Lady Of The Press" in episode ten of "The Picture of Death."

MUSIC: (UP AND UNDER)

ANNCR: "LADY OF THE PRESS" is written by Dwight Hauser, and produced by Gordon T. Hughes, and is brought to you each day, Monday through Friday, at this same time by the makers of ALKA SELTZER.

MUSIC: (TO FILL)

ANNCR: [Dick Cutting speaking] This is CBS. THE COLUMBIA BROADCASTIG SYSTEM.

# EPISODE #10

# "PICTURE OF DEATH"

| | | |
|---|---|---|
| SPONSOR: | ALKA SELTZER | MAY 12, 1944 |
| AGENCY: | WADE 4:00—4:15 PM, PWT | |

ANNCR: The makers of Alka Seltzer present—"LADY OF THE PRESS"

MUSIC: (STING) (QUICK PUNCTUATION)

ANNCR: The adventures of Sandra Martin, radio's newest romantic-mystery serial!

MUSIC: (THEME-ESTABLISH AND FADE OUT)

(OPENING ANNOUNCEMENT)

CUTTING: Say mother, have you noticed that so many of the foods you know your family should have foods such as butter, eggs, cream, cheese, liver, carrots, and green vegetables—are either hard to find in the markets or are expensive, either in terms of money or ration points? Yet, your family needs these foods because, for one reason, they are among the best sources of vitamins A and D. Now, ~~they~~ [your family] must get vitamin A from some source—for ~~its aid~~ [it aids] in preventing night blindness and in keeping up normal resistance to colds—and vitamin D for helping maintain strong healthy teeth and bones. So mother, make sure your family gets ample amounts of these two so-called cod liver oil vitamins by supplementing their diets with One-A-Day-Brand Vitamin A and D Tablets. They're so rich in these vitamins that a single pleasant-tasting-tablet daily does the job. That makes for economy as well as convenience. So start now to give your family the protective benefits of ample vitamins [A and D]. Your druggist has One-A-Day-Brand Vitamin A and D Tablets. Look for the brand with the big "One" and the name Miles Laboratories on the yellow package.

MUSIC: *(THEME ESTABLISH AND FADE DOWN UNDER)*

ANNCR: And now, "Lady Of The Press," and episode ten in, "The Picture of Death".

MUSIC: *(STING-QUICK FIGURATION FADING OUT UNDER)*

ANNCR: Sandra Martin has been taken into custody on suspicion of an accessory after the fact in the murder of Frances Evers. The only tangible evidence The Chief of the Homicide Bureau has against her is the fact that she was present in the room at the time of the murder. Plus the unexplainable fact that a mushroomed bullet fell out of Sandra's purse at the feet of inspector McDaniels. Sandra claims to have no idea how the bullet got there, but the inspector feels that this is sufficient evidence to warrant holding her until it can be explained.

SOUND: *CLICK OF INTER COM SWITCH*

VOICE: *(FILTER)* Yes, Chief.

CHIEF: Do you have Miss Martin out there?

VOICE: Yes, Chief.

CHIEF: Well, send her in here, will you?

VOICE: Sure, Chief.

| | |
|---|---|
| SOUND: | CLICK OF INTER COM SWITCH DOOR OPENS |
| CHIEF: | Ah. Good. Come in Miss Martin. |
| SANDRA: | Well, have you finally decided to see me? |
| CHIEF: | Sorry for the delay, but, I wanted all the facts I could get. Come in and close the door please. |
| SOUND: | DOOR SLAMS-FOOTSTEPS IN FAST |
| SANDRA: | I'll give you some facts. In fact, I've been waiting all night, in the custody of that goon you call a police matron, for a chance to give you some facts . . . and, I don't think you're going to like them. |
| CHIEF: | Now, Miss Martin, let's not loose our temper. That will get neither of us anyplace. |
| SANDRA: | On the contrary, my temper has a place all picked out for you . . . and it's not on the city payroll. |
| CHIEF: | Miss Martin, are you here to tell me what's on your mind or to answer some questions? |
| SANDRA: | I'll answer some questions, and I'll ask some, too. In the first place, who do you think you are? Is it a habit of yours to go around arresting innocent people and holding them overnight without counsel? |
| CHIEF: | Unfortunately, it was upon the advice of Lieutenant Taggart that you were held last night. |
| SANDRA: | Lieutenant Taggart? Why, that—what's the idea anyway? |
| CHIEF: | He felt it would be better not to give any publicity to the fact that you'd been picked up until we were a little more certain of our ground. |
| SANDRA: | Then why don't you ask Hack Taggart for the truth? |

| | |
|---|---|
| CHIEF: | Miss Martin, are you insinuating that the Lieutenant has not been telling me the truth? |
| SANDRA: | Not all of it, he hasn't. |
| CHIEF: | Please explain what you mean by that. |
| SANDRA: | Just this . . . Hack Taggart knows that I had no more to do with that crime than he had. Two unfortunate coincidences point toward me as an accomplice. But, if the Lieutenant would only tell the rest of it, those two coincidences would be fully explained. |
| CHIEF: | This is a serious accusation you're making against Taggart, Miss Martin. |
| SANDRA: | And I suppose you think facing an indictment by the Grand Jury is going to be a pink tea party for me? Well, I don't intend to be humiliated in the eyes of the public simply because Hack Taggart wants to play around with an idea. |
| CHIEF: | Just what is it that Lieutenant Taggart knows that he hasn't told me? |
| SANDRA: | The identity of Frances Evers Murderer. |
| CHIEF: | What? |
| SANDRA: | Exactly. If you want to know who did, ask Taggart. He has plenty of proof. |
| CHIEF: | If this is true, Miss Martin, you know what will happen to Taggart? |
| SANDRA: | Right now, I'm interested in what will happen to me. Well why don't you ask him . . . if you really want the truth? |
| CHIEF: | Of course I do. I'll call him. |
| SOUND: | *CLICK OF INTER COM SWITCH* |

| | |
|---|---|
| VOICE: | *(FILTER)* Yes? |
| CHIEF: | Send Lieutenant Taggart into my office at once. |
| VOICE: | Yes, sir. |
| SOUND: | *CLICK OF INTER COM SWITCH* |
| CHIEF: | I should like you to remain. Since you're made this accusation, I think it only fair to Taggart that you face him with it. |
| SANDRA: | I'll be happy to. I've been pushed around in this case by him just about all I intend to be. |
| CHIEF: | There's one thing I don't understand . . . you're a newspaper woman. If you are in possession of information which hasn't been brought to our attention, why didn't you make it public? |
| SANDRA: | I wanted to, but, Lieutenant Taggart talked me out of it on the grounds that publicity would warn the criminal and interfere with his apprehension. |
| CHIEF: | I can understand that, but, when he carries it to the extent of involving other people, that's going too far. |
| SOUND: | *KNOCK ON DOOR* |
| CHIEF: | Come in. |
| SOUND: | *DOOR OPENS* |
| CHIEF: | Oh, Taggart, come in. Close the door after you, please. |
| SOUND: | *DOOR CLOSE FOOTSTEPS FADE IN* |
| HACK: | Yes, Chief. Good morning, Sandra.<br>*(PAUSE)*<br>Well, not a very warm reception, What's up? |

| | |
|---|---|
| CHIEF: | Taggart, I'm going to ask you a question and I want the truth. |
| HACK: | All right, if I know the answer. |
| CHIEF: | Who murdered Frances Evers? |
| HACK: | *(TO SANDRA)* Oh, so you told, did you? |
| SANDRA: | Yes, I did. If you think I'm going to spend my time in jail just so that you can play around with some fool theory, you're crazy. |
| CHIEF: | That hasn't answered my question, Taggart. Who killed her? |
| HACK: | Guy by the name of Hoagan. Society Editor for the Courier. |
| CHIEF: | How long have you known this? |
| HACK: | Ever since the day of the murder. We have a picture of him. Skip Williams shot a picture just as he fired the gun. His reflection is quite clear in the window. It shows up plainly along with that of the dead girl. |
| CHIEF: | And perhaps you can also explain why you've seen fit to keep this evidence secret. |
| HACK: | Certainly. Hoagan is still at large. He doesn't know that we have the picture. Any publicity would make him that much harder to catch. |
| CHIEF: | That's all well and good, but, in withholding this evidence you're implicated this innocent girl. |
| HACK: | I wonder. |
| CHIEF: | What do you mean? |
| HACK: | She was present at the murder. The Grand Jury is going to want to know who got Frances Evers into a position where she'd be murdered. |

SANDRA: Why you—

HACK: Ah, ah, just a minute. Regardless of who actually pulled the trigger on the murder gun, the Grand Jury is going to ask questions of all those involved. That includes Miss Martin and Skip Williams. Especially Miss Martin, since we found that bullet in her purse.

SANDRA: Hack Taggart…You're a—a—I'll bet if the truth were known you planted that bullet there yourself.

HACK: You know better than that. I'm trying to help you. If you had any sense you could see that.

SANDRA: Inspector, am I free to go now?

CHIEF: Well, as Taggart says, the Grand Jury is going to want some answers. However, I don't think you'll run away. You're at liberty pending the hearing, but, keep in contact with me.

SANDRA: I'm willing to do anything I can. I shall gladly appear before the Grand Jury . . . as a witness. But, now, if you don't mind, I've seen about enough of the man who wants to place me there as a suspect.

SOUND: *FOOTSTEPS TO DOOR-DOOR OPEN-SLAM*

HACK: She can really get her dander up, can't she?

CHIEF: If you ask me, Taggart, she has a right to. Of all the low-down tricks I've ever seen in this department, this latest of yours just about tops them all.

HACK: Now, just a minute, Chief, I know what I'm doing. It may be a bit unorthodox, but it'll work.

CHIEF: I'm warning you, Taggart, you're flirting with a dismissal.

HACK: How come? I told you that I knew who killed Frances Evers.

CHIEF: I know you did, but I thought you meant you had a good idea. I didn't suppose you had a picture of him. What more evidence do you want?

HACK: Having a picture of him and having him are two different things. If the people are back of this that I suspect, Hoagan's going to be a mighty tough baby to catch, and, publishing that picture wouldn't help any.

CHIEF: But it would clear Sandra Martin.

HACK: How do you figure that?

CHIEF: Well, at least it would clear her of any suspicion of the actual murder. Don't you see how this thing is going to look if we don't publicize it?

HACK: Maybe I do.

CHIEF: ~~Well, I'll tell you...~~ While we sit here with a picture of the guy who murdered Frances Evers, Sandra Martin will face the Grand Jury as one of the only two known people present at the time. Honestly, Taggart, I give you an inch and you take a mile. When you said you knew the identity of the murderer, I thought you were basing it on suspicious clues. Instead, I Find you're carrying around a picture of the guy.

HACK: I don't see that that changes things any.

CHIEF: I had her arrested. Don't you realize that? Held her in jail all night. I thought I could stall her when she came in here this morning, when she started telling me you knew a lot of stuff I didn't. I let her think she was right. Now, I find out that she was. What kind of a dunder head does that make me?

HACK: I dunno.

CHIEF: Oh, you don't? Well, I'll tell you. It's put me in the position of having arrested an innocent girl, when this department was in possession of evidence which proves her innocence.

HACK: Oh no it doesn't. I told you. It only clears her of the actual murder, not of complicity.

CHIEF: ~~You mean to say that you still think she had something to do with it?~~

HACK: ~~What I think isn't important...The facts are And the facts certainly don't look too good for her.... She got Evers in the room...She was present when the act took place. And, we found the missing bullet in her purse.~~

CHIEF: ~~Yes...That's right...Say, and by the way.....Did I give you that bullet?~~

HACK: ~~Why no, Chief.....What's the matter...(SMIRK) Have you lost it?~~

CHIEF: ~~Funny...I'd swear I brought it back here to the office and put it in this drawer...Somebody must have stolen it.~~

HACK: ~~Oh that's too bad...I wonder who would have done such a thing...Say...Mind if I use your phone, Chief...I want to call the D. A. I think he should be in possession of all the evidence we have before the Grand Jury sits on Monday.~~

HACK: ~~She can really get her dander up, can't she?~~

CHIEF: ~~If you ask me, Taggart.....She has a right to. Of all the low tricks I've ever seen in this department...this latest of yours just about tops them all.~~

HACK: ~~Now...Just a minute Chief...I know what I'm doing...It may be a bit unorthodox...but it'll work...~~

CHIEF: ~~I'm warning you Taggart.~~ You're flirting with a dismissal.

HACK: Mind if I use your phone, Chief?

CHIEF: What for?

HACK: I want to call the D.A.'s office. I think there's some information he should have before the hearing on Monday.

| | |
|---|---|
| MUSIC: | (BRIDGE) |
| SOUND: | NEWSPAPER OFFICE |
| SOUND: | HURRIED FOOTSTEPS |
| SKIP: | Well, if it isn't our lady detective. |
| SANDRA: | Hi, Skip. |
| SKIP: | Just for the record, would you mind telling me where you've been? |
| SANDRA: | I spent the night in the custody of a police matron. |
| SKIP: | You what? |
| SANDRA: | That's right. And Lieutenant Taggart finally went too far. I told the Chief Inspector all we know about the case and he let me go, and if I'm not mistaken, Mr. Hack Taggart is now sitting on the same hot seat he warmed up for us. |
| SKIP: | Oh that's great. You finally came to your senses and let him have it, huh? |
| SANDRA: | I'll say I did. |
| SKIP: | Well, where do we go from here? |
| SANDRA: | Now that we can stop worrying about the Grand Jury we can go back to uncovering the evidence against those Black Market Operators. |
| SKIP: | You just can't let well enough alone, can you? |
| SANDRA: | I'm still convinced they were behind the death of Frances Evers. And I'm going to prove it. What about those license numbers I told you to get? |
| SKIP: | Right here. I got eight of them, and then I came back here. You weren't here, so I went ahead and had them checked. |

Episode #10 • 139

|  |  |
|---|---|
|  | Here's the list together with the names and addresses of the owners. |
| SANDRA: | Good work, Skip. You're coming right along in this detective business. |
| SKIP: | I don't see what good they're going to do you. |
| SANDRA: | That attendant at the service station asked to see our card. That means that some of the customers have some kind of a card. Now, there's no need for such a thing in a legitimately operated service station, so maybe if we can trace one of these cards. We might find something interesting. |
| SKIP: | Yes, and we might find ourselves in a lot more trouble than we are now. |
| SANDRA: | That's not the point. The point is getting some evidence on that ring. |
| SKIP: | If they killed Frances Evers for having evidence against them, doesn't it occur to you that they might do the same to you if you get it? You're sticking your neck out. |
| SANDRA: | Maybe so, but, this thing is too important to stop now. |
| MAN: | *(FADE IN)* Say, Miss . . . Miss . . . is your name Martin? |
| SANDRA: | Yes. |
| MAN: | Sandra Martin? |
| SANDRA: | Yes. Why? |
| MAN: | Little paper here that might interest you. Here you are. |
| SANDRA: | [Thanks.] Well, what is it? Who's it from? |
| MAN: | *(CHUCKLES)* Open it up. You'll understand. *(CHUCKLES-FADES)* |

| | |
|---|---|
| SOUND: | FOOTSTEPS FADE OFF |
| SANDRA: | Well, what— |
| SKIP: | You better summon all your courage. |
| SOUND: | TEARING ENVELOPE |
| | (PAUSE) |
| SKIP: | Well? |
| SANDRA: | It's a summons to appear before the Grand Jury on Monday. |
| SKIP: | Well, we expected it. |
| SANDRA: | Yes, in a way, but, I expected it to be as a witness. |
| SKIP: | Well, isn't that what it is? |
| SANDRA: | No, Skip, it isn't. They are ordering my appearance as a suspect. |
| MUSIC: | (TO TAG) |
| | (CLOSING ANNOUNCEMENT) |
| CUTTING: | Tell me, mother—do you give your children cod liver oil? And, do they LIKE it? Well, I'll tell you something they WILL like—One-A-Day-Brand Vitamin A and D Tablets, for they taste like candy. And yet in spite of their pleasant taste, each single One-A-Day-Brand Vitamin A and D Tablet supplies exactly the same amounts of vitamins A and D as one and one-half teaspoons full of minimum USP cod liver oil. That makes it so easy—just one tablet each day—and that's all. And the cost? Only a trifle over a penny a day, per person, if you buy the large package—so little, in fact, you'll want to give the whole family their protective benefits. But remember, there are now THREE different kinds of One-A-Day Brand Vitamins. When you want |

the kind containing the so-called cod liver oil vitamins, ask your druggist for One-A-Day-Brand Vitamin A and D Tablets. They come in the yellow package with the big "One".

MUSIC: *(THEME ESTABLISH AND FADE)*

ANNCR: Apparently, Sandra's pleas to Hack have fallen on deaf ears. Although she believed Hack would protect her from this humiliation, it appears now that he had no intention of doing so from the beginning. How could this man, who once loved her, be so brutally cruel now? Listen again Monday, when our "Lady of the Press" stands before the Grand Jury to defend herself from this accusation in episode eleven of "The Picture of Death".

MUSIC: *(UP AND UNDER:)*

ANNCR: "LADY OF THE PRESS" is written by Dwight Hauser, and produced by Gordon T. Hughes, and is brought to you each day, Monday through Friday at this same time by the makers of Alka Seltzer.

MUSIC: *(THEME TO FILL)*

ANNCR: [Dick Cutting speaking]
This is CBS. The COLUMBIA BROADCASTIG SYSTEM.

# EPISODE #11

# "PICTURE OF DEATH"

| | |
|---|---|
| SPONSOR: | ALKA SELTZER    MAY 15, 1944 |
| AGENCY: | WADE  4:00—4:15 PM, PWT PN |

---

ANNCR: The makers of Alka Seltzer present—"LADY OF THE PRESS"

MUSIC: *(STING) (QUICK PUNCTUATION)*

ANNCR: The adventures of Sandra Martin, radio's newest romantic-mystery serial!

MUSIC: *(THEME-ESTABLISH AND FADE OUT:)*

CUTTING: All of you folks remember, I'm sure, the "three r's"—readin'—'ritin' and 'rithmetic. Well, here's a little problem concerning one of the "r's"—see if you know the answer. It's a question of one and one. One Alka-Seltzer Tablet dropped in a glass of water plus lots of rest, sensible eating and general care equals what? That's right. It equals comforting relief for the dull, achy misery of a cold. So keep this solution in mind if you have a cold now or next time one threatens. Remember too, that if a sore throat is a part of your cold distress, Alka-Seltzer makes a mighty soothing, comforting gargle. Try it. You know, of course, that you can get effervescent, comfort-bringing Alka Seltzer Tablets at all drug stores in thirty and sixty cent size packages.

## 144 • Lady of the Press

| | |
|---|---|
| MUSIC: | (THEME-ESTABLISH AND FADE DOWN UNDER) |
| ANNCR: | And now, "Lady of the Press", and episode eleven in, "The Picture of Death". |
| MUSIC: | (STING AND QUICK FIGURATION FADING DOWN UNDER) |
| ANNCR: | In view of the absence of Elbert Hoagan, the real murderer of Frances Evers, together with implicating circumstances and the face that a mushroomed bullet was found in her purse, Sandra Martin has been subpoenaed to appear before the Grand Jury under suspicion as an accomplice to the crime. Just when she believe Hack Taggart's hard shell of bitterness had been softened by memories, he seems to have turned completely against her. Hack could have saved her this humiliating experience, and she is at a loss to understand why he insists on doing everything in his power to implicate her. But, Sandra is not easily beaten. And, it is obvious that she intends pulling no punches in her efforts to absolve herself of guilt. We find her now, shortly after having received the summons in the office of Bruce Elliot, one of the city's most brilliant young attorneys. |
| BRUCE: | I appreciate your position, Miss Martin. Your need for legal representation is dire. But, on such short notice, I don't see how I could possibly do a good job for you. |
| SANDRA: | I've watched your rise in this town. I saw how you battered down the prosecution on that Grimm case. I know your ability. |
| BRUCE: | Walter Grimm was innocent. |
| SANDRA: | Are—are you inferring that you think I'm not? |
| BRUCE: | No. I'm simply saying that I don't know that you are. |
| SANDRA: | But, I've told you . . . I had nothing to do with the murder of Frances Evers. |

| | |
|---|---|
| BRUCE: | And, as just another person, I believe you. As a client upon whose word I must face a jury, I can't accept merely your personal word. |
| SANDRA: | But, there's every reason to believe I didn't do it or even have anything to do with it. |
| BRUCE: | Not unless there's proof. |
| SANDRA: | But there is. There's the picture of Hoagan. |
| BRUCE: | Which you say is in Lieutenant Taggart's possession. |
| SANDRA: | That's right. |
| BRUCE: | You also stated that you believe he would not make use of that evidence for fear it would clear you completely. |
| SANDRA: | Oh, I don't know what he'll do. Frankly, Mr. Elliot, I don't know what to expect from him. |
| BRUCE: | Then, you can't base your case upon a development you're not certain of. |
| SANDRA: | No, I suppose you're right. |
| BRUCE: | Even if the picture is produced, if what you say about it is true, it would only establish Hoagan as the man who pulled the trigger. As I understand it, you're suspected of aiding him. |
| SANDRA: | That's what the subpoena says. |
| BRUCE: | You admit that you were responsible for Frances Evers presence in the room at the time of the murder? |
| SANDRA: | *(SLIGHTLY EXASPERATED)* Yes. I told you. I'd arranged for her to sit for some pictures. |
| BRUCE: | You expect me to believe that, don't you? |

| | |
|---|---|
| SANDRA: | Certainly! *(ANGRY)* If I hadn't expected your trust and cooperation, why would I have come to you? |
| BRUCE: | You should be more capable of answering that than I. |
| SANDRA: | *(ICY)* I'm sorry, Mr. Elliot, I guess I've made a mistake. I shouldn't have attempted to judge your character from your court record. Good day! |
| SOUND: | A FEW STEPS |
| BRUCE: | Just a minute, Miss Martin. I've not said that I don't believe you. |
| SANDRA: | No, but, you intimated as much, and I didn't come here to be cross examined by you. |
| BRUCE: | Then what did you come for? |
| SANDRA: | Because I hoped you'd see my position and help me. |
| BRUCE: | Have I said I wouldn't? |
| SANDRA: | No. But from what I've seen so far, your help is just what I need to be found guilty. |
| BRUCE: | I think you will be. |
| SANDRA: | Oh, thanks, awfully. Good bye. |
| BRUCE: | By the Grand Jury, I mean. I'm almost certain you'll be forced to stand trial, that is, unless there's something you haven't told me. |
| SANDRA: | I've certainly told you all that I intend telling you. |
| BRUCE: | Than you can scarcely blame me for looking at is as I think a jury would, can you? |
| SANDRA: | I'm not interested in blaming anyone. I was just hoping you'd be able to stop them from blaming me. |

| | |
|---|---|
| BRUCE: | Well, I haven't said I wouldn't. |
| SANDRA: | Your enthusiasm overwhelms me. I want an attorney, but, I want one in whom I can place some confidence. |
| BRUCE: | Well, I'm sorry, if you feel you've made a mistake in coming here. But, you really couldn't expect me to ask a jury to believe something which I don't. |
| SANDRA: | Excuse me if I seem repetitious, Mr. Elliot. I believe I bid you good day once before. |
| BRUCE: | Good day, Miss Martin. |
| SOUND: | *FOOTSTEPS TO DOOR-DOOR OPEN-SLAM* |
| MUSIC: | *(BRIDGE)* |
| SOUND: | *NEWSPAPER OFFICE* |
| ~~SOUND:~~ | ~~*FOOTSTEPS FADE IN*~~ |
| SKIP: | Oh, San, gee, I'm glad you're back. Well, how'd you do with Elliot? |
| SANDRA: | That guy's the biggest stuffed shirt I ever saw. |
| SKIP: | You mean, he—he won't take your case? |
| SANDRA: | I don't want him to. |
| SKIP: | Oh, fine. You're just up as an accomplice to murder, so you don't want the best defense attorney in town. Have you lost your marbles? |
| SANDRA: | No, but, I've lost the good opinion I had of Bruce Elliot. Why do you know what he had the nerve to ask me? |
| SKIP: | No. What? |
| SANDRA: | Whether or not I was really innocent. How do you like that? |

SKIP: And after the swell pictures I ran of him after that Grimm Case.

OPERATOR: ~~(OFF) Miss Martin…Oh Miss Martin?~~

SANDRA: ~~Oh, yes…Betty…What is it?~~

OPERATOR: ~~I have a call for you…will you take it at Mr. William's desk.~~

SANDRA: And the support this paper gave him.

SKIP: Gee, you'd think the guy would have some gratitude.

SANDRA: I'm learning to rely less and less on what you'd think people would do, Skip. Oh well, no use worrying over what Bruce Elliot won't do. The important thing is what we're going to do.

SKIP: And what have you got in mind?

SANDRA: I don't know for sure, but, come in and talk it over. I don't want the whole office staff in on everything.

SKIP: Okay.

SOUND: *FOOTSTEPS*

SKIP: All I can say is that both Hack and this Bruce are darned inconsiderate.

SOUND: *DOOR OPEN*

SANDRA: And, as a consequence, I'm in a fine spot.

SOUND: *DOOR CLOSE OFFICE NOISES OUT*

SANDRA: That's better. Maybe we can think a little more clearly without all that racket.

SKIP: Just where do we stand?

| | |
|---|---|
| SANDRA: | Well, so far, I'm subpoenaed. You're not, yet? |
| SKIP: | But, I'm a cinch to be. |
| SANDRA: | Yes, I think you are. |
| SKIP: | I still think we ought to forget Taggart's wishes and use that picture. |
| SANDRA: | That's one thing we don't dare do now. Up to now it's been a matter of choice, but not any longer. |
| SKIP: | How come? |
| SANDRA: | Because Hack happens to be in possession of a mushroomed bullet. |
| SKIP: | What's that got to do with it? |
| SANDRA: | Nothing except that the bullet fell out of my purse. |
| SKIP: | What? |
| SANDRA: | That's right. Oh, don't ask me how it got there. I haven't the faintest idea. But I do know that it would be mighty hard to explain to the Grand Jury, and I also know that if we go against Hack's wishes about the picture, he'll present that bullet as evidence. |
| SKIP: | How do you know he won't anyway? |
| SANDRA: | I don't, but, at least there a chance he won't. There's none if we print the picture. Oh, Skip, I don't know what to do. I'd relied so much on the help of Bruce Elliot. I felt certain he'd ~~help~~ [take the case]. |
| SKIP: | Well, after all, he's not the only lawyer in town. There must be plenty of lawyers just as good as he is. |
| SANDRA: | Are there? Name me one. |

| | |
|---|---|
| SKIP: | Yeah. I see what you mean. So what do we do? |
| SANDRA: | Skip, I'm just about at the end of my rope. I just don't know where to turn next. |
| SOUND: | PHONE RINGS. FOOTSTEPS. RECEIVER OFF HOOK. |
| SANDRA: | Hello? Sandra Martin, speaking. |
| BRUCE: | *(FILTER)* Oh, Miss Martin, this is Bruce Elliot. |
| SANDRA: | Who? |
| BRUCE: | Bruce Elliot. |
| SANDRA: | *(S.V. TO SKIP)* It's him . . . Bruce Elliot. Yes, what is it? |
| ~~SANDRA:~~ | ~~Who's it from?~~ |
| ~~OPERATOR:~~ | ~~I don't know….Some fellow with a very romantic voice.~~ |
| ~~SANDRA:~~ | ~~I could use that about now—I better take it in re-write….. Switch it in there, will you?~~ |
| ~~OPERATOR:~~ | ~~Okay.~~ |
| ~~SOUND:~~ | ~~FOOTSTEPS~~ |
| ~~SANDRA:~~ | ~~See you in a minute, Skip.~~ |
| ~~SKIP:~~ | ~~(OFF) Yeah. Sure. (FADES) Romance at a time like this.~~ |
| ~~SOUND:~~ | ~~FOOTSTEPS UP TO DOOR-DOOR OPEN-CLOSE- OFFICE SOUND OUT- FOOTSTEPS TO PHONE- RECEIVER OFF HOOK~~ |
| ~~SANDRA:~~ | ~~Hello, Betty?~~ |
| ~~OPERATOR:~~ | ~~(ON FILTER) Yes…..~~ |
| ~~SANDRA:~~ | ~~I'm ready for that call…Switch it in, will you?~~ |

OPERATOR: ~~All right....Here is your party...Go ahead.~~

SANDRA: ~~Sandra Martin, speaking~~

BRUCE: *(FILTER)* Miss Martin, I hope you'll forgive my taking the liberty to call you.

SANDRA: It seems to me we covered our business rather thoroughly a few minutes ago.

BRUCE: That's only your opinion, Miss Martin. You see, I have to be rather careful of the cases I take.

SANDRA: You don't have a thing to worry about. Your caution is beyond improvement.

BRUCE: That's fortunate for my clients. The public and the juries are more apt to be favorable if they think I represent only innocent clients.

SANDRA: What about the innocent clients that you don't represent?

BRUCE: There are none . . . that I know of.

SANDRA: What about me?

BRUCE: That's what I called to tell you. I've decided to take your case.

SANDRA: What?

BRUCE: You see, I had to be sure. The way you walked out without a pressure argument convinced me. If you really were guilty you'd have tried to reason with me.

SANDRA: Oh, psychology, huh?

BRUCE: Or just common sense. Well, do you still want me to represent [you]?

SANDRA: Yes, if you're convinced that I'm innocent.

| | |
|---|---|
| BRUCE: | I told you, I've never defended anyone about whom I had the slightest doubt. |
| SANDRA: | Well, okay. That's what I wanted in the first place. |
| BRUCE: | Fine, but, we haven't much time. We'll have to work fast on this case. You try to figure out all the circumstances which might have a bearing on the case. I'll be over there within ten minutes and we'll put it together. |
| SANDRA: | Thanks, Mr. Elliot. You've no idea what a lift you've given me. |
| SOUND: | RECEIVER ON HOOK |
| MUSIC: | (BRIDGE) |
| BRUCE: | Now, you're certain that you've told me everything? |
| SANDRA: | I can't think of anything we've left out, can you, Skip? |
| SKIP: | No. |
| BRUCE: | All right. As I see it, our biggest stumbling block is this Lieutenant Taggart. |
| SKIP: | You can say that again. |
| SANDRA: | Well, Mr. Elliot, in view of what we've told you, what in your opinion, are our chances? |
| BRUCE: | I don't want to sound pessimistic, Miss Martin, but, I'd say there's small chance of the Grand Jury doing anything except indicting you. |
| SANDRA: | But . . . the evidence . . . it's insufficient. |
| BRUCE: | You must understand that actually the action of the Grand Jury is not really important or conclusive. You see, the D.A's office will present the evidence they have, just enough of it to establish the possibility that you were an accomplice of Hoagan. |

SANDRA: But we weren't.

BRUCE: I know, but you must admit that you could have been. The job of the Grand Jury isn't to determine your guilt; it's only to decide whether or not there is a possibility of your guilt.

SKIP: But, Holy Cats! Aren't we going to try and convince them that we're innocent?

BRUCE: If you retain me as your legal representative, then my advice is that we do not present our case to the Grand Jury. I believe the evidence you've given me—on the surface—is just as incriminating as any the D.A. may present.

SKIP: Then what do you suggest?

BRUCE: If the Grand Jury indicts you, there will be an arrest, and then an arraignment before a magistrate. Our defense can then be presented to the magistrate . . . and, if he sees fit, he can dismiss the charges.

SANDRA: But, if the Grand Jury indicts us on the basis of the same evidence, won't he be apt to sustain them?

BRUCE: Probably.

SANDRA: Then—?

BRUCE: Look, Miss Martin, through innuendo and implication, you have become involved in a serious crime. The fact that the D.A.'s office and the local police have failed to apprehend the real criminal makes it that much worse for you.

SKIP: Yeah, ~~Well~~ [But] if we depend on the efforts of the homicide squad we'll spend the rest of our lives in the clink.

BRUCE: We'll not depend entirely upon them. It would be much simpler if they'd apprehend the criminal.

SANDRA: But suppose they don't? Suppose they never catch him? What happens to us then?

| | |
|---|---|
| BRUCE: | Miss Martin, the D.A.'s office will do everything in it's power to fasten the guilt for this crime upon the most logical suspect. We might as well face it. Next to Hoagan himself, you and Mr. Williams here are the most logical suspects. I might say the only logical suspects. |
| SANDRA: | But we can't just accept that idea as some all-powerful fate about which we can do nothing. |
| BRUCE: | Certainly not. Just as it is the D.A.'s job to convict, it's my job get an acquittal. If we can't do it by bringing Hoagan to justice, then we'll have to try it in another way. |
| SANDRA: | And what is this other way? |
| BRUCE: | I'm not certain just yet, but, from what you've told me so far, I'm beginning to get a pretty good idea. |
| MUSIC: | (TO TAG) |
| CUTTING: | Say, how are all you Victory Gardeners coming along these days? Are you keeping pretty well ahead of the weeds and pests you have to fight? Well, that takes a lot of work, so I wouldn't be a bit surprised but what every now and then around supper time—after a strenuous day in the garden—your muscles get kinda stiff and sore. Right. Well, whenever this happens, just remember that Alka-Seltzer offers a kind of fast relief for muscular aches and pains that's mighty hard to beat. It's a fact, friends—Alka-Seltzer is just as effective at a time like this as it is for a simple headache, or for occasional acid indigestion. Try it, won't you—whenever unusually strenuous physical work in the garden, or yard, or around the house, makes your muscles stiff and sore. You can get effervescent, pain-relieving Alka-Seltzer Tablets at all drug stores. |
| MUSIC: | (THEME—ESTABLISH AND FADE UNDER) |
| ANNCR: | Will Bruce Elliot's idea save Sandra from a Grand Jury Indictment? Or, failing this, from conviction later on? And will Sandra be able to place her trust in another man after |

her disillusionment in Hack Taggart—the man who once loved her? Listen tomorrow when our "Lady of the Press" hears the verdict of the Grand Jury, in episode twelve of "The Picture of Death".

MUSIC: (UP AND UNDER)

ANNCR: "LADY OF THE PRESS", is written by Dwight Hauser and produced by Gordon T. Hughes and is brought to you each day, Monday through Friday at this same time by the makers of—ALKA SELTZER.

MUSIC: (UP TO FILL)

ANNCR: [Dick Cutting speaking] This is CBS. THE COLUMBIA BROADCASTING SYSTEM.

# EPISODE #12

# "PICTURE OF DEATH"

| | | |
|---|---|---|
| SPONSOR: | ALKA SELTZER | MAY 16, 1944 |
| AGENCY: | WADE 4:00—4:15 PM, PWT PN | |

---

ANNCR: The makers of Alka Seltzer present—"LADY OF THE PRESS"

MUSIC: *(STING) (QUICK PUNCTUATION)*

ANNCR: The adventures of Sandra Martin, radio's newest romantic-mystery serial!

MUSIC: (THEME-ESTABLISH AND FADE OUT:)

CUTTING: If there are children in your family, friends, you'll certainly be interested in One-A-Day Brand Vitamin A and D Tablets. You parents all know, of course, how important cod liver oil has always been for babies and growing children. But DO you know that just ONE candy-like One-A-Day Brand Vitamin A and D Tablet contains the same amount of these two vitamins as one and one-half teaspoonfuls of minimum USP cod liver oil? It's a fact. So, from the time your kiddies are old enough to appreciate the difference, give them One-A-Day Brand Vitamin A and D Tablets. Not only are they pleasant to taste but also mighty economical—just slightly more than a penny a day when you buy the large size package. Thus, you can hardly afford not to make yours a One-A-Day family by giving every member—young and old alike—the protective benefits of ample A and D vitamins. Your druggist has them—One-A-Day Brand Vitamin A and D Tablets, by Miles Laboratories. They're the ones in the yellow package with the big one.

MUSIC: *(THEME ESTABLISH AND FADE FOR:)*

ANNCR: And now, "Lady of the Press", and episode twelve in, "The Picture of Death."

MUSIC: *(STING AND QUICK FIGURATION FADES OUT UNDER)*

ANNCR: Sandra Martin, held on suspicion as an accomplice in the murder of Frances Evers, has placed all her hopes for acquittal on the talent of the brilliant young attorney, Bruce Elliot. Together with the aid of Skip Williams, they have spent most of the night piecing together every tiny bit of evidence which may have a bearing on the case. But now, today, even Bruce Elliot is extremely doubtful as to the outcome after hearing the District Attorney's presentation of the evidence to the Grand Jury. We find the three at lunch during a recess before the decision of the Grand Jury is announced.

SOUND: *RATTLE OF DISHES. FADE BACKGROUND*

SANDRA: Well, regardless of the outcome, I want to thank you for all your trouble, Bruce.

SKIP: Oh. So, already it's "Bruce" huh?

BRUCE: *(CHUCKLING)* Well, I call you Skip. Is there any reason why Sandra and I shouldn't address each other by first names?

SKIP: Oh no, no, no, no. Only you're certainly flirting with danger.

SANDRA: How on earth could using first names be dangerous?

SKIP: It's not only that, but you two have been seeing a lot of one another in the last thirty-six hours. All you need to do now to tighten the noose around our necks is to make Hack Taggart jealous.

SANDRA: Skip! Please! Your suggestion is most embarrassing.

BRUCE: Oh, I don't mind. As a matter of fact I rather like the idea. It isn't everyday one has the privilege of representing so charming a client.

SKIP: You see what I mean?

SANDRA: You've been very kind, Bruce, and I realize what a risk it is for you.

SKIP: Oh sure. Great risk. He may lose a client. We lose our freedom and maybe our necks.

BRUCE: Don't worry, Sandra. I'll do all I can, and you can rely on that.

SANDRA: Seriously, Bruce, how does it look?

BRUCE: Not good. If I were on that Grand Jury, I'd bring in an indictment.

SANDRA: The D.A. did a good job all right, didn't he?

BRUCE: He had everything in his favor.

~~SANDRA: Say…It's ten minutes of one. We better be getting back. Even if it is bad news—we'll have to face it.~~

~~BRUCE: Right….But, don't feel too discouraged…Just remember this….no Grand Jury has ever convicted anyone yet.~~

~~MUSIC: (BRIDGE)~~

~~SOUND:	COURT ROOM BUZZ—GAVEL~~

~~CLERK:	(DOUBLE) Order...Order in the court.~~

~~SOUND:	BUZZ DOWN~~

~~JUDGE:	(OFF) (DRONE) In the matter of the state versus, Sandra Martin and James W. Williams...The Jury finds the evidence sufficient for arrangement on the charge as presented.~~

~~SANDRA:	(SLIGHT GASP)~~

~~SKIP:	Steady baby.~~

SANDRA:	Yes. Hack Taggart certainly gave him all he needed.

BRUCE:	But, don't forget he could have given him a lot more information than he apparently did.

SANDRA:	What?

BRUCE:	You don't think he'd have kept from the Grand Jury the fact that a spent bullet had dropped from your purse? Together with the fact that the bullet which killed Frances Evers hasn't been found, if he'd know it, do you?

SANDRA:	No, I don't suppose so. Evidently Hack didn't tell him about the bullet.

BRUCE:	No, I'm sure he didn't. It was the fact that you made the arrangements for Frances Evers to be in that room at the time of the murder.

SANDRA:	But I didn't know there was going to be a murder.

BRUCE:	Certainly not. But, that's what we have to prove. And that's why in my estimation you'll have to stand trail. You see, look at it this way: by your own arrangements, Frances Evers was brought to the scene where she would be in close proximity to someone who wished to kill her.

| | |
|---|---|
| SANDRA: | If we could only use that picture as evidence, then we could prove it was Elbert Hoagan. |
| BRUCE: | Yes, but you yourself believe he murdered her at the behest of the Black Market Operators whom she was about to expose. |
| SANDRA: | I'm sure of it. There couldn't have been any other motive. |
| BRUCE: | Then, let me ask you this: how can the Grand Jury be certain you weren't mixed up with the Black Market? |
| SANDRA: | I don't suppose they can. |
| BRUCE: | Exactly. That's why I say that if I were on that Jury I'd bring in an indictment. |
| SANDRA: | Well, it's ten minutes to one. We better get back and face it. Even if it is bad news. |
| BRUCE: | Right, but don't feel too discouraged. Just remember this: no Grand Jury has convicted anyone. |
| *MUSIC:* | *(BRIDGE)* |
| *SOUND:* | *GAVEL* |
| JUDGE: | *(OFF) DRONE*—In the matter of the accusation of Sandra Martin and James W. (SKIP) Williams. The jury finds sufficient evidence for arraignment on the charge as presented. |
| *SANDRA:* | *(GASP)* |
| SKIP: | Steady, baby. |
| JUDGE: | The court hereby orders the arrest of Sandra Martin and James Williams on the charge of— |
| BRUCE: | Your honor— |

JUDGE: You wish to say something, Mr. Elliot?

BRUCE: If your honor please, I represent the defendants in this case, and I beg a hearing of the defense evidence before proceeding with this case.

JUDGE: Are you prepared at this time to argue the case?

BRUCE: I am.

JUDGE: Step to the bench please.

BRUCE: Thank you.

SOUND: FOOTSTEPS

SANDRA: (ALMOST SOBBING) Oh, Skip, somehow I just didn't think they'd really do it.

SKIP: Never mind, baby. We're in good hands. This guy Elliot knows what he's doin'. You do a good job of pickin' baby.

SANDRA: Oh, I hope he can convince the Judge. I just can't stand it, Skip. The humiliation! Think of it—being charged with murder!

SKIP: He'll do his best. I'm sure of that.

SANDRA: It's so unfair.

SOUND: GAVEL

JUDGE: Very well, Mr. Elliot. The court will hear your remarks..

BRUCE: Thank you. Your honor, I submit that this arrangement has been entered without a consideration of sufficient evidence. Only those facts pointing toward the possibility of Miss Martin's and Mr. William's involvement have been presented. No evidence has been offered to throw light on the possibility that Miss Martin and Mr. Williams are innocent.

| | | |
|---|---|---|
| JUDGE: | | One, moment, Mr. Elliot. This is not a trial; this is neither the time nor the place to present arguments regarding the guilt or innocence of these two people. If you have evidence which will disqualify that previously presented, and upon which the Grand Jury based its decision, the court will be pleased to hear it. Otherwise . . . . |
| BRUCE: | | But, your honor, I hold that all the evidence has not been presented. |
| JUDGE: | | I must remind you again, Mr. Elliot, this is only a hearing; this is not the time for a complete presentation of all the facts. The Grand Jury has reached the decision that sufficient evidence has been presented to warrant these two people standing trial. Can you refute the evidence upon which they based that decision? |
| BRUCE: | | I—no, your honor, I cannot. |
| JUDGE: | | You admit that the facts as presented by the District Attorney are true. |
| BRUCE: | | Yes. I do. It is true that Sandra Martin, and Mr. Williams, were in the room at the time of the murder. And, it is true that Miss Evers was in that room at the behest of Miss Martin. ~~It is also true that a fired bullet was seen to drop from Miss Martins purse...~~ But, these are all circumstances which can be explained if proper consideration is given the defense. |
| JUDGE: | | You shall have recourse to the due process of law in that respect. In the meantime, unless you can refute the evidence previously given, I have no choice but to sustain the verdict of the Grand Jury and to hold these defendants for trial. |
| BRUCE: | | Then, as a gesture of protest, I move for a dismissal of the charges. |
| JUDGE: | | Is your motion substantiated by any further grounds? |

BRUCE: No, your honor, it is merely a protest.

JUDGE: Motion denied.
(PAUSE)
It is not the mind of this court to condemn or to judge the suspects. It is, however, the duty of this court to carry out the decision of the Grand Jury. Warrant is hereby issued for arrest of the defendants. They will remain in the custody of the proper authorities in lieu of bail in the amount of $5,000 each until the fifteenth day of July, 1944, at which time they will appear in the Circuit Court of this district before a jury of their peers and answer to the charges entered against them.

SOUND: *GAVEL*

JUDGE: Next Case.

MUSIC: *(BRIDGE)*

SOUND: *TINKLE OF GLASSES*

SANDRA: Well, here's to our life of crime, Skip.

SKIP: Yeah.

BRUCE: Don't consider everything entirely lost, Sandra.

SANDRA: No. I guess it's not so bad, but I'm wondering what the reaction of my managing editor and my readers is going to be to this Sandra Martin bound over by the Grand Jury on a five thousand dollar bail.

BRUCE: You must try to forget it Sandra. Worrying will do you no good, and, of course, there are a good many things I'll have to take up with you between now and the trial.

SANDRA: Well, seeing you may prove a welcome relief.

BRUCE: It will to me, I assure you, but I'm really concerned over the things you do between now and the trial to keep it off your mind.

| | |
|---|---|
| SANDRA: | Don't worry about that. My work in the next few weeks is pretty well cut out for me. |
| BRUCE: | Oh? What? |
| SANDRA: | I started this whole thing in order to bring that Black Market Ring to justice. The fact that I've been indicted isn't going to change that. |
| SKIP: | Here we go again. |
| BRUCE: | Nonsense. Skip, that's exactly the kind of spirit that will help her see this thing through. You know, I'm glad you asked me here to your apartment, Sandra. I'm happy to see your spirit in action. I've learned to have a great deal of admiration for you in the last few days. |
| SANDRA: | Thank you, Bruce. I hope you'll stick around to help sustain it. |
| SOUND: | *PHONE RINGS* |
| SANDRA: | Excuse me, please. |
| SOUND: | *FOOTSTEPS. RECEIVER OFF HOOK.* |
| SANDRA: | *(IN PHONE)* Yes? |
| HACK: | *(FILTER)* Hello, Sandra? |
| SANDRA: | Hack! Well, this is a surprise. What did you do, call me up in order to gloat? |
| HACK: | I want to see you. It's important. |
| SANDRA: | Anything of importance between us ceased as of day before yesterday. |
| HACK: | Listen to me, Sandra. I know how you feel, but that's beside the point as far as our relationship in this case is concerned. If you'll listen to reason we can help each other. |

| | |
|---|---|
| SANDRA: | That's all I need. A little more of your help and I'll be shot at sunrise. |
| HACK: | Now, listen to me. I'm down stairs . . . and I'm coming up to see you . . . because there are a few things in which I, and I alone, can help you. I'll be right up. |
| SOUND: | *CLICK OF RECEIVER (FILTER)* |
| SANDRA: | Well! How do you like that? |
| SKIP: | WHAT? |
| SOUND: | *RECEIVER ON HOOK* |
| SANDRA: | Our minion of the law is on his way up to see us! |
| SKIP: | Taggart? |
| SANDRA: | None other. |
| SKIP: | Oh! I can't even celebrate my conviction without that guy pokin' his nose in. |
| BRUCE: | Perhaps I better go. From what I've heard, my presence here might prove embarrassing. |
| SANDRA: | Oh no. By all means stay. We don't want to withhold any of our plans from Hack. The poor District Attorney might not have any evidence if we did. |
| SOUND: | *KNOCK ON DOOR FOOTSTEPS DOOR OPENS* |
| SANDRA: | Come in, Hack, come in. We're just celebrating our initiation into the San Quentin Social Order. |
| HACK: | Cut it, will you? |
| SANDRA: | You mean you want to join in the fun? How would you like to be master of ceremonies at this little gathering? |

HACK: You don't understand a lot of things, Sandra, but, most especially, you don't understand that it's sometimes necessary for a man to do things he doesn't want to do.

SANDRA: Like building up a case against innocent people?

HACK: Maybe. Sometimes that's the way to learn the truth.

SANDRA: Let's not get started on the truth. I don't want to have to tell you the truth about yourself just now. Oh, by the way, I don't think you've met my attorney. Lt. Taggart, this is Bruce Elliot.

TAGGART: Hello.

BRUCE: I've heard a lot about you, Lt.

HACK: All bad, I presume.

BRUCE: Well, you could hardly expect our mutual friends to be character witnesses for you. Not after your stand in this matter.

HACK: No. I suppose not, but, just remember this, Elliot, the best time to catch a criminal is when his guard is down.

SANDRA: Just what do you mean by that?

HACK: You'll understand when the time comes. In the meantime, take it any way that is best suits you.

MUSIC: *(TO CURTAIN)*

CUTTING: Remember that old saying, "An ounce of prevention is worth a pound of cure?" Well, how true that is, particularly as far as colds are concerned. Now, if you would like help in avoiding colds (and who wouldn't), why don't you do as countless thousands of others are—help keep up your vitamin A guard by taking a single One-A-Day Brand Vitamin A and D Tablet each day. That single One-A-Day Brand Vitamin A and D Tablet will supply you with twenty-five per cent MORE than your basic daily requirements of BOTH of these vitamins (and the so-called "sunshine vitamin D" is important to you too, and hard to get regardless of the season). Not only are One-A-Day Brand A and D Tablets high in vitamin content, but they're also surprisingly low in cost—just slightly more than a penny a day, when you buy the large $2.15 package. And, of course, they're really pleasant to take. Better be sure of your vitamin A guard against colds. Ask your druggist for One-A-Day Brand Vitamin A and D Tablets right away. Look for the brand with the big one and the name Miles Laboratories on the yellow package.

MUSIC: (THEME ESTABLISH AND FADE DOWN UNDER)

ANNCR: What can be Hack's motive for continuing his persecution of Sandra? Will the introduction into Sandra's life of this brilliant, handsome young lawyer serve to widen the gulf between Hack and Sandra? Listen tomorrow, as our "Lady Of The Press" prepares herself for the interim between now and the murder trial in episode thirteen in "The Picture Of Death".

MUSIC: (THEME UP AND UNDER)

ANNCR: "Lady of the Press" is written by Dwight Hauser and produced by Gordon T. Hughes and is brought to you each day, Monday through Friday at this same time, by the makers of ALKA SELTZER!

MUSIC: (UP TO FILL)

ANNCR: [Dick Cutting speaking] This is CBS, the COLUMBIA BROADCASTING SYSTEM.

# EPISODE #13

# "PICTURE OF DEATH"

| | | |
|---|---|---|
| SPONSOR: | ALKA SELTZER | MAY 10, 1944 |
| AGENCY: | WADE 4:00—4:15 PM, PWT PN | |

---

ANNCR: The makers of Alka Seltzer present—"LADY OF THE PRESS"

*MUSIC:* (STING ...QUICK PUNCTUATION)

ANNCR: The adventures of Sandra Martin, radio's newest romantic-mystery serial!

*MUSIC:* (THEME-ESTABLISH AND FADE OUT:)

CUTTING: You know, this war has taught us all that there are many things we CAN get along without when we have to. Yet there are still many others that are indispensable, and right up at the top of this list is a well-balanced diet. We can't DO our best unless we FEEL our best. So for your own sake and your country's, as well, eat wisely. And for general, all-around vitamin protection—to guard against a vitamin deficiency that can cause you to lack your normal energy, nerves and digestion, and resistance to colds—we suggest that you bolster up your diet with a single One-A-Day Brand Multiple Vitamin Capsule each day. Think of it, friends, by taking just a single One-A-Day Brand Multiple Vitamin Capsule each day, you are sure of getting your full, basic daily requirements of ALL the vitamins whose requirements are known. And quality? One-A-Day Brand Multiple Vitamin Capsules are as fine as can be made—they're laboratory tested and potency guaranteed by Miles. Your druggist has One-A-Day Brand Multiple Vitamin Capsules. Look for the brand with the big one and the name Miles Laboratories on the new blue package.

MUSIC: (THEME.....ESTABLISH AND FADE UNDER)

ANNCR: And now, "Lady Of The Press" and episode thirteen—in, "The Picture of Death."

MUSIC: (STING AND QUICK FIGURATION-FADE DOWN AND OUT UNDER)

ANNCR: The Grand Jury has indicted Sandra Martin, and she must stand trial on suspicion as an accomplice in the murder of Frances Evers. As the city's outstanding newspaper reporter living under the stigma of indictment during the next few weeks will not be pleasant for her. [For] many are bound to condemn her prematurely. Regardless of this, she's determined to proceed with her investigation of the Black Market. Well now, it is the morning after the hearing, and we find Sandra just putting in her first appearance at the paper after her indictment. That facing her friends and co-workers will be humiliating, there can be no doubt... but Sandra Martin is not easily beaten. She enters the office with head high and a smile on her lips.

SOUND: NEWSPAPER OFFICE SOUNDS-FOOTSTEPS-SOUND DIES DOWN QUICKLY FOOTSTEPS COME TO STOP

SANDRA: Hi' gang!

CAST: (AD LIB) (QUIETLY .EMBARRASSED) Morning, Miss Martin. Hi, Hello, Sandra, etc., etc.

SANDRA: (POISE) Now look, let's get one thing straight: this is not to become the demonstration of the penitents. Let's cut out the funeral silence and act like a newspaper office.

BETTY: We—we're all terribly sorry, Miss Martin. We—

SANDRA: Sure, I know how all of you feel, but I don't see a face in the room that looks as though it's owner thought I was guilty—and I'm not—and as long as you believe that, I'll be alright.

MAN: We're for you San.

CAST: *(AD LIB)* You bet we are, one hundred percent. You're okay, Sandra.

SANDRA: Then, let's not have any sobbing until it's time for tears. This fight hasn't really started yet. I may need your help, but you can bet on one thing . . . I'm going to win it.

CAST: *(ENTHUSIASTICALLY)* Thata, girl, Sandra. Don't let 'em kick you around, etc., etc.

SANDRA: Okay, now that we understand each other, let's get back to running a newspaper.

SOUND: *OFFICE SOUNDS BACK UP. CAST AD LIBS-FOOTSTEPS UP AND STOP*

SANDRA: Well, what's the crepe hanging on your face for, Skip?

SKIP: I don't know why I had to be the one to tell you.

SANDRA: Tell me what?

SKIP: The Chief, he came in early. He's boilin' mad! Wanted to see you. Told me to tell you to come to his office the minute you came in.

SANDRA: Oh. Well, maybe this is the time for tears after all.

SKIP: I—if you go—I'm goin' with you, Sandra.

SANDRA: Hmmmm. Good old, Skip. I really believe you're just that dumb.

| | |
|---|---|
| SKIP: | Dumb, nothin! I mean it. |
| SANDRA: | Sure. I know you do. But, forget it. I can take my own medicine. |
| SKIP: | From the look on the Chief's face, it's going to be pretty bitter. |
| SANDRA: | Well, I guess I better go right in before I work up a case of sympathy for myself. |
| SKIP: | I'm sorry, Sandra. |
| SANDRA: | Don't be. Just . . . wish me luck, Skip. |
| SKIP: | You know I do that. |
| SANDRA: | Well, it's not very good policy to keep the boss waiting when he wants to fire you, is it? |
| SKIP: | I guess not. |
| SANDRA: | Keep you're fingers crossed. |
| SKIP: | Tight! |
| SOUND: | *FOOTSTEPS-KNOCK ON DOOR* |
| EDITOR: | *(MUFFLED) (ANGRILY)* Come in! |
| SOUND: | *DOOR OPEN* |
| EDITOR: | *(OFF)* Oh, it's you. Come in. |
| SOUND: | *A FEW STEPS* |
| EDITOR: | Close the door. |
| SOUND: | *DOOR CLOSE* |
| EDITOR: | Now, Miss Martin, will you please tell me the meaning of this disgraceful business? |

SANDRA: I wish I knew the meaning of it.

EDITOR: Well, just what do you intend doing about it?

SANDRA: I got into it by trying to break a black Market Ring, and I intend to go right on with that little job until it's finished.

EDITOR: Well, this is a fine time for a thing like this to happen, a campaign in the offing and nobody that I can put in your place.

SANDRA: Oh. That's really too bad!

EDITOR: Yes, it is. The whole thing's an out and out disgrace.

SANDRA: I'm sorry about the way you feel! I rather expected something a little different from you.

EDITOR: Oh? What did you think I'd do?

SANDRA: I had rather hoped you would stand by me.

EDITOR: Stand by you? Why, my dear young lady, that's exactly what I am doing. Here—read this. It goes on today's [the] editorial page [today] under my personal signature.

SOUND: *RATTLE OF PAPER*

SANDRA: *(READS)* The disgraceful attempt, on the part of certain local groups or individuals, to smear the good name of the Couriers star reporter, will be met, challenged, and fought with all the weapons at the command of this newspaper. Sandra Martin stands indicted by the Grand Jury, but she remains innocent in the eyes of this paper and her fellow workers. This time, somebody has gone too far. To frame Sandra Martin is going to mean breaking this paper first. This fight has—

SANDRA: *(CHOKING TEARS)*

EDITOR: There, there, Sandra. Now, don't you worry. Everything is going to be all right. They can't do a thing like this to you. You've nothing [haven't a thing] to worry about.

SANDRA: It's not that; It's just that everyone's faith in me. Well, it's—it's—

EDITOR: Why shouldn't we have faith in you? You're innocent. ~~aren't you.~~

SANDRA: Of course.

EDITOR: Well, alright, we'll prove it.

SANDRA: Then—what did you mean by putting some one in my place?

EDITOR: Just this: from this minute on, I want you to devote every ~~minute~~ [second] of your time to cracking this case—and ~~that~~ [exposing the] Black Market. I don't want you to worry about ~~one more~~ [any other] story . . . until this thing is in the bag.

SANDRA: You mean . . . you want me to stay on the payroll and just work on that?

EDITOR: That's exactly what I want. Now, get on out of here and get busy.

SANDRA: Well . . . oh, I don't know what to say except that—that—gee, you're a swell boss.

EDITOR: And you're my best reporter. Now, go on and get busy. Oh, and when you go by accounting, stop in and tell them I said to boost your expense account by $20 a week.

MUSIC: (BRIDGE)

~~SOUND: DOOR BELL~~

~~SANDRA: (OFF) See who it is, will you, Dovey.~~

~~DOVEY: Sure.~~

~~SOUND: FOOTSTEPS TO DOOR—...DOOR OPEN~~

SKIP: ~~Hi, Lovey-Dovey.....Sandra here?~~

DOVEY: ~~(IGNORING HIM) (CALLS) Sandra...~~

SANDRA: ~~Yes......?~~

DOVEY: ~~Sompin' outa the comics is here to see you.~~

SKIP: ~~Aw, now Dovey.....You hadn't ought to talk that way about me. ... People all quit readin' those heart throbs of yours if you don't practice what you preach....You ought to be nice to me.~~

DOVEY: ~~Look, menace.....I'll never forgive you for the moniker you hung on me.~~

SANDRA: Gee, Dovey, it's nice to be home ~~The let down in suspense is wonderful.~~ [To let your hair down.]

DOVEY: Are you going to stay home tonight?

SANDRA: I think it would be nice and restful.

DOVEY: Swell. You can keep me company. I have some work to do. After dinner!

SANDRA: I never knew you to work at home. What's up?

DOVEY: Look . . . rubber bands, a whole sack full. I got 'em from the butcher.

SANDRA: Well, what are you going to do with them?

DOVEY: Sew 'em into my girdle. That thing is like sheet metal cast the way it is now.

SANDRA: *(CHUCKLES)* You know, Dovey, you expect too much from a girdle. You ought to know by now that no matter how much you squeeze yourself in one place, it's bound to come out in another.

| | |
|---|---|
| SOUND: | *DOOR BELL* |
| SANDRA: | *(OFF)* See who it is, will you, Dovey. |
| DOVEY: | Sure. |
| SOUND: | *FOOTSTEPS TO DOOR. DOOR OPEN* |
| SKIP: | Hi, Lovey-Dovey. Sandra here? |
| DOVEY: | *(IGNORING HIM) (CALLS)* Sandra. |
| SANDRA: | Yes. |
| DOVEY: | Sompin outa the comics is here to see you. |
| SKIP: | Aw, now Dovey, you hadn't ought to talk that way about me. People will quit readin' those heart throbs of yours if you don't practice what you preach. You ought to be nice to me. |
| DOVEY: | Look, menace, I ought to destroy you. I'll never forgive you for the moniker you hung on me. |
| SKIP: | You mean Lovey-Dovey? Aw, I think it's sweet. It's an expression of the way ~~we~~ all [of us down at the paper] feel about you. |
| DOVEY: | So, for the rest of my life, everybody forgets there's such a person as Marian Lang. An' I even get so all I answer to is "Dovey." |
| SANDRA: | *(FADING IN)* Oh, hello, Skip. What brings you here? |
| SKIP: | Well, we sorta got into this thing together, an' after you left the Chief's office, you beat it without sayin' anything. I sorta wondered where we go from here. |
| DOVEY: | Get him! I actually believe he's jealous because the Grand Jury ~~left him out of the indictment~~ [indicted him 2nd]. |

| | |
|---|---|
| SKIP: | Aw, go pull a heart string. [Well, what happened, baby?] |
| SANDRA: | Well, the chief boosted my expense account and put me on my own case exclusively. |
| [SKIP: | Well how about that? |
| SANDRA: | So, I started by spending the day with my attorney. |
| SKIP: | No sooner do I get that dumb cop outa the way than, Bing! I walk smack into a bright attorney for competition. |
| SANDRA: | Don't be silly, Skip. I had business with him. |
| SKIP: | Yeah, and from the look in his eye, I'd say there was going to be a lot of that business from now on. |
| SANDRA: | He's a fine attorney, and I admire him. |
| SKIP: | ~~Yeah~~ [Uh-huh]. Well, you're goin' to need a good one. |
| SANDRA: | I know. |
| ~~SKIP:~~ | ~~Seriously San… What do we do next?~~ |
| ~~SANDRA:~~ | ~~We go to work tooth and nail tryin' to get at that Black Market.~~ |
| ~~SKIP:~~ | ~~We gonna forget about Hoagan?~~ |
| ~~SANDRA:~~ | ~~They're one and one and the same as far as I'm concerned… Once we crack one… we'll have the other.~~ |
| ~~SKIP:~~ | ~~Fine… Where do we start?~~ |
| ~~SANDRA:~~ | ~~With those license numbers you took the other day.~~ |
| ~~SKIP:~~ | ~~Good… I still got 'em.~~ |
| ~~SANDRA:~~ | ~~First thing in the morning… We'll get on it…~~ |

SKIP: ~~Swell~~ Then, [in the meantime] how about a movie tonight? Sorta get things off your [our] mind[s].

SANDRA: You know, I think that's a good idea. Dovey and I were just ready to go out to dinner. You can come along and then take us to a movie afterward.

SKIP: Oh great. Nothin' like havin' a love expert ~~right~~ along with you when you're on a date.

DOVEY: Come on, stupid, I'll be watchin' the picture.

SOUND: FOOTSTEPS TO DOOR. DOOR OPENS

SANDRA: You know, I'm glad the decision finally came. It's put an end to the suspense. Now I can relax with the complete knowledge that I'm a suspect.

HACK: Hello Sandra.

SANDRA: Hack . . . where did you come from?

HACK: I was just on my way to see you. Going out?

SANDRA: Well, yes, that is, I was—

HACK: I'd like to talk to you . . . if you can postpone your date.

SANDRA: Is there really anything we can talk about, Hack?

HACK: I think so. And . . . it'll be good for both of us.

SANDRA: Seems to me you've pretty much had your say . . . in court.

HACK: I know. That's over now, for a while at least. Now, it's time for us to get back to working together on this thing..

[SANDRA: No, Hack.

HACK: I'm asking you to come back in and talk. I've some pretty important things to say.

| | |
|---|---|
| SANDRA: | Well, Skip, do you mind? You and Dovey go ahead. I'll try and join you later. |
| SKIP: | I am a sucker, and, brother, am I being taken. Come on, sweetheart, this romance is even beyond you. |
| SOUND: | *FOOTSTEPS FADING* |
| HACK: | Well, aren't you going to ask me in? The hall isn't a very good place to talk. |
| SANDRA: | All right. Come on in. But this talking your going to do better be grade "A". |
| HACK: | Don't worry. It will be. Grade "A" and ration free. |
| SOUND: | *FOOTSTEPS-DOOR CLOSE* |
| HACK: | Mind if I sit down? |
| SANDRA: | No, of course not. |
| HACK: | It's been a long time since we sat in this room . . . alone. |
| SANDRA: | *(WELLING TEARS)* Now look, Hack, if you think you can play on my memories of what we once meant to one another just to get me to forget the rotten thing ~~you did~~ [you've done to me] you're crazy. |
| ~~HACK:~~ | ~~Didn't mean it that way at all…I just thought I'd mention that it was nice to be back here alone with you.~~ |
| ~~SANDRA:~~ | ~~I wanted you to come here often when you first came back from overseas…But, you have too hard a head for memories.~~ |
| ~~HACK:~~ | ~~Let's not bicker Sandra…I came here to talk to you seriously…Not about what we used to be…Not even about us…Except as regards this mess your in.~~ |
| SANDRA: | And just who got me into this mess? |

| | |
|---|---|
| HACK: | I had a lot to do with it, I'll admit. But, suppose now I were to tell you that I can clear you of the whole thing? |
| SANDRA: | I know you can! You know I'm innocent. |
| HACK: | And suppose I were to tell you that proving your innocence is exactly what I'm trying to do? What would you say? |
| SANDRA: | I'd say . . . you were lying. |
| MUSIC: | (TO CURTAIN) |
| CUTTING: | You know, friends, millions of people in this great land of ours are enjoying healthier, more active lives these days because they are getting sufficient vitamins. How about you? Are you getting enough vitamins each day to help keep up your normal resistance to colds, and to help you maintain normal energy, nerves and digestion, and strong bones and teeth? Well, a mighty easy, economical way to be sure you get your FULL basic daily requirements of ALL the vitamins whose requirements are known, is to bolster your diet every day with a single One-A-Day-Brand Multiple Vitamin Capsule, the kind that has eight different vitamins, all in one easy-to-take capsule. Think of it, friends—just one One-A-Day-Brand Multiple Vitamin Capsule each day and the job is done. And the cost is unbelievably low. Why, then, allow a vitamin deficiency to make you, or any of your family feel fagged out, nervous, irritable or troubled with poor digestion or colds, when a single One-A-Day-Brand Multiple Vitamin Capsule each day can do so much for you? Ask YOUR druggist for One-A-Day-Brand Multiple Vitamin Capsules, in the blue package with the big one and the name Miles Laboratories. |
| MUSIC: | (THEME-ESTABLISH AND FADE DOWN UNDER) |
| ANNCR: | What do you suppose is Hack's reason for taking this new tactic? Has he experienced a change of heart, and does he honestly wish to help Sandra now? Or, will his apparent interest in her welfare take the same course as his past actions? Listen tomorrow as our "Lady of the Press" faces |

|        |                                                                                                                                                                    |
|--------|--------------------------------------------------------------------------------------------------------------------------------------------------------------------|
|        | this new development in her relation with Hack Taggart in episode fourteen of "The Picture of Death."                                                              |
| MUSIC: | (UP AND UNDER)                                                                                                                                                     |
| ANNCR: | "Lady of the Press" is written by Dwight Hauser, and produced by Gordon T. Hughes, and is brought to you each day, Monday through Friday at this same time, by the makers of—ALKA SELTZER. |
| MUSIC: | (UP TO FILL)                                                                                                                                                       |
| ANNCR: | [Dick Cutting speaking] This is CBS, THE COLUMBIA BROADCASTING SYSTEM.                                                                                             |

# EPISODE #14

# "PICTURE OF DEATH"

| | |
|---|---|
| SPONSOR: | ALKA SELTZER    MAY 18, 1944 |
| AGENCY: | WADE  4:00—4:15 PM, PWT PN |

---

ANNCR: The makers of Alka Seltzer present—"LADY OF THE PRESS"

MUSIC: *(STING...QUICK PUNCTUATION)*

ANNCR: The adventures of Sandra Martin, radio's newest romantic-mystery serial!

MUSIC: *(THEME-ESTABLISH AND FADE OUT:)*

CUTTING: You know, friends, we had some folks out to the house the other night and while we were sitting around talking, one of them complained about "not being able to take it like he used to" (as he put it). So, I asked him what about his eating habits, and he told me just as I suspected—he doesn't have enough time to eat as he should. When he does eat, it's more frequently than not just a sandwich, a piece of pie, and a cup of coffee. Well, these are good foods but, unfortunately, they are very likely to be seriously lacking in B-vitamins—those vitamins we need all the more these days for normal nerves, energy and digestion. Now, how about you? Are YOU getting enough of the B-vitamins out of your food to "keep up to par?" Well, why take chances when now, by taking a single One-A-Day Brand Vitamin B-Complex Tablet each day, you can be sure of getting your full basic daily requirements of ALL the B-vitamins whose requirements are known. You can't beat that single table convenience. What's more, One-A-Day Brand B-Complex Tablets are mighty economical for the same reason. So don't put it off. Ask your druggist for One-A-Day Brand Vitamin B-Complex Tablets right away. They come in the gray package with the big one and the name Miles Laboratories.

MUSIC: *(THEME-ESTABLISH AND FADE)*

ANNCR: And now, "Lady Of The Press", and episode fourteen—in— "THE PICTURE OF DEATH."

MUSIC: *(STING AND QUICK FIGURATION FADES OUT UNDER)*

ANNCR: Following Sandra Martin's indictment by the Grand Jury, due largely to the evidence presented or with held by him, Hack Taggart has now come to Sandra offering his aid and cooperation. Sandra has been deeply hurt by Hacks action since his return to civilian life on a medical discharge. Her efforts to rehabilitate this man who she once loved so completely have led only to tears and heartbreak for her. Conflicting emotions fill her heart and mind as she glimpses once more at a fleeting indication of the man she once loved, in this new attitude of Hacks.

SANDRA: Why have you done this to me, Hack? Is it, that your bitterness has crowded out all kindness, all compassion? Or is it that you honestly believe I might be guilty?

HACK: I know you're not guilty.

SANDRA: Then, why?

HACK: Perhaps you'll understand, sometime, Sandra. In the meantime, all I can do is ask you to trust me. I cannot explain things just now.

| | |
|---|---|
| SANDRA: | That's asking a great deal of a person whom you've helped to convict. |
| HACK: | Sandra, how often must you be told that you've not been convicted? You've been indicted. You'll stand trial and be given an opportunity to prove your innocence. |
| SANDRA: | But, what about the humiliation, in the meantime? |
| HACK: | You happen to be living in a country where you are considered innocent until proven guilty. |
| SANDRA: | Oh, don't be naive, Hack. There are thousands of people to whom the mere connection of my name with the suspicion of murder will condemn me. |
| HACK: | Only narrow minded bigotry would react that way. |
| SANDRA: | But unfortunately, there's an awful lot of bigotry in this world. |
| HACK: | I know it's unfortunate. I don't suppose it will do any good to tell you that there was no other way. But, you'll see. This way is the only right way, no matter how wrong it looks at present. |
| SANDRA: | I can't understand you anymore, Hack. If you were the same person I fell in love with, I'd know what to say to you now, but, as things stand, the only thing I can say is that what you've done has hurt, and I don't intend to let myself in for any more of the same. |
| HACK: | All right. Sorry, you feel that way. Then, let's put in on a purely business basis. You're going to need some evidence with which to clear yourself. |
| SANDRA: | You already have enough to clear me. |
| HACK: | I don't think so. You're going to need evidence against the Black Market, and you're going to need the person of Hoagan. I know that you realize that, and I know you'll try and get it. |

SANDRA: And if I do?

HACK: If you do, you're going to get into a lot of trouble. You're going to need help, and, when that time comes, I'll be around to offer it.

SANDRA: Hack, I—

HACK: You can take what help I'll give any way you like. You may think it's because of our personal relationship, or you may consider it part of my job. It's entirely up to you.

SANDRA: I, think you better go now. You've put so many obstacles in the way of my trusting you that, even though that's what I'd rather do than anything else in the world, it's going to take some thinking over. I think I'll arrive at a more sane decision if I do that thinking by myself.

HACK: Okay. Sorry I spoiled your evening, but, I wanted you to know.

SANDRA: It doesn't matter. Skip and Dovey will be back later. In the meantime, I think it will be better for me to be alone.

HACK: Good night.

SANDRA: Good night, Hack.

SOUND: *FOOTSTEPS. DOOR OPEN*

HACK: Just one thing more . . . if things don't look straight to you right now, try and postpone your judgment until all the ends are tied up. It'll be better that way . . . for both of us.

SOUND: *DOOR CLOSE*

SANDRA: *(CHOKING SOB)* Oh, Hack, Hack.

~~MUSIC:~~ ~~*(BRIDGE)*~~ *[BOARD FADE]*

SOUND: *TRAFFIC*

| | |
|---|---|
| SKIP: | Flicker me eyelids, if that wasn't the longest, dullest movie I ever saw. |
| DOVEY: | There's one thing I've never been able to figure out. |
| SKIP: | Oh, baby, did you leave yourself wide open. But, I'll skip it. What's that? |
| DOVEY: | How can a fourth-rate quickie be an added attraction to a second rate B picture that isn't any attraction in the first place? |
| SKIP: | *(CONFUSED)* What did you say? |
| DOVEY: | Thinking back, it doesn't make sense to me, either. |
| SKIP: | Hey, here's a cab. We better hop it and get you home. We been gone over four hours, and Sandra's alone. |
| DOVEY: | So? |
| SKIP: | Well, after yesterday, it doesn't seem right to leave her all by herself. |
| DOVEY: | What gives you the idea that she's alone? We left her in charge of the pride of the homicide squad. |
| SKIP: | Yeah, but after what he pulled on her, she's not going to keep him around long. My guess is that she gave him the brush off and sent him home to bed. |
| DOVEY: | You really do have a weak mind, don't you? |
| SKIP: | Cab? Hey, Cab! |
| DRIVER: | *(DUB SKIP)* Yeah. Hop in. |
| SOUND: | DOOR OPEN |
| SKIP: | After you, me proud beauty. |

DOVEY: What?

SKIP: Oh well, you're proud, anyway.

SOUND: DOOR CLOSE

DRIVER: Where to?

SKIP: 777 Elmwood Drive.

SOUND: STARTER-MOTOR START-CAB PULLING OUT

SKIP: Ah, at last. The last map of a wasted evening, if I ever had one.

DOVEY: Yes, Sandra was lucky to stay home. Wonder what she's doing with her evening?

~~MUSIC: (BRIDGE)~~ [BOARD FADE]

SOUND: DOOR BELL (SANDRAS) FOOTSTEPS-DOOR OPEN

SANDRA: Well, you two certainly—(STARTS)

MAN: Expecting somebody else, Miss Martin?

SANDRA: You—what are you doing here? What do you want?

MAN: Just a little talk. I enjoyed our conversation so much the other day at Miss Evers house, I thought I'd like to see more of you.

SANDRA: You get out of here! There are plenty of people who can hear me if I scream . . . and believe me I will.

MAN: One yelp out you, lady and you'll be pickin' lead out your pretty head. Now, get back in there.

~~SOUND: FOOTSTEPS~~

~~SANDRA: You seem to be a very brave man...I notice you always have a gun to bolster your bravery.~~

| | |
|---|---|
| ~~MAN:~~ | ~~Yeah…I like it that way.~~ |
| SOUND: | *DOOR CLOSE* |
| SANDRA: | Just what is it that you want? |
| MAN: | Well, I like you. You're a nice girl, an' beside that, your pretty. I wouldn't want to see anything happen to you. |
| SANDRA: | So, you've set yourself up as my personal protector, I suppose? |
| MAN: | In a manner of speakin', I guess you could call it that. You see, I know a lot about you. That's part of my business. |
| SANDRA: | Oh? Who pays you for that? |
| MAN: | Well, now that's going to have to remain a secret, but, here's somethin' that ain't. You're in a sweet little mess already. Now, if you just lay off a few ideas that you have, there are some friends of mine that can help straighten things out for you. |
| SANDRA: | In what way? |
| MAN: | Well, these friends of mine have a little business. They, don't like to have people pokin' their noses into it. Especially newspaper people who try to connect that business up with a murder. |
| SANDRA: | I suppose you're going to tell me next that there is no connection? |
| MAN: | As a matter of fact there ain't, but, that's beside the point. These friends of mine don't want you snoopin' around in regardless. |
| SANDRA: | You can tell your friends that I'll snoop wherever I please. |
| MAN: | All right. I'll tell em', but I don't think they'll like it. |

SANDRA: I didn't expect them to.

MAN: An' if they don't like what you do, then they might decide not to help you outta the jam your in. As a matter of fact, they might even decide to make it even tougher.

SANDRA: That would take a genius.

MAN: Not necessarily. As a matter of fact, all they have to do is sit tight. They got the thing that will make it tougher.

SANDRA: Meaning Hoagan?

MAN: You're a good guesser.

SANDRA: Do you think you can bluff me into giving up the fight against these Black Market rats in order to get Hoagan into court?

MAN: It'd be the smart thing to do, if Hoagan doesn't show up. It's going to be that much tougher on you.

SANDRA: But, how do I know you have him? How do I know this isn't a bluff you're pulling?

MAN: You don't. That's why I come to see you personally. I'd like for you to take a little trip with me. I'd like for you to meet Hoagan personally . . . then you can see for yourself.

SANDRA: You mean that you'd take me to Hoagan?

MAN: If you'll play ball. That's the whole idea.

SANDRA: But, how do I know this isn't a trap?

MAN: Lady, we already got you in a trap. We just want you to see how tight it can spring.

SANDRA: All right. I'll go with you on one condition.

MAN: What's that?

| | |
|---|---|
| SANDRA: | That you guarantee my safe return to this apartment within twenty-four hours. |
| MAN: | Oh sure, baby. You got my word for it. |
| SANDRA: | Yes, but I want a little bit more solid guarantee than that. |
| MAN: | Don't you trust me? |
| SANDRA: | No. I trust facts. [Now] Here is only one condition upon which I'll go with you. |
| MAN: | Okay, Lady? ~~State your terms.~~ |
| ~~SANDRA:~~ | ~~(FADING) Good—Now here is what I want....~~ |
| ~~SOUND:~~ | ~~FOOTSTEPS DOWN HILL~~ [BOARD FADE] |
| ~~SOUND:~~ | ~~FOOTSTEPS~~ |
| SKIP: | Well, here we are, back to your little nest, Dovey. |
| DOVEY: | Ring for Sandra, will you? My key is under a lot of stuff in my purse. |
| SKIP: | Sure. |
| SOUND: | DOOR BELL (MUFFLED) |
| DOVEY: | I hope we aren't disturbing a tryst. |
| SKIP: | A what? |
| DOVEY: | A tryst. A moment of divine love. A fleeting emotion of lovers enthralled. |
| SKIP: | Save it for your column. Well, what's holding up the parade? |
| DOVEY: | Ring it again. |

[SOUND:	DOOR BELL]

SKIP:	Okay. I suppose we could stand out here ringin' door bells all night before you condescend to dig for that key.

DOVEY:	Okay, never mind. Here it is.

SKIP:	Allow me.

SOUND:	KEY IN LOCK

DOVEY:	My, such chivalry. It's not natural to you, Skip.

SKIP:	Oh no, ya' think I took a correspondence course?

DOVEY:	Maybe.

SOUND:	DOOR OPEN

DOVEY:	Hi San. Sorry we're so late. Hey, San—

SKIP:	Maybe she's in the kitchen. I hope so. I'm hungry.

DOVEY:	Take a look. I'll look in the bedroom.

SOUND:	FOOTSTEPS—DOOR OPEN

SKIP:	Hey, San. You out here?
	(CALLS)
	She's not in here, Dovey.

DOVEY:	(OFF) Not in the bedroom either. I guess she and Hack must have gone out.

SKIP:	Yeah. Well, they'll be back before long. I want to see her before I go home. Suppose you brew me up a cup of java while we're waitin'?

MUSIC:	TO CURTAIN.

CUTTING:	Say, here's some information that will probably come as a big surprise to all you ladies who pride yourselves on serving well balanced meals at your house. Do you know just how difficult it is to be sure that your family gets enough of the B-vitamins from their foods? Well, the B-vitamin content of food varies with its age—the kind of soil it's grown in—the way it's cooked. Now, since the B-vitamins are so essential for grownups and children alike—for normal energy, digestion and nerves—it will pay you to supplement your family's diet by giving them each a single One-A-Day Brand Vitamin B-Complex Tablet each day. That single One-A-Day B-Complex Tablet is so rich in these important vitamins that it supplies their full basic daily requirements of ALL the B-vitamins whose requirements are known. That single table convenience is important to you because it's far easier to remember to take one tablet each day than it is three or four—and of course, the vitamins you forget to take can't possibly do you any good. That single table makes for economy, too. So, for the kind of vitamins that help you maintain normal energy, nerves and digestion, ask for One-A-Day Brand Vitamin B-Complex Tablets. Look for the big one and the name Miles Laboratories on the gray package.

MUSIC: *(THEME-ESTABLISH AND FADE UNDER)*

ANNCR: Has Sandra let herself be led by this strange man into a position from which she cannot return? Or, did she know of a way to guarantee her safe return? How long will it be before Skip and Dovey realize that she did not go out with Hack? Listen tomorrow ~~as our "Lady of The Press" enters a house of mystery with the strange man in~~ [when the whereabouts of our "Lady of The Press" becomes more of a mystery in] episode fifteen of "THE PICTURE OF DEATH."

MUSIC: *(STING AND FADE UNDER)*

ANNCR: "Lady Of The Press is written by Dwight Hauser, and produced by Gordon T. Hughes and is brought to you each day, Monday through Friday at this same time by the makers of—ALKA SELTZER.

MUSIC:      (TO FILL)

ANNCR:      [Dick Cutting speaking] This is CBS. The COLUMBIA BROADCASTING SYSTEM.

# EPISODE #15

# "PICTURE OF DEATH"

| | | |
|---|---|---|
| SPONSOR: | ALKA SELTZER | MAY 19, 1944 |
| AGENCY: | WADE 4:00—4:15 PM, PWT PN | |

---

ANNCR: The makers of Alka Seltzer present—"LADY OF THE PRESS"

MUSIC: *(STING) (QUICK PUNCTUATION)*

ANNCR: The adventures of Sandra Martin, radio's newest romantic-mystery serial!

MUSIC: *(THEME-ESTABLISH AND FADE OUT)*

CUTTING: I wonder how many of you listeners are letting a vitamin deficiency keep you from feeling like your own normal self, sapping your vitality, robbing you of steady nerves and good digestion, making you more susceptible to colds? Well, Nature intended you to enjoy good health and through no fault of Hers, it is pretty hard nowadays for you to be sure you get enough vitamins from natural sources. So, why run the risk of a vitamin deficiency and its consequences when now, by taking a single One-A-Day Brand Multiple Vitamin Capsule each day, you can get your full basic daily requirements of all the vitamins whose requirements are known? Now, what could be easier? And, of course, One-A-Day Brand Multiple Vitamin Capsules are economical—a sixty day supply of sixty capsules only costs two dollars. Yet in spite of their low cost, they offer you the very highest quality in vitamins that money can buy. So start now to give your family the protective benefits of ample vitamins by giving them each a single One-A-Day Brand Multiple Vitamins Capsule each day. Your druggist has them. Look for the brand with the big one and the name Miles Laboratories on the new <u>blue</u> package. That's the "one" to buy.

MUSIC: (THEME-ESTABLISH AND FADE DOWN)

ANNCR: And now, "Lady Of The Press" and episode fifteen—in— "THE PICTURE OF DEATH".

MUSIC: (STING AND QUICK FIGURATION FADES OUT UNDER)

ANNCR: Arriving back at the girls' apartment after attending a late movie, Skip and Dovey find Sandra missing. At first, they believe she has gone out with Hack Taggart with whom they left her. However, after waiting several hours, their suspicions turn to fear as they realize that something is amiss. They have no way of knowing that Sandra has gone willingly with the strange man who promised her an audience with Elbert Hoagan. Did they know with whom she left their fear for her safety would increased? For, they do not know, as we do, that Sandra had a plan whereby she believed she could guarantee her safe return to the apartment.

SKIP: I don't like this, Dovey. Somethin's wrong. It's after three a.m.

DOVEY: I know. Sandra's not in the habit of staying away so long without letting anyone know.

SKIP: Of course, leaving her to the protection of that Taggart is just the same as turning her over to a Jap Prison camp. We should have known better.

DOVEY: Well, what are we going to do? Sit here and think of all the things we shouldn't have done? Or, are we going to start looking for her?

SKIP: You got any ideas where to start?

DOVEY: No.

SKIP: Well, much as I hate to, I suppose we better begin with Taggart. He was the last one to see her . . . that we know of.

DOVEY: Yes. You better call him.

SKIP: The only part of calling him that gives me any pleasure is that it's so late. Probably get him out of bed.

SOUND: *A FEW FOOTSTEPS*

DOVEY: Why she can't just stick to reporting and forget this crusading is more than I'll ever figure out.

SKIP: That's probably why you're writing advice to the love sick while she's the Star reporter.

SOUND: *DIALING OF PHONE*

DOVEY: I write that column because I like it, not because I want to do something better and can't.

SKIP: Well, it's nice to be able to recognize ones own limitations.

DOVEY: Oh, go pop a flash bulb.

SKIP: *(TO HIMSELF)* Come on, Taggart. Wake up. The best thing you do is sleep. Come on, will ya? *(TRANSPOSITION)* Hello? Hello, Hack? This is Skip. Yeah. What? Look, Boy Scout, I'm not calling you in order to visit; I'm calling to find out what you've done with Sandra. That's right. No, she's not here! Would I be callin' and askin' you, if she was? Well, when did you leave? *(TO DOVEY)* He says he only stayed about half an hour. *(BACK IN PHONE)* An' you haven't seen her or heard from her since? Oh. Well, then in that case, I think you better get off the dime and start lookin' for her. Yeah. That's right. And look, let me know what you find out. Oh, never mind about me, I got a few plans about findin' her myself.

SOUND: *RECIEVER ON HOOK*

DOVEY: Well?

SKIP: He only stayed half an hour. That means she was alone, from eight until we came in at 12:30. Holy smoke, anything might have happened to her in that length of time!

DOVEY: Wait a minute. I've got an idea. Maybe the landlady saw her go out, or somebody else come in.

SKIP: That's a good idea. You check with her, while I call the paper. We gotta get goin'. In the spot she's in, she wouldn't be safe in the Mayor's office.

MUSIC: *(BRIDGE)*

SOUND: *DOOR OPEN*

SKIP: Yeah? What'd 'ya find out?

DOVEY: Plenty! .Although I don't know how much good it will do.

SKIP: Well, come on, spill it, will you?

DOVEY: Well, the landlady said Taggart left early.

SKIP: We already know that.

DOVEY: Then, she says she didn't see any more of Sandra until about eleven o'clock. Then, she went out of here with a man.

SKIP: A man . . . a man . . . what man? Did she know him? Who was he?

DOVEY: She never saw him before. She said he was medium height, dark skin, wore a thin black mustache, and had a black hat, which he wore low over his left eye.

SKIP: The mug! That's who it was. The same guy that stole Frances Evers file from us and then knocked me cold in the Alto. Ohhhhh! If he's got Sandra, no telling what might happen to her.

DOVEY: How about doing away with the speculation getting down to action.

SKIP: How? How do we know where they are?

DOVEY: We don't, but you haven't let me finish telling you what I found out from the Landlady.

SKIP: You know more? Well spill it.

DOVEY: Fine, if I can keep you quiet long enough. She said she thought it was kinda late for Sandra to be going out with a strange man. And so she watched them. There was a sedan parked in front, but they walked on by it down to the corner mail box. She said it looked as though they mailed a letter and then they came back and got in the car and drove off.

SKIP: Did she get the license number?

DOVEY: No. It was pretty dark. And besides, she said if looked to her as though the license plates were covered with mud.

SKIP: That's it! The same car! Come on.

DOVEY: Where?

SKIP: I don't know if it's any good or not, but, the only thing I can think of right now is to have a look in that mail box.

*MUSIC:* (BRIDGE)

| | |
|---|---|
| SOUND: | HEAVY POUNDING ON METAL |
| DOVEY: | Honestly, Skip, you are just about the most ignorant character in town. |
| SKIP: | (STRUGGLING WITH MAIL BOX) What do you mean I got to get it open haven't I? |
| DOVEY: | I don't know, but, I do know that breaking into a post box is a Federal Offense. |
| SKIP: | So it's a Federal Offense. You don't see any G men around do you? |
| DOVEY: | No, but, any cop could arrest you for it, and that little detail carries a mighty stiff rap. |
| SKIP: | Right now, I'm interested in only one thing: finding out what Sandra put in this mail box. And, I'm going to do it if I have to bust the thing into (GRUNTS WITH BLOWS) a thousand (GRUNTS) pieces! |
| DOVEY: | Why don't you try the lock? |
| SKIP: | Have you lost your marbles? They wouldn't leave one of these things unlocked. |
| DOVEY: | But a little tap on the padlock might. |
| SKIP: | Okay, cracksman. Why don't you have a try at it? Here's the hammer. |
| DOVEY: | All right. Hold the padlock up edgewise, will ya? |
| SKIP: | (SARCASTICALLY) We could also do it with nitro. |
| SOUND: | RATTLE OF LOCK |
| DOVEY: | Keep quiet and hold the lock still. |
| SOUND: | RATTLE OF LOCK |

| | |
|---|---|
| SKIP: | Okay, go ahead. |
| *SOUND:* | *BLOW* |
| SKIP: | DOOOOOOO! You stupid—you hit m' finger! |
| DOVEY: | Did I? Sorry. |
| SKIP: | You're sorry. . |
| DOVEY: | Slightly, but it was worth it. |
| SKIP: | What do ya mean? |
| DOVEY: | Look what you're holding in your hand? |
| SKIP: | Huh? *(TAKE)* The padlock! All right, you win. Look out. Stand back while I open it up. |
| *SOUND:* | *STEEL MAIL BOX DOOR OPENING* |
| DOVEY: | Hurry it up will you? If we get caught— |
| SKIP: | Hey, will you look at this thing? |
| DOVEY: | Yes. What is it? |
| SKIP: | It's empty, that's what. What's eatin' that landlady? Sandra never mailed any letter in this box. |
| DOVEY: | Wait a minute, I just happened to think . . . isn't there a card telling the pick up times? |
| SKIP: | I guess so. Yeah. Here it is. |
| DOVEY: | What's the latest one? |
| SKIP: | *(READING)* Twelve thirty . . . a.m. |
| DOVEY: | Oh great! You couldn't have thought of that before beating the box to pieces, could you? |

| | |
|---|---|
| SKIP: | Did you? |
| DOVEY: | Come on, Watson, let's get out of here. |
| SOUND: | *FOOTSTEPS ON PAVEMENT* |
| SKIP: | I don't get it. What would she be going to the mail box for anyway? |
| DOVEY: | Why does anyone go to a mail box? |
| SKIP: | To mail a letter, but . . . if she was with that mug, I don't imagine he was in favor of her launching on any communication. |
| DOVEY: | So, where do we go from here? |
| SKIP: | You go back in and wait. Maybe we'll hear from her, or from the mug. In the meantime, I'm going over to the department for a talk with Taggart. I'll be by here the first thing in the morning. |
| DOVEY: | It's morning now, sweetheart. |
| SKIP: | All right. Whatever you do, don't leave the apartment, just in case there's some attempt made to contact us. I'll be by after nine. |
| MUSIC: | (BRIDGE) |
| SOUND: | *DOOR BELL* |
| SKIP: | (YAWNS) |
| SOUND: | *DOOR OPEN* |
| SKIP: | Morning, Dovey. Hear anything? |
| DOVEY: | Not a word. |
| SOUND: | *DOOR CLOSES* |

| | |
|---|---|
| DOVEY: | How about you? |
| SKIP: | Been with Hack all night. He's started a search. Boy, I'm so groggy, I don't know if I'd even recognize Sandra. |
| DOVEY: | By the time that mug gets through with her, probably none of us will. Look, we've got to do something . . . and quick. |
| SKIP: | I know it, but we're at a dead end. There's just nothing to start with. |
| DOVEY: | There has to be. |
| SKIP: | Trouble is that it takes so long to check up on any clues. I got a picture of that mug the day he stole the file from us. Sandra and I were planin' on usin' it for a story, but, I turned it over to Hack. He's checkin' that. Outside of that, we're at a stand still. |
| DOVEY: | It doesn't seem possible that anyone as well known as Sandra could just disappear completely. |
| SKIP: | No. |
| SOUND: | *TELEPHONE RING. A FEW STEPS.* |
| SKIP: | Answer it quick. Maybe it's San. |
| DOVEY: | Don't get your hopes up too high. |
| SOUND: | *RECIEVER OFF HOOK.* |
| DOVEY: | Hello? Oh, yes, he's here. *(TO SKIP)* It's Taggart. Wants to talk to you. |
| SKIP: | Okay. |
| SOUND: | *A FEW FOOTSTEPS* |
| SKIP: | Yeah? Yeah. Oh, you did, huh? Find out anything? No record of the guy? Aw nuts! I was hopin' that picture would do us some good. Sure, sure, I'll get the Courier to run it, |

but what for? Yeah, somebody might see him and recognize him. Yeah, okay. Anything else some up? Well, look, sonny, you better get your merit badges on get out lookin' for her.

| | |
|---|---|
| SOUND: | *RECIEVER ON HOOK* |
| DOVEY: | No trace of her? |
| SKIP: | Naw. |
| SOUND: | *DOOR BELL RING* |
| DOVEY: | Somebody at the door. |
| SKIP: | Yeah we'll open it. Don't just stand there. |
| DOVEY: | *(SCARED)* Suppose it's . . . it's one of them? |
| SKIP: | Okay. Okay. I'll open and I hope it is one of them. |
| SOUND: | *DOOR OPEN* |
| SKIP: | Oh, mail. |
| SOUND: | *DOOR CLOSE* |
| SKIP: | Couple of letters. Here you are. |
| DOVEY: | Thanks. Hey! |
| SKIP: | What's the matter? |
| DOVEY: | This one in the brown envelope, it's addressed to you, and it's got Sandra's name in the left hand corner. |
| SKIP: | What? Gimme it. |
| DOVEY: | Open it. Maybe it's— |
| SOUND: | *TEARING PAPER* |

SKIP: I am, I am, can't ya see?

SOUND: *RATTLE OF PAPER*

DOVEY: What's it say? What—

SKIP: Be quiet and let me see, will ya? *(READING)* Skip, I am sending you this letter along with another to myself. *(TO DOVEY)* Is that other one to Sandra.

DOVEY: Yes.

SKIP: *(READING)* If I am not back by twelve o'clock noon on Monday, take the letter addressed to me and turn it over to the police. In that envelope is information which will lead to my captors if I fail to return. Don't worry until then, and under no condition open the other letter before twelve. Signed, Sandra. *(TO DOVEY)* Now ain't that a lulu? We gotta sit on the hot seat until noon before we can find out what's in that letter.

MUSIC: *(CURTAIN)*

CUTTING: You know, friends, everywhere you go these days you hear folks talking about the amazing new vitamin product of the Miles Laboratories—One-A-Day Brand Multiple Vitamin Capsules, multiple because they contain eight vitamins all in one single capsule. And it's no wonder either that One-A-Day Brand Multiple Vitamin Capsules are growing so fast in popularity because they have everything you could want in a vitamin product. Certainly they're convenient to take. Just a single One-A-Day Brand Multiple Vitamin Capsule each day supplies you with your full basic daily requirements of ALL the vitamins whose requirements are known—helping you to guard against a vitamin deficiency which could cause you to be tired out, nervous, irritable, subject to frequent colds. And because a single capsule each day does the job of three or four lower potency capsules, that brings the cost way down. So, if you want eight different vitamins in one capsule for general all around vitamin protection, ask your druggist for One-A-Day Brand Multiple Vitamin Capsules. Look for the big one on the <u>blue</u> package.

| | |
|---|---|
| MUSIC: | (THEME ESTABLISH AND FADE UNDER |
| ANNCR: | Within that envelope is there contained a sure means of guaranteeing Sandra's safe return, or will twelve o'clock arrive without further word from her? If so, what will Skip find in the letter? And, will Hack now be brought to realize what his attitude in the matter has achieved? Listen again Monday, as Skip and Dovey postpone until twelve o'clock their vigil for "Our Lady Of The Press." in episode sixteen of—<br>"THE PICTURE OF DEATH!" |
| MUSIC: | (STING AND QUICK FIGURATION FADE UNDER) |
| ANNCR: | "LADY OF THE PRESS" is written by Dwight Hauser, and produced by Gordon T. Hughes and is brought to you each day Monday through Friday at this same time by the makers of—<br>ALKA SELTZER |
| MUSIC: | (UP TO FILL) |
| ANNCR: | This is CBS. THE COLUMBIA BROADCASTING SYSTEM. |

# EPISODE #16

# "PICTURE OF DEATH"

| | |
|---|---|
| SPONSOR: | ALKA SELTZER    MAY 22, 1944 |
| AGENCY: | WADE 4:00—4:15 P.M. PWT PN |

---

ANNCR:     The makers of Alka Seltzer present—"LADY OF THE PRESS"

MUSIC:     *(STING) (QUICK PUNCTUATION)*

ANNCR:     The adventures of Sandra Martin, radio's newest romantic-mystery serial!

MUSIC:     *(THEME-ESTABLISH AND FADE OUT)*

CUTTING:     Remember that old saying, "We dig our graves with our teeth?" Well, that's exactly what a lot of folks are doing these days, and maybe you are one of them. Perhaps you're so busy, you can't always seem to find the time to eat properly and when you do eat, the chances are you choose the foods which please your appetite and not the needs of your body. This is especially true, I believe, with the selection of foods that contain the B-vitamins—those vitamins so necessary for normal energy and "staying power", for nerves and digestion. But now that it costs so little to be sure of your B-vitamins, you can hardly afford to run the risk of a deficiency and its consequences. Now, by taking a single One-A-Day Brand Vitamin B-Complex

|          |   |
|----------|---|
| | Tablet each day, you are sure of getting your full basic daily requirements of ALL the B-vitamins whose requirements are known. And the cost—mighty low—much less than you'd expect to pay for other kinds which require you to take three or four tablets daily to do the same job. So, for the help they can give you in maintaining normal energy, nerves and digestion, ask your druggist for One-A-Day Brand Vitamin B-Complex Tablets. Look for the big "one" and the name Miles on the GRAY package. |
| MUSIC: | (THEME ESTABLISH AND FADE) |
| ANNCR: | And now, "Lady Of The Press" and episode sixteen—in "THE PICTURE OF DEATH!" |
| MUSIC: | (STING AND QUICK FIGURATION FADES UNDER FOR) |
| ANNCR: | Returning to Sandra Martin's apartment following a movie, Skip Williams and her roommate, Dovey, found Sandra missing. Hopefully, Skip and Dovey awaited word from her, but, as the hours dragged on, they became desperate. Then, early this morning in the first mail, two letters arrived: one addressed to Skip and one to Sandra, but both were addressed in Sandra's handwriting. Enclosed in Skip's letter was the information that the one addressed to Sandra contains information concerning her whereabouts. However, the note was extremely definite on one point! The letter addressed to Sandra is not to be opened unless she fails to return by twelve noon. Well, by now, Dovey has gone to the Courier Office, and Skip has remained behind. It is now ten minutes of twelve and a large black car with muddy license plates is pulling to the curb before Sandra's apartment. |
| SOUND: | CAR PULLING TO STOP. CAR DOOR OPENS |
| MAN: | Well, sister, here we are, back safe and sound. You see? My word is better than you seemed to think. |
| SANDRA: | You're word! My chances of getting back wouldn't have been worth much if I hadn't insisted on that little guarantee. |

| | |
|---|---|
| MAN: | Yeah. Speaking of that, if you don't mind, I'd like to get it back and get out of here. I have a strange feeling that there are safer places for me. |
| SANDRA: | At least more welcome ones. All right, come on in and you'll get back your guarantee. |
| MAN: | Okay, but just in case you have any ideas, remember the little persuader I got in my pocket. |
| SANDRA: | Never without a gun, are you? I told you if you got me back you'd get the letter. My word *does* happen to be good. |
| MAN: | All right, let's go. |
| SOUND: | *CLIMBING OUT OF CAR. CAR DOOR CLOSE [TRAFFIC]* |
| MAN: | Okay. Walk ahead of me. Oh, just a little. We don't want to make it appear that we ain't on friendly terms. |
| SOUND: | *FOOTSTEPS* |
| SANDRA: | Just how would you put it? |
| MAN: | Well, you're a nice gal. And you got plenty of guts. I got a lot of admiration for you. Too bad we happen to be on different teams. |
| SANDRA: | Is it? |
| MAN: | Sure. I might be able to do you lot of good, if I didn't happen to have other connections. |
| SOUND: | *DOOR OPEN AND CLOSE FOOTSTEPS CONTINUE ON CARPET* |
| SANDRA: | I have no doubt that you could be hired if I wanted to stoop to those tactics. |
| MAN: | You mean, you got no respect for my ethics? |

SANDRA: Exactly.

MAN: I think you do me a great injustice. After all, you did get to see Hoagan, didn't you? *[Cut footsteps]*

SANDRA: A lot of good it did me.

MAN: Well, all you wanted was to be sure I wasn't lyin'. *[Keys Rattle]*

SANDRA: That would take more than I've seen so far.

SOUND: KEY IN LOCK

MAN: Oh, just a minute, sister. I'll open the door.

SANDRA: What's the matter? Afraid someone is waiting for us?

MAN: In my business, you can't be too careful. All right, stand back a little, just in case I have to blast my way out of here.

SOUND: DOORS FLUNG OPEN
(PAUSE)

SANDRA: See? No hidden policeman.

MAN: Okay. Get inside.

SANDRA: Well, thanks for asking me in.

SOUND: A FEW STEPS [DOOR CLOSE]

MAN: Now, get me that letter, and step on it!

SANDRA: All right. Here. This looks like it, here on the table.

MAN: Gimme.

SANDRA: All right. All right. Here.

MAN: I'll just have a look, if you don't mind.

| | |
|---|---|
| SOUND: | TEARING PAPER |
| SANDRA: | Go ahead. It's your drivers license. |
| MAN: | I just want to make sure it's here. |
| SANDRA: | Well? |
| MAN: | Yeah, it's here. Okay, now, this little note with my thumb print. We'll just burn that up if you don't mind. *[Burn paper]* |
| SANDRA: | Not at all. It's served my purpose I'm back home safely. |
| MAN: | Clever little idea you had. |
| SANDRA: | I don't think for a minute that's your name on the license, but I did notice the prints were the same. |
| MAN: | Smart girl. That was a perfect guarantee. I wouldn't have dared to let anything happen to you with this stuff here waitin' for the cops. |
| SANDRA: | RIGHT. |
| MAN: | But, now, well, the little note's burned up. My license is back in my pocket, an' there ain't a trace of evidence. |
| SANDRA: | What does that mean? |
| MAN: | You didn't really think we'd let you in so deep and turn you lose again, did you? |
| SANDRA: | Why you— |
| MAN: | *(CHUCKLES)* You seen Hoagan all right. That's what you wanted. Okay, now I'll tell you what we want. |
| SANDRA: | I thought there was a catch to it, but just telling me won't get it. |

MAN: I'll lay you odds it will. You see, now that you know we got Hoagan, you'll probably be more receptive to our ideas.

SANDRA: Why?

MAN: Cause you know we'll hold him until you clear us of any implication in that murder.

SANDRA: And just how do you think I can do that?

MAN: I'll show you.

SOUND: *FOOTSTEPS-RECEIVER OFF HOOK*

SANDRA: Just what are you up to?

MAN: What's the number of your paper?

SANDRA: Cumberland 8-600 [1231]

MAN: Let's see if it is.

SOUND: *DIALING PHONE*

SANDRA: Where do you think you'll get by calling my paper?

MAN: I'll tell you after I see who answers that number. *(IN PHONE)* What? Just a minute. *(TO SANDRA)* That's right, sister, it's the Courier. Now look, you get on this phone and give 'em the straight stuff on Hoagan.

SANDRA: What do you mean?

MAN: You know what I mean . . . that Hoagan killed Frances Evers on his own, and that all this poppycot about Black Market Operators being behind it is phony.

SANDRA: Sorry. I don't believe that.

MAN: Now, look, sister, I ain't foolin! You give the city desk that story. As soon as it breaks, Hoagan will be turned loose, and that will clear you.

SANDRA: I'm not that much interested in [getting] an acquittal.

MAN: Okay, let me put it this way: do it and you're cleared; refuse and you're dead. Take your choice. *(IN PHONE)* Okay, Operator, gimme the city desk. All right, sister, you got about five seconds to start spieling' that story into that phone.

SANDRA: I—

MAN: I ain't in no mood to play around! Get over there, or get a slug in ya' pretty head!

~~SOUND: A FEW STEPS~~

~~MAN: And no funny stuff.~~

SANDRA: *(IN PHONE)* Hello, City Desk? Sandra Martin. Take this copy. Mark it for three star. Right. Having seen and talked with Elbert Hoagan, admitted murderer of Frances Evers, this reporter is now convinced that Hoagan acted solely in his own capacity and was in no way influenced by other illegal circles previously suspected.

MAN: *(S.V.)* That's fine, sister, keep talking.

SANDRA: It is the opinion of this paper that—

SKIP: All right, Mug, reach!

SANDRA: Skip!

MAN: What? Who—

SKIP: Never mind the cracks. Get those mitts up and keep 'em up. And don't turn around. .

MAN: *(LAUGHS)* Can't you see I've got a gun on your girl friend?

SKIP: Use it and see how quick you check out. Hold up that call, Sandra.

| | |
|---|---|
| SANDRA: | *(IN PHONE)* Kill that copy! And hang onto the wire! |
| SKIP: | Now, drop that gun.<br>*(PAUSE)* |
| MAN: | Okay, you win. |
| SOUND: | *GUN DROPPING TO FLOOR* |
| SKIP: | That's better. Finally, we're gettin' a little cooperation out of you. ~~Pick up his gun, Sandra.~~ [Give me his gun, Sandra.] |
| SOUND: | *A FEW STEPS* |
| SANDRA: | Where on earth did you come from, Skip? |
| SKIP: | I been waitin' here ever since the mail came this morning. When I saw you coming, I ducked into the closet. I thought I better wait for the right opportunity, but I couldn't see that story going through. |
| SANDRA: | Good boy! Then, you heard what's been going on? |
| SKIP: | Yeah, I heard, which reminds me . . . I'll take that drivers license of yours, wise guy. |
| MAN: | Okay, but it won't do you any good. The only real threat she had against me was that paper I signed. The drivers license won't identify me. |
| SKIP: | Where you're going, you'll be your own identification. San, get Hack over here right away. |
| SANDRA: | Right. Hello, City Desk? Just kill that story and call Lieutenant Taggart at the Homicide Squad. Tell him to get over to my apartment now! Yes. Tell him it's urgent. |
| SOUND: | *RECEIVER ON HOOK* |
| SKIP: | Okay. Now, let's have that license. |

| | |
|---|---|
| MAN: | Okay. |
| MAN: | I gotta admit you caught me off guard, but I ain't so dumb as to argue with a guy when he's got a gun on me. You ask for it, so— |
| SANDRA: | Skip! Look out! |
| MAN: | Here you are! |
| SOUND: | *BLOW* |
| SOUND: | *RUNNING* |
| SKIP: | Stop him, San! Don't let him pass you! |
| SOUND: | *DOOR OPEN* |
| SANDRA: | Shoot, Skip. |
| SKIP: | Where is it? He knocked the gun out of my hands. |
| SOUND: | *DOOR SLAM* |
| SANDRA: | Ohhhhhh! We can't let him get away. |
| SKIP: | Here's the gun. I'll go after him. |
| SANDRA: | No, Skip, not that way. Out the window! You can see his car from here. He'll have to come into full view. Wait for him. |
| SKIP: | Yeah. Good! Gimme a chance to aim. I'm not too hot with one of these things. |
| SANDRA: | Take your time and make sure. |
| SKIP: | Yeah. I'm just waitin' for him to come into sight. |
| SANDRA: | There he comes. |
| SKIP: | I see him.<br>*(PAUSE)* |

| | |
|---|---|
| SOUND: | SHOT |
| SANDRA: | You missed. |
| SOUND: | TWO SHOTS |
| SANDRA: | You should have a shot gun. Here, give me that gun. |
| SKIP: | Here. |
| SOUND: | MOTOR STARTS OFF |
| SANDRA: | He's in the car! |
| SKIP: | Well, try and get one of the tires. |
| SOUND: | SHOT |
| SOUND: | CAR PULLING AWAY |
| SOUND: | SHOT |
| SANDRA: | Well, looks like we missed our big chance. |
| SKIP: | Yeah. He's too far away now. Even if one of us could shoot straight. |
| MUSIC: | (BRIDGE) |
| SKIP: | Well, now that all the excitement is over and the crook has gotten away we're honored with your presence. Why is it that you're always around when you're not wanted and never when you are? |
| HACK: | You should talk. Stand there with a loaded gun and let a guy get away. |
| SKIP: | Well, the dumb cluck! How'd I know he was stupid enough to take a poke at me? |
| HACK: | Stupid? Hah! Look who's talking. He got away didn't he? |

SKIP: Sure, but, that was a chance I wouldn't have taken. How'd he know I wouldn't shoot him?

HACK: The only thing you can shoot is a camera.

SANDRA: Lay down your swords, boys. What's the important thing, for you two to take cracks at each other or try to figure out what to do with the information I got?

HACK: I'd have a lot better chance doing something with it if you'd let me in on it from the start instead of just calling on me when you're in trouble.

SANDRA: Well, your previous attitude hasn't exactly been indicative of cooperation.

HACK: I told you the reason.

SANDRA: Sure, that this was your way of helping, but, that explanation is pretty vague.

HACK: Skip, do you have any pictures to take?

SKIP: Naw. Can't think of a thing that. Oh, I get it, you want me to go take pictures, Sandra?

SANDRA: I—well—I would like to discuss a couple of things with Hack. Do you mind, Skip?

SKIP: I refuse to answer that. But, okay. I guess I can find something to shoot.

HACK: Be careful it isn't yourself.

SKIP: Don't worry. I gotta see it that there's somebody around to protect Sandra . . . from you.

SOUND: *FOOTSTEPS—DOOR OPENS*

SKIP: Take my advice, honey, and don't let that flat foot talk you into a spot where you'll believe him.

| | |
|---|---|
| SOUND: | DOOR CLOSE |
| SANDRA: | Is he right, Hack? Should I ever believe you again? |
| HACK: | That depends on how badly you want to, Sandra. |
| MUSIC: | (TO CURTAIN) |
| CUTTING: | Say, folks, how are you feeling these days? Are your energy and nerves and digestion what they should be? Well, if you don't seem to have your old "get up and go", if your nerves are jumpy, or if you're having digestive upsets, it's possible that your three square meals a day aren't supplying you with enough B-vitamins. And if such is the case, you are just the person who should start now to supplement your diet with One-A-Day Brand Vitamin B-Complex Tablets. By taking just a single One-A-Day Brand Vitamin B-Complex Tablet each day, you can be sure of getting your FULL basic daily requirements of ALL the B-vitamins whose requirements have been established. And because a single tablet each day does the job, that makes One-A-Day Brand B-Complex mighty reasonable—far less than you'd expect to pay for other brands that require you to take three or four tablets daily. So for a mighty convenient, economical way to get your extra B-vitamins, ask your druggist for One-A-Day Brand Vitamin B-Complex Tablets. They come in the GRAY package and are made by Miles. Look for the big "1" on the GRAY package—that's the "one" to buy. |
| MUSIC: | (THEME ESTABLISH AND FADE FOR:) |
| ANNCR: | Does Sandra really want to place her happiness at the disposal of a man whom she feels has already betrayed her once? Can Hack persuade her to follow blindly and believe in him? And, if he can will she open her heart once more to anguish in an attempt to rehabilitate this man whom she once loved? Listen tomorrow when our "LADY OF THE PRESS" makes her decision in episode seventeen of—"THE PICTURE OF DEATH"! |

| | |
|---|---|
| *MUSIC:* | *(THEME UP AND UNDER:)* |
| ANNCR: | "Lady of the Press" is written by Dwight Hauser, and produced by Gordon T. Hughes, and is brought to you each day, Monday through Friday at this same time by the makers of ALKA SELTZER. |
| *MUSIC:* | *(UP TO FILL)* |
| ANNCR: | [Dick Cutting speaking] This is CBS. The COLUMBIA BROADCASTIG SYSTEM. |

# EPISODE #17

# "PICTURE OF DEATH"

| | | |
|---|---|---|
| SPONSOR: | ALKA SELTZER | MAY 23, 1944 |
| AGENCY: | WADE 4:00—4:15 PM, PWT PN | |

ANNCR: The makers of Alka Seltzer present—"LADY OF THE PRESS"

MUSIC: *(STING) (QUICK PUNCTUATION)*

ANNCR: The adventures of Sandra Martin, radio's newest romantic-mystery serial!

MUSIC: *(THEME...ESTABLISH AND FADE OUT)*

CUTTING: Friends, do you ever come to the end of a hard day's work, saying to yourself, "What a day! I never thought I'd get through this one." Well, I guess most of us have days like that every once in a while. And haven't you noticed that when you go through one, it frequently leaves you feeling headachy and upset? Well, why feel that way for long—why ruin the pleasure of the few hours of relaxation you get—when a glass of sparkling, refreshing Alka-Seltzer can help set you right with the world again, in a hurry. You see, Alka-Seltzer contains the analgesic you need to ease a dull headache and the alkalizing properties necessary to settle an upset, acid stomach. Try it the very next time a busy day leaves you feeling pretty "down in the mouth." Your druggist has Alka-Seltzer by the glass at his soda fountain and also sells it by the sixty and thirty cent size package for home and work use. Get wise to Alka-Seltzer, folks—you'll be glad you did.*

MUSIC: (THEME ESTABLISH AND FADE FOR)

ANNCR: And now, "Lady Of The Press" and episode seventeen—in—"THE PICTURE OF DEATH"

MUSIC: (STING AND QUICK FIGURATION FADES UNDER)

ANNCR: After going with the strange man who seems to plague her every move to see Elbert Hoagan Sandra Martin has returned to her apartment. In order to assure her safe return, she had insisted upon the man surrendering his drivers license. This she had mailed to herself together with instructions to Skip to open it if she failed to return by twelve o'clock noon. This guarantee served its purpose, but it also made it necessary for the strange man to return with her in order that he might recover this positive identification of himself. After the license was returned to him, he drew a gun and tried to force Sandra into giving her newspaper a story absolving the Black Market Ring in the murder of Frances Evers. However, Skip, hiding in a closet, interrupted the proceedings and foiled the man's attempt, but neither he nor Sandra were able to prevent the strange man's escape. Now, Lieutenant Hack Taggart has arrived, and Sandra has asked Skip to leave them alone....

SANDRA: You must know how badly I want to believe you, Hack.

HACK: Well, there's nothing stopping you.

SANDRA: But there is. The way you've acted in connection with this whole case.

HACK: I told you once Sandra that I was handling things in the way I thought would prove best for everyone concerned.

SANDRA: Well, I'm concerned. More than I care to be. Thanks to you. Is casing suspicion on innocent people the best way of handling it?

HACK: Possibly;

SANDRA: I can't understand you, Hack.

HACK: I don't expect you to.

SANDRA: But, don't you care whether I do or not?

HACK: Yes.

SANDRA: Then what is it? Is there something else more important to you?

HACK: Right now, there is.

SANDRA: Can't you tell me what it is?

HACK: No, I can't. I would like to think you had faith in me. I've told you that I have a reason for doing this the way I have. It's a good reason, but it's a reason that can't be discussed just yet.

SANDRA: And in the meantime, you're asking me to have pure blind faith.

HACK: I'm not asking you. You're the one who brought it up. You want proof of my faith. I can't give you that. So, if my word isn't good enough, I'm afraid you're out of luck.

SANDRA: But Hack, your word. It's up against some pretty strong facts. You've done everything in your power to cast suspicion on Skip and me. Every possible bit of evidence you've presented in the most incriminating light. Put that against the fact that you say you're helping me and it just doesn't add up.

HACK: Sometimes you get the right answer by division rather than addition.

SANDRA: I don't follow you?

HACK: You will. In the meantime, don't be so sorry for yourself.

SANDRA: I'm not sorry for myself, Hack. I'm sorry for us.

HACK: Us?

SANDRA: Yes for us, and for the thing we've lost. There's an acute shortage in the world of the kind of love and beauty we once had. There isn't enough to waste the way we're wasting it.

HACK: Beauty isn't very high on the world market at present.

SANDRA: All the more reason we should have held on to what we had.

HACK: Sandra, you should learn to face things the way they are, not the way you'd like them to be.

SANDRA: What do you think I'm doing? Do you suppose my heart is breaking because I've turned my back on the way things are? Don't you know that all the pain and anguish in my soul is there because I'm facing the cold bitter fact that our love is gone?

HACK: Sandra, please . . . .

SANDRA: Don't you think it would be easier if I said to myself, "Well, that's what war does to a man. He's through. We're through. Nothing can be done about it. Forget it and try something new"? Wouldn't that be easier than trying to bring it back?

HACK: Sometimes it's better to leave the lights off when there isn't anything left to see, Sandra.

SANDRA: But I don't believe there is nothing but darkness. I remember a glowing beauty, Hack, and somehow I can't accept the premise that there isn't still a tiny flicker left. A flicker that might be fanned into a bright burning fire again.

| | |
|---|---|
| HACK: | Sandra, listen to me a moment. I love you. I've never stopped loving you. I love you so much that I can't let you go on loving me. |
| SANDRA: | *(TEARFULLY)* That's a strange kind of love. |
| HACK: | I know, but it's because you're still in love with a memory, and, unfortunately, the house that memory lived in isn't the same. You're in love with what I was before I went away. I know that I could still have you on that basis, but I can't be unfair. Until, if ever, I can become again the man you're really in love with, things will have to stay the way they are. |
| SANDRA: | Why, Hack, why? |
| HACK: | Because I like the pre-war Hack Taggart a lot better than I like this one, and I don't intend becoming an imposter in your memory. |
| SANDRA: | That leaves me nothing but ashes, doesn't it? |
| HACK: | All I can say is that I hope you won't mistrust me too much until you've seen the end of the play. I know there isn't much solid ground on which to place your trust, but I'm hoping it's enough. Believe me, Sandra. |
| *MUSIC:* | *(BRIDGE)* |
| SOUND: | NEWSPAPER OFFICE |
| SANDRA: | *(CALLS)* Skip! Skip! |
| SKIP: | Yeah, San? |
| SANDRA: | Come in to rewrite for a minute, will you? |
| SKIP: | Coming. |
| *SOUND:* | *FOOTSTEPS* |

| | |
|---|---|
| SKIP: | What's up? |
| SANDRA: | Something I want to talk over with you . . . alone. Come in. |
| SOUND: | *DOOR CLOSE. SOUND OUT* |
| SKIP: | Yeah, what is it? |
| SANDRA: | Skip, we've got a job on our hands, and we've got to go to work on it right now. |
| SKIP: | Somethin' new come up? |
| SANDRA: | No. It's just that I've gotten straightened out a little. |
| SKIP: | How do you mean? |
| SANDRA: | Well, the hearing is over, and the case doesn't go to trial ~~until July 18th~~ [for several weeks]. In the meantime, we've got to devote every minute to building up evidence against the Black Market. |
| SKIP: | What brought about this sudden recurrence of enthusiasm? |
| SANDRA: | Well, for one thing, I think we'll be able to rely a little more on help from Hack. |
| SKIP: | ~~Oh sure....~~I need help from him like I need a hole in the head. |
| SANDRA: | It may seem strange to you, but I really believe Hack has our interest at heart. |
| SKIP: | After all he's done? I knew he'd talk you into it. |
| SANDRA: | *(LAUGH)* He hasn't really talked me into anything, but I just have a hunch, Skip. We've got to play along with him anyway. Now, here's where we start. |
| SKIP: | I can tell you where we'll finish if we trust him. |

| | |
|---|---|
| SANDRA: | We'll have to take a chance. First thing we're going to check up on those license numbers you got at that service station. |
| SKIP: | Look, San[dra], I'm in this thing pretty deep with you, right? |
| SANDRA: | Well sure, Skip. Why? |
| SKIP: | Then, don't you think I oughta know where we stand? |
| SANDRA: | You mean you think you don't? |
| SKIP: | Not about one thing, I don't. |
| SANDRA: | What's that? |
| SKIP: | You know I overheard the conversation between you and ~~the man~~ [that gunman] at your apartment. |
| SANDRA: | Yes. |
| SKIP: | And I heard you admit you'd seen Hoagan. |
| SANDRA: | Yes. I saw him. |
| SKIP: | Well, don't you think I ought to know about it? |
| SANDRA: | Oh! Sure, Skip. I forgot. You see, the fellow told me they intended holding Hoagan until I took the heat off them. I pretended not to believe they had Hoagan. So, in order to persuade me he agreed to let me see him. |
| SKIP: | And he went through with it? |
| SANDRA: | Yes. |
| SKIP: | Then you know where he is? |
| SANDRA: | No. I don't. This man took me out to ~~Glencaren~~ [Smuggler's] Cove. |

| | |
|---|---|
| SKIP: | You mean the spot where the rum runners used to land? Back in the Prohibition days? |
| SANDRA: | Yes. We waited there for several hours. Finally, another car drove up and parked beside us. They had Hoagan tied up in the back seat. |
| SKIP: | And you talked to him? |
| SANDRA: | Yes. |
| SKIP: | Well, what did he say? |
| SANDRA: | He pleaded with me to follow their advice. He insisted they had nothing to do with his killing Frances Evers. |
| SKIP: | What do you know! |
| SANDRA: | He said he wanted to be free to give himself up and confess. |
| SKIP: | He did? But why? |
| SANDRA: | I don't know, unless they've tortured him so much he's willing to say anything they want him to say. |
| SKIP: | So, what happened then? |
| SANDRA: | Nothing. They took Hoagan away and the man brought me back. So, I didn't really learn anything. I was hoping I'd find out where they were keeping him, but they're too slick for that. [So, that's the whole story, Skip.] |
| SKIP: | Okay. As long as I know where we stand, I'm ~~willing to play along~~ [with you all the way]. |
| SANDRA: | Good. Now, we've got to start checking the evidence on this ring by beginning with the customers. Unless I miss my guess, they'll lead us to the operators, and the operators will lead us to the big shots, and when we find the big shots, we'll know who it is that's holding Hoagan. |

| | |
|---|---|
| SKIP: | That's a long way around. |
| SANDRA: | I know, but it's the only way. Now, what's the first name we have on the list? |
| SKIP: | J. Tully Whitley. |
| SANDRA: | Address? |
| SKIP: | 7765 Portland Drive. |
| SANDRA: | Hmm. Good neighborhood. Well, come on Skip, let's get out there and have a little talk with J. Tully. |
| MUSIC: | (BRIDGE) |
| SOUND: | CAR RUNNING |
| SANDRA: | Slow down, Skip. This is the seventy-seven block. |
| SOUND: | CAR SLOWS |
| SANDRA: | Should be right along here. |
| SKIP: | There it is. That big white one. 7765. |
| SANDRA: | Okay. Park just beyond the drive way. |
| SKIP: | Right. |
| SOUND: | CAR PULLS TO STOP |
| SANDRA: | All right. Come on. Let's have a look. |
| SKIP: | What are you going to tell this guy, Whitley? He can't just bust up there and tell him you suspect him of patronizing a Black Market. |
| SANDRA: | I know that, silly, but I think I know a way to get what we want. |

| | |
|---|---|
| SKIP: | We keep messin' with this kinda stuff and we're goin' to get something we don't want. |
| SANDRA: | Maybe, but we won't get either if we don't take a chance. Come on. |
| SOUND: | *CLIMBING OUT OF CAR. CAR DOOR SHUT* |
| SKIP: | Someday, I'm going to buy myself a chicken ranch and settle down to a life of ease. |
| SOUND: | *FOOTSTEPS* |
| SANDRA: | If you ever owned a chicken, it would lay flash bulbs instead of eggs. |
| SKIP: | Very funny, Miss Martin. |
| SANDRA: | *(LAUGHS)* Okay, let's stop the foolishness and concentrate on the task ahead of us. |
| SKIP: | Whata we gonna tell the guy? |
| SANDRA: | We'll tell him we're from the gas station and we've come to pick up his card. |
| SKIP: | [OK. Fine.] And I suppose he'll just up and hand it over? |
| SANDRA: | We'll tell him that we've had to change the code. That we'll bring him back a new one. |
| SKIP: | I think we're skatin' on pretty thin ice. |
| SANDRA: | Possibly, but do you know a better way to get a hold of one of those cards? |
| SKIP: | No. |
| SANDRA: | Okay. |
| SOUND: | *FOOTSTEPS STOP* |

| | |
|---|---|
| SKIP: | Want me to ring? |
| SANDRA: | Yes. Go ahead. |
| SOUND: | DOOR (OFF) CHIMES<br>(PAUSE) |
| SKIP: | I don't mind tellin' you this gives me the jitters. How do we know what kind of trap we might be walkin' into? |
| SANDRA: | We don't. Ring again, will you? |
| SOUND: | DOOR BELL (CAR APPROACHING) |
| SKIP: | Doesn't seem to be anyone here. |
| SANDRA: | There's bound to be. An estate like this wouldn't be left empty. |
| SOUND: | TWO SHOTS AS CAR SPEEDS BY |
| SKIP: | Duck, San, duck! Somebody's shootin' at us! |
| MUSIC: | (TO CURTAIN) |
| CUTTING: | In these busy times, there are few of us who get to enjoy as many evenings of recreation with friends as we used to. Right? But if you're looking forward to a good time tonight—or some night soon—a movie, a game of cards, or just a good old "gabfest" with friends—we hope you won't forget to have a package of Alka-Seltzer Tablets handy in your home. Then, if you happen to have TOO good a time—stay up late and eat too much of a midnight snack—you'll be prepared, with sparkling refreshing Alka-Seltzer, to help yourself to quick relief for the headache or the acid upset stomach which may result. So now's the time to check up on your supply of Alka-Seltzer, and if it's running low, get another sixty or thirty cent package from your druggist right away—because it's far better to be safe than sorry. |

MUSIC:     (THEME ESTABLISH AND FADE)

ANNCR:     Sandra and Skip seem to have walked into a trap. Could it be that they have been followed once more by the strange man who has caused them so much trouble before? And as the bullets whined past Skip, did they miss Sandra? Listen tomorrow as our "Lady Of The Press" faces new and increasing danger in episode eighteen of—The Picture Of Death."

MUSIC:     (UP AND UNDER)

ANNCR:     "Lady Of The Press" is written by Dwight Hauser, and produced by Gordon T. Hughes, and is brought to you each day, Monday through Friday at this same time by the maker of—ALKA SELTZER.

MUSIC:     (UP TO FILL)

ANNCR:     [Dick Cutting speaking] This is CBS. THE COLUMBIA BROADCASTING SYSTEM

# EPISODE #18

# "PICTURE OF DEATH"

| | | |
|---|---|---|
| SPONSOR: | ALKA SELTZER | MAY 24, 1944 |
| AGENCY: | WADE  4:00—4:15 P.M., PWT PN | |

---

ANNCR: The makers of Alka Seltzer present—"LADY OF THE PRESS"

MUSIC: *(STING. QUICK PUNCTUATION)*

ANNCR: The adventures of Sandra Martin, radio's newest romantic-mystery serial!

MUSIC: *(THEME ESTABLISH AND FADE OUT)*

*(OPENING ANNOUNCEMENT)*

CUTTING: I wonder how many of you ladies are absolutely sure that the food you serve your family each day supplies them with enough A and D vitamins - vitamin A to help maintain their normal resistance to colds and vitamin D (the so-called sunshine-vitamin) for the aid it gives in the formation and maintenance of bones and teeth? Well, why guess? Instead, be sure by supplementing their daily diet with a single One-A-Day Brand Vitamin A and D Tablet each day. That single One-A-Day A and D Tablet is so rich in these vitamins that it supplies twenty-five percent more than their full basic daily requirements of both A and D. One-A-Day Brand Vitamin A and D Tablets are really pleasant to taste too—even though each tablet does contain the same amount of these vitamins as one and a half teaspoonfuls of minimum USP cod liver oil. And of course, they're really economical—because one One-A-Day Brand Vitamin A and D Tablet does the work of two or three lower potency kinds. So ladies, if you aren't already doing so, give your family the protective benefits of ample amounts of vitamin A and D. Just ask your druggist for One-A-Day Brand Vitamin A and D Tablets, in the YELLOW package with the big "one", and the name Miles.

MUSIC: (THEME ESTABLISH AND FADE)

ANNCR: And now, Lady Of The Press" and episode eighteen in THE PICTURE OF DEATH!

MUSIC: (STING AND QUICK FIGURATION FADES UNDER)

ANNCR: Realizing that their only hope of clearing themselves of guilt when their case comes to trial will lie in proving the Black Market Ring accomplices in the murder of Frances Evers, Sandra Martin and Skip Williams have taken up a trail which they believe will lead them to the evidence. Asked for a special card at a service station, they became suspicious of this business as a Black Market outlet. Consequently, Sandra had Skip remain nearby to check the license numbers of the customers. With a long list of the owners of these cars at their disposal, they have now set out to contact them hoping to learn something from them. But, as they stood ringing the doorbell at the first house, shots rang out! And bullets whizzed toward them as a large black sedan sped past.

SOUND: CAR SPEEDING OFF

SKIP: Are you all right, San? Did they get you?

SANDRA: No. I'm all right.

SKIP: Stay down. Those babies meant business.

| | |
|---|---|
| SOUND: | *POLICE CAR (SIREN?)* |
| SKIP: | Hey, listen . . . do you hear what I hear? |
| SANDRA: | I don't know. What do you hear? |
| SKIP: | A police car. |
| SANDRA: | Then in that case, we're hearing the same thing. |
| SOUND: | *SIREN UP* |
| SKIP: | Here it comes. |
| SANDRA: | Look Skip, it's a squad car. |
| SOUND: | *SQUAD CAR SPEEDS BY* |
| SKIP: | Yes, and if I'm not mistaken, that was our boy detective in the front seat. |
| SANDRA: | He's tailed us! |
| SKIP: | I knew he would. |
| SANDRA: | Come on, Skip, let's go. |
| SOUND: | *RUNNING FOOTSTEP* |
| SKIP: | Where we goin'? |
| SANDRA: | Not only is this apt to be one of the biggest news breaks in a long time but it's also definite proof that Hack <u>is</u> on our side. Hurry! |
| MUSIC: | *(BRIDGE)* |
| SOUND: | *SPEEDING CAR SIREN IN DISTANCE* |
| SANDRA: | Hurry, Skip! Can't we go any faster? |

| | |
|---|---|
| SKIP: | Baby, if I push any harder on this throttle, I'll be draggin' my foot on the pavement. |
| SANDRA: | Are we gaining on them? |
| SKIP: | If we're not, the army ought to have a look at their motor. We're doin' eighty-five. |
| SANDRA: | I can still see the black sedan up ahead of Hack, but I think the gap is closing. |
| SKIP: | Why the heck doesn't he shoot? He could at least try for a tire. |
| SANDRA: | (SCREAM) Look out, Hack! Skip, that other car! Hack! Look out! |
| SOUND: | CRASH OFF |
| SANDRA: | (STUNNED) Hack. Oh, Hack! |
| SKIP: | They hit that light post tryin' to dodge that car. |
| SANDRA: | Oh, Skip, Skip! Hurry! We've got to get to him. |
| SKIP: | This ain't goin' to be easy, baby. You're gonna need plenty of stuff to face what we're about to see. |
| SANDRA: | Just hurry! The important thing now is get to him. |
| SKIP: | Yeah. Okay, baby. |
| SANDRA: | Oh, Hack. Why did you have to follow us? |
| SOUND: | CAR SLOWS |
| SKIP: | Looks like a bad wreck, Sandra. |
| SANDRA: | I know. |
| SOUND: | CAR SKIDS TO STOP |

SANDRA: Come on, Skip, give me a hand.

SOUND: *CAR DOORS OPEN-FOOTSTEPS RUNNING ON PAVEMENT*

SKIP: You see him.

SANDRA: Not yet.

SOUND: *FOOTSTEPS STOP*

SKIP: There—there he is—crumpled up in front.

SANDRA: Oh no! Oh, Hack, my darling.

SKIP: Come on. We gotta get him out of there.

SOUND: *RATTLING OF METAL*

SANDRA: He's—he's all crushed down between the seat and the motor.

SKIP: Yeah. Lemme see if I can't knock this door off.

SOUND: *POUNDING ON DOOR.  DOOR FALLING.*

SKIP: Now, that's better. Maybe I can get in there to him.

SANDRA: Hurry, Skip! Every minute may mean the difference between life and . . . .

SKIP: Yeah. I know, baby. I'll hurry.

SOUND: *CRAWLING INTO WRECKAGE*

SANDRA: Can you see? Is he . . . .?

SKIP: He's unconscious at least. He's pretty badly cut up.

SANDRA: *(SOB)*

| | |
|---|---|
| SKIP: | *(SLIGHTLY OFF)* Now, if I can wriggle back out, I think I can pull him with me. |
| SANDRA: | Be careful, Skip. There may be broken bones. |
| SKIP: | Yeah. Get a hold of my feet and see if you can help, will ya? |
| SANDRA: | Sure. |
| SKIP: | That's a girl. |
| SOUND: | *CRAWLING FROM WRECKAGE* |
| SKIP: | There. That's better. Now, lemme get a hold of him and I can lift him out. |
| SANDRA: | Let me help. |
| SKIP: | Sure. Raise his arm. |
| SOUND: | *LIFTING BODY FROM WRECK* |
| SANDRA: | Oh Hack, Hack, my darling. |
| SKIP: | Here—put him down here on the grass. |
| SOUND: | *LYING BODY ON GROUND* |
| SKIP: | See how his pulse is. I'm going after the driver. |
| SANDRA: | All right. |
| SOUND: | *FOOTSTEPS OFF* |
| SANDRA: | *(PRAYERFULLY)* Dear God, please let him be all right. Don't let him—I'll do anything, only don't let him—die! *(PAUSE) (ALMOST SCREAMING)* Skip! Skip! Come back! |
| SOUND: | *FOOTSTEPS RUNNING IN* |
| SKIP: | Yeah? What is it? |

| | |
|---|---|
| SANDRA: | Skip, I can't feel any pulse beat. Oh, Skip! *(CRIES)* |
| SKIP: | Wait a minute, baby. You're too upset to find his pulse if it is beating. Here, let me try. |
| SANDRA: | *(CRYING)* Oh, Skip, I'm scared. I— |
| SKIP: | Be quiet. *(PAUSE) (COUNTING UNCERTAINLY)* One-two-three-four-five-six— |
| SANDRA: | Is he--? |
| SKIP: | *(COUNTING MORE STEADILY)*—eight- nine- ten- eleven. Yeah, he's okay, at least his heart's still beating. |
| SANDRA: | *(BREAKS)* |
| SKIP: | Well, this is no time for that. I said he's all right. It's beating. Pretty strong, too. |
| SANDRA: | Thank heaven! *(GAINING CONTROL)* I'll take care of him, Skip. You can go back to the driver. |
| SKIP: | No use going back to him, Sandra. He was the unlucky one. |
| SANDRA: | Oh. Oh, that's horrible. Someone probably loved him just as much as I love Hack. |
| SKIP: | Yeah, well, we gotta get the Lieutenant to the hospital. We don't want the same thing happening to him. Poor, guy! |
| SANDRA: | Why, Skip, you— |
| SKIP: | Yeah, I know, but you can't fight with a guy as much as I have with him and not have a soft spot for him. [Dope!] Come on. |
| MUSIC: | *(BRIDGE)* |
| SANDRA: | May I see him now, Nurse? |

| | |
|---|---|
| NURSE: | I don't think the doctors are allowing visitors. |
| SANDRA: | I'm—I was—his fiancé. Please? |
| NURSE: | Well, I'll check. |
| SOUND: | DIAL INTER HOUSE PHONE |
| NURSE: | Pailey, Emergency ward. Lieutenant Taggart's fiancé wishes to see him. Is it all right? What? All right. Yes, I'll see to it. Thank you. |
| SOUND: | RECEIVER ON HOOK |
| NURSE: | The Doctor says you may go in, if you're very quiet and don't upset him. You may stay five minutes. Fourth door to your right. |
| SANDRA: | Thank you. |
| SOUND: | FOOTSTEPS DOWN CORRIDOR STOP HOSPITAL. DOOR OPEN-CLOSES. FOOTSTEPS SOFTLY |
| HACK: | (HEAVY STEADY BREATHING) |
| SANDRA: | (GENTLY) Hack? |
| HACK: | (SPASMOTIC BREATHING) |
| SANDRA: | Hack? Hack, dear, don't you know me? |
| HACK: | (INCREDULOUSLY) Sandra? Why, Sandra, what are you doing here? |
| SANDRA: | I brought you here. I haven't left the hospital. You didn't suppose I wouldn't come to see you, did you? |
| HACK: | Well, no, but how did you get here? Join the WACS? |
| SANDRA: | (SLIGHT START) What? What do you mean, dear? |

| | |
|---|---|
| HACK: | Not in uniform. How'd you get here? |
| SANDRA: | They just said I could come up and see you for a few minutes, Hack. I came as soon as they'd let me after you were hurt. |
| HACK: | How did you know so soon? How did you get up? |
| SANDRA: | In the elevator. |
| HACK: | No, Sandra dear. Don't kid. How'd you get through the lines? |
| SANDRA: | The lines? |
| HACK: | The firing is so heavy. |
| SANDRA: | *(REALIZING DELIRIOUS)* Oh, my darling, no! |
| HACK: | Nobody's safe in that hell out there, especially a woman. I don't know what the army is thinking of . . . letting you come up here. Go back, Sandra. It's not safe for you here. Nurses don't even come up this far. |
| SANDRA: | Hack, darling, don't excite yourself. You—you're not at the front anymore. You're safe in a quiet peaceful hospital . . . back home. |
| HACK: | No! No safe peaceful place in Sicily. It's too dangerous for you! You shouldn't have come, but—but I'm glad you did. |
| *MUSIC:* | *(BRIDGE)* |
| *SOUND:* | *DOOR BELL—DOOR OPEN* |
| SKIP: | Hello, Dovey. Sandra, here? |
| DOVEY: | No. |
| SKIP: | Oh. Where is she? |

DOVEY: She's at the hospital, I guess. She went to see if they'd let her see Hack.

SKIP: Oh. Yeah. I guess I should have expected that.

DOVEY: Look, you big dope, why don't you get onto yourself?

SKIP: ~~Huh? What are you talkin' about?~~

DOVEY: ~~You know what I'm talking about….About Sandra.~~

SKIP: ~~Well what about her?~~

DOVEY: ~~Just how much of a wallop is necessary for you to tumble.~~

SKIP: ~~I don't get you?~~

DOVEY: ~~Can't you see how she feels about Hack?~~

SKIP: ~~Sure…I've always known that…~~

DOVEY: ~~Then…What are you hanging around for.~~

SKIP: You probably wouldn't understand this, Dovey, being an expert on love. ~~But, it just happens that I think just as much of Sandra as she does of Hack….And until he rates that kind of love…I'm stickin' see…~~

DOVEY: ~~No….I don't see….Don't you think it's tough enough on her to realize that he's in the hospital because he was trying to protect her…Do you think you make it any easier for her?~~

SKIP: ~~Yes, I do….Right now, Sandra needs all the help she can get….Strong help…And, it's a cinch the boy scout isn't in any shape to help her. And, whether you agree or not….I'm stickin' around to do what I can.~~

DOVEY: ~~Even though she doesn't want you?~~

SKIP: Sandra may not love me, but she doesn't hate me either, and regardless of how she feels about me, I'm going to help her.

|  | I'm going to because I want to, not because of any change that I think it might make in her feeling toward me. I'm pretty nuts about her, and that's all that's necessary. I'll do all I can for her, and if she wants it that way—for her and Hack. |
|---|---|
| DOVEY: | You know, if I thought you really meant that, I'd have a lot more respect for you. |
| SKIP: | That I could do without. |
| DOVEY: | Well, even a lot more wouldn't be a great deal. So, don't let it worry you. |
| SKIP: | It doesn't. What worries me is what's keepin' Sandra. |
| DOVEY: | I told you she was at the hospital. She's apt to stay there for a week. |
| SKIP: | No, she won't. They won't let her. I was up there this afternoon myself, and there no lettin' anybody see Hack. |
| DOVEY: | You mean you went to call on <u>him</u>? |
| SKIP: | In a moment of weakness. I did. |
| DOVEY: | Now, I've heard everything. All I need now is for Hack and Sandra to get married with you as best man. |
| SKIP: | Well, don't think I wouldn't be. |
| DOVEY: | That's not the way I heard it. |
| SKIP: | Well, you been listenin' at the wrong key holes, baby. |
| DOVEY: | Are you insinuating that the only way I can judge a man is by hearsay? |
| SKIP: | Oh, I don't know. Some of the best remarks I've heard on mankind are hearsay. And speakin' of that, what do you call that column you write? |

| | |
|---|---|
| DOVEY: | That, Romeo, is bread and butter. |
| SKIP: | Yeah, even you couldn't have all that experience. |
| DOVEY: | Why, you— |
| SOUND: | DOOR OPEN |
| SKIP: | San, I've been waitin' for you. |
| SANDRA: | Hello, Skip. Hello, Dovey. |
| DOVEY: | Hello, baby. How is it? |
| SANDRA: | Bad. |
| SKIP: | You mean, Hack—did—did they let you see him? |
| SANDRA: | For a minute. |
| SKIP: | Well . . . how is he? Has he come too yet? What'd he say? |
| SANDRA: | He thought he was still at the front in Sicily. He thought I'd come there to him and—(*SOBS*)—he was glad. |
| SKIP: | Well, he'll probably be all right. I wouldn't feel too bad yet. |
| DOVEY: | Shut up. |
| SANDRA: | It's not that so much; it's just that the only time he has seemed really glad to have me near him since he got back is when he's delirious. |
| *MUSIC:* | *(CURTAIN)* |
| | *(CLOSING ANNOUNCEMENT)* |
| CUTTING: | Say, mother, when you think of cod liver oil for your children, do you also think of sticky spoons, and a bit of a fuss and bother? Well, here's a way to solve these problems. When you think of vitamins A and D (they're the ones contained in cod liver oil), just think of One-A-Day Brand |

Vitamin A and D Tablets—a really pleasant way of giving the children their so-called cod liver oil vitamins. And while it's hard to believe, it's true—each single candy-like One-A-Day Brand Vitamin A and D Tablet gives a child twenty-five percent MORE than his established minimum daily requirement of these two protective vitamins—actually, it would take one and one-half teaspoonfuls of minimum USP cod liver oil to supply that same amount. Remember though, your druggist now has THREE different kinds of One-A-Day Brand Vitamins. When you want the so-called cod liver oil vitamins, A and D, look for the big "one" and the name Miles on the YELLOW package.

MUSIC: *(THEME ESTABLISH AND FADE UNDER)*

ANNCR: Can Hack's irrational response to Sandra's presence be an indication of a return to the former relationship between them? Does an unconscious man say the things which are really in his heart and mind? Can Sandra accept this delirious reaction as a basis upon which their love can be rebuilt if and when Hack recovers? Listen tomorrow, as our "Lady Of The Press" takes up the vigil over her injured lover in—episode nineteen of "THE PICTURE OF DEATH."

MUSIC: *(PUNCTUATION AND UNDER)*

ANNCR: "Lady Of The Press", is written by Dwight Hauser, and produced by Gordon T. Hughes, and is brought to you each day, Monday through Friday at this same time by the makers of ALKA SELTZER.

MUSIC: *(UP TO FILL)*

ANNCR: [Dick Cutting speaking] This CBS. The COLUMBIA BROADCASTING SYSTEM.

# EPISODE #19

# "PICTURE OF DEATH"

| | | |
|---|---|---|
| SPONSOR: | ALKA SELTZER | MAY 25, 1944 |
| AGENCY: | WADE  4:00—4:15 PM, PWT PN | |

---

ANNCR: The makers of Alka Seltzer present—"LADY OF THE PRESS"

MUSIC: *(STING...QUICK PUNCTUATION)*

ANNCR: The adventures of Sandra Martin, radio' newest romantic-mystery serial!

MUSIC: *(THEME-ESTABLISH AND FADE OUT)*

*(OPENING ANNOUNCEMENT)*

CUTTING: How about it, friends—are you letting a vitamin deficiency keep you from feeling like your old normal self? Well, if you are not sure that your three square meals a day are supplying you with enough vitamins for normal energy, nerves and digestion, resistance to colds, strong bones and teeth, then you are just the person who ought to know about One-A-Day Brand Multiple Vitamin Capsules— called multiple because each capsule contains eight different vitamins. In fact, One-A-Day Brand Multiple Vitamin Capsules are so rich in vitamins that a single tablet each day will supply you with your FULL basic daily requirements of ALL the vitamins whose requirements have been established. Yet in spite of their high vitamin content and their unsurpassed quality, One-A-Day Brand Multiple Vitamin Capsules are surprisingly low in cost—because it takes only one capsule daily to do the job. How then can you or any member of your family run the risk of a vitamin deficiency? Better ask your druggist for One-A-Day Brand Multiple Vitamin Capsules right away, and help yourself to their protective benefits every day. Look for the brand with the name Miles and the big "1" on the BLUE package—that's the "one" to buy. At all drug stores.

MUSIC: *THEME ESTABLISH AND FADE*

ANNCR: And now, "Lady Of The Press", and episode nineteen—in "THE PICTURE OF DEATH!"

MUSIC: *PUNCTUATION AND DOWN FADE OUT UNDER*

ANNCR: Injured in an accident while pursuing Sandra Martin's assailant, Hack Taggart now lies in a hospital in a state of coma. The strange man, who seems destined to plague Sandra's every move, has once more escaped. Sandra has been keeping an almost constant vigil in the emergency ward, waiting and hoping for the moment when Hack will regain consciousness. She has become nearly exhausted from loss of sleep and through emotional strain, for no one realizes better than Sandra that Hack's condition can be traced to his desire to protect her from harm. Well now, we look in on Hack as he lies on the hospital bed. A nurse has just entered his room.

~~NURSE: Are you awake, Mr. Taggart?—Mr. Taggart?~~

~~HACK: (IRRATIONAL) Sandra.....Sandra you've come....I'm glad..~~

~~NURSE: Please, Mr. Taggart.....I'm is Miss....Emmons....Your nurse.~~

HACK: Sandra . . . you've come to help me. You must . . . you mustn't let them send me back.

| | |
|---|---|
| NURSE: | [No,] Mr. Taggart, I'm your Nurse, and you're not going to be sent anyplace. |
| HACK: | But, they're trying to—they're trying to discharge me. |
| NURSE: | Hmm. Delirious. ~~Oh……You don't have to worry about that Mr. Taggart.~~ |
| HACK: | But, they mustn't, Sandra. I'll be all right now . . . now that they've taken the shrapnel out, won't I? ~~They have taken it out, haven't they?~~ |
| NURSE: | Yes, Mr. Taggart. You're going to be all right. |
| HACK: | Don't call me Mr. Taggart, Sandra. They mustn't send me back. I've earned the right to stay here and fight. ~~Earned it by a baptism of hell.~~....Did—did they tell you how I got it, Sandra? ~~Did I tell you?~~ |
| NURSE: | No, ~~you~~ [they] didn't. |
| HACK: | It was right after the landing. Several of us were lying on the beach. |
| TECH: | *BEGIN B.F.* |
| HACK: | The Jerries were layin' down a barrage of machine gun fire like a solid steel sheet above our heads. |
| TECH: | *B.F. TO ZERO* |
| SOUND: | *GUNFIRE* |
| SOLDIER: | *(SHOUTS)* Stay down! Taggart! You fool! Stay down! |
| TAGGART: | Can't get any Jerries that way. I'm goin' after that machine gun nest. |
| SOLDIER: | No, Taggart! You'll be killed! Stay down! |
| TAGGART: | Sorry. I didn't come here to lie on the beach! |

| | |
|---|---|
| SOUND: | WHISTLING SHEEL |
| SOLDIER: | Get down! Get— |
| SOUND: | EXPLOSION |
| MUSIC: | (TRANSITION) |
| DOCTOR: | All right, who's next? |
| SERGEANT: | This man, Doctor. He's full of shrapnel. |
| DOCTOR: | Is he ready? |
| SERGEANT: | Yes. The anesthetic has been given. |
| DOCTOR: | Hmm. Pretty bad. Well, we'll see what we can do, but this boy has seen the last of his fighting days. |
| MUSIC: | (TRANSITION) |
| SOUND: | TINKLE OF SURGICAL INSTRUMENTS |
| DOCTOR: | All right. That's about all we can do for him here. I think most of the metal is out. See that this man gets priority passage back to the base hospital. |
| MUSIC: | (TRANSITION) |
| COLONEL: | Well, Taggart, you're a lucky young man. |
| HACK: | You mean . . . because I'm still alive? |
| COLONEL: | Yes. You had a pretty bad time. |
| HACK: | I know. |
| COLONEL: | I suppose you realize what a wonderful job of surgery was done on you. |
| HACK: | I think so. |

COLONEL: ~~Why, when they brought you in here....I wouldn't have given ten cents for your chances of pulling through. Let alone coming back to practically normal.~~

HACK: ~~What do you mean, sir....."Practically normal?"~~

COLONEL: ~~Well....A man just can't have his body pumped full of sharpnel and ever be exactly the same again....However.. To all appearances...You're just as good as new....I don't see any XXX worry....~~ You should stand up under ordinary civilian life just as well as before.

HACK: Civilian life?

COLONEL: Yes. Taggart, I've got good news for you. Here—

SOUND: *RATTLE OF PAPER*

HACK: Why, this is a discharge. Physically unfit for further military service.

COLONEL: That's right, Taggart. You've done your part. Now, it's all set for you to go home.

HACK: Well, I beg your pardon, sir, but I guess I'm not as duly impressed as I should be.

COLONEL: But you're going home, Taggart. You'll be back inside of a month.

HACK: Don't I have anything to say about this?

~~COLONEL:~~ ~~Well...I don't know...Do you?~~

~~HACK:~~ ~~Yes...I think I might at least have been consulted...to find out whether I wanted this or not.~~

COLONEL: Taggart, when a man has done as much as you have, and when his medical report reads like yours, the army knows what to do without consulting him.

HACK: But, I don't want this, Sir.

COLONEL: You don't want—Taggart, do you feel all right?

HACK: I did before you handed me this discharge.

COLONEL: But, don't you see, Taggart, you're not in shape for fighting.

HACK: Look, you told me yourself I was practically as good as new.

COLONEL: ~~Certainly~~ [Not quite Taggart, but] you'll be alright once you're away from the front.

~~HACK: I didn't join this army to quit when the job was half done...I enlisted because I wanted to do my part.~~

~~COLONEL: Well...I'd say you've done your part, Taggart.~~

~~HACK: No...Nobody's done his part until it's over...This is the biggest show on earth....And everybody's got a part in it....Anyone who quits before the show's over.....is letting himself and his country down.~~

~~COLONEL: You're not quitting, Taggart...You're being discharged.~~

~~HACK: Is there any possibility of getting a review of my case?~~

~~COLONEL: With a view toward what?~~

~~HACK: Toward staying in...Sir...I...I don't want to go back. I want to stay here.~~

~~COLONEL: Not a chance, Taggart.~~

HACK: How do you think I'll feel going home before it's over? I'm all right. I look all right. Do you think I can go home and see the same people and do the same things I did before and not cringe over quitting?

COLONEL: I've told you, Taggart, you're not quitting. You're still a soldier, and you'll follow orders. Your last orders happen to be acceptance of this discharge and return to America.

|          | You'll find someway to continue helping. There are still important things to do on the home front. |
|---------|---|
| HACK: | *(DISDAINFULLY)* Important things? After this butchering murder of the battle front, do you think anything can seem important except actively trying to put an end to this? |
| COLONEL: | Certainly. Why there are thousands of jobs back home that are just as important as any up here. |
| HACK: | Sorry, sir, but I can't see it that way. Look, I left a girl back home, a girl that I want to marry someday. I want to marry her, maybe even have a family, but I want my wife and my kids to live in a decent world, a world that I helped to make. |
| COLONEL: | For heavens sake, Taggart, do you think you have to personally kill Hitler to help? Why, you've done more already than ninety percent of the population. |
| HACK: | Nobody's done his equal share until he's done all he can. We're not going to win this war by guys quittin' when the job's half done. |
| COLONEL: | You're job is done, and that's final, Taggart. If you want me to put it bluntly, I will. The fact is that the army can't take a chance on men like you. You're not in perfect physical condition. If you go on and get into some important action, you're apt to fold up at the crucial moment. You'd be a liability to the army from now on, Taggart. |
| HACK: | I—I see. So, I'm supposed to go back and sit around while a lot of other guys fashion the world for me, my wife, and my kids to live in, huh? |
| COLONEL: | I wouldn't put it that way, Taggart. |
| HACK: | No? Well, that's the way I put it, except for one thing: there won't be any wife or kids. It'll be hard enough to face people I don't care anything about, but it will be impossible to pretend anything I can do back there is very important, not in comparison to what I've seen here. |

COLONEL: You shouldn't feel that way, Taggart. You really shouldn't. After a man has given as much of himself to his country as you had, he shouldn't go back with a heart filled with bitterness.

HACK: Maybe not, but I don't seem to have much control over that just now.

TECH: *BEGIN B.F.*

HACK: I can't help it if I feel that I belong here instead of being shipped back to lie and rot on a home front that seems unimportant to me.

TECH: *B.F. TO ZERO*

HACK: ~~That's why~~ [So] you gotta help me, San. You can't let 'em send me back. You can't! ~~They…They're trying to! But, I won't let them…I won't let them I tell you. You understand…I won't let them.~~

NURSE: ~~Please~~ Mr. Taggart, you mustn't excite yourself. Your condition is very uncertain at best. ~~This excitement can only make it worse…~~ You must try and sleep.

MUSIC: *BRIDGE*

SOUND: *FOOTSTEPS UP AND STOP*

SANDRA: Is it possible to see Lieutenant Taggart now?

NURSE: Well, I hardly think so. I was just with him and he's delirious. He seems to think he's at a war front in Sicily.

SANDRA: Please, I really think I should see him. ~~I know him very well~~ I—I might possibly be able to help him. The association of ideas. Maybe seeing me, he'll—

NURSE: ~~What is your name, please?~~ [Oh, you must be Sandra.]

SANDRA: ~~Sandra, Sandra Martin…~~ [Yes] I was his—

| | |
|---|---|
| NURSE: | ~~Oh, yes...~~ [I know. Nurse Paley told me.] Perhaps seeing you might help. As a matter of fact, he thought you were with him. He was delirious and he thought I was you. He seems to think a great deal of you. |
| SANDRA: | He does? You mean he was happy that he thought it was I? |
| NURSE: | Very hap. He's been through a lot, Miss, but he's fortunate to have someone like you to come back to. Yes, you may go in. ~~You know the room...~~ |
| SANDRA: | Yes, thank you, and thank you for telling me. |
| NURSE: | You're welcome. I thought you should know. |
| SANDRA: | Yes. |
| SOUND: | FOOTSTEPS DOWN CORRIDOR. .DOOR OPEN |
| HACK: | (OFF-MUMBLING) |
| SANDRA: | Oh, Hack, Hack, darling, please, you must try to be quiet. |
| HACK: | Don't let them send me back. But, you don't belong here. I don't see why they let you come here. They had no right to let you come. Promise me you'll go back. Go back and wait for me? |
| SANDRA: | I'm not in Sicily, Hack, and neither are you. |
| HACK: | They can't send me back. |
| SANDRA: | Hack, listen to me. Try to understand. You are back, and so am I. You're dreaming, Hack. You're not in Sicily anymore. You're at home. You're hurt, but you'll be alright. |
| HACK: | You mean they did send me back? Sandra, I— |
| SANDRA: | It's all right, darling. Just be quiet. You've had a bad time, but you're going to be all right. |

| | |
|---|---|
| HACK: | Sandra, *(COMING OUT OF IT)* where, am I? Hospital? What's wrong? That car. Man shot at you. Didn't I get him? |
| SANDRA: | *(CHOKING BACK TEARS)* No, Hack, he got away. |
| HACK: | Well, we gotta get him. Come. *(PAINFULLY)* Oh! |
| SANDRA: | You must lie quietly, Hack. |
| HACK: | What's wrong? My head, it— |
| SANDRA: | You had a smash up, Hack. You got hurt. |
| HACK: | Yes. I remember now. I was chasing that car. I followed you and Skip. Then that car came by and they started shooting at you. |
| SANDRA: | I know, Hack, but don't think about that now. You must rest. |
| HACK: | No, I'm all right, now. Just a little groggy. Guess I must have hit something. Remember when I was chasing him? It reminded me of a time back in Sicily just before a big push. We were chasin' a Jerry staff car in a jeep. First time since I got back that anything seemed really important. Oh, but I guess you wouldn't understand that, would you? |
| SANDRA: | As I've never understood before, Hack. Seeing you like this makes me realize more than ever how much you mean to me. |
| HACK: | You shouldn't talk that way, Sandra. I'm not the same. I've tried to tell you that. |
| SANDRA: | And in trying, you've told me that that somehow down underneath you are the same. You just don't think so. Now, you must go back to sleep, Hack. |
| HACK: | Sandra, I— |
| SANDRA: | Quiet. You're in no condition to argue with me, darling. You just rest and sleep. I'm going now. I'll come back later. |

|  |  |
|---|---|
|  | But, don't worry, darling. Everything is going to be all right again. Everything. |
| MUSIC: | (BRIDGE) |
| SANDRA: | Oh, Doctor? Doctor? |
| DOCTOR: | Yes, Miss Martin? |
| SANDRA: | I've just come from Lieutenant Taggart. Could you tell me if he's going to be alright? |
| DOCTOR: | It's hard to say, just yet, Miss Martin. He's had a severe blow. Some concussion. Can't tell how he's going to come along until he's had some more rest. |
| SANDRA: | But that's what I wanted to tell you. He's— |
| DOCTOR: | These cases are rather touchy. You see, the coma is produced by nervous shock. It's really a good thing in a way. Keeps the patient quiet. They mustn't be brought out of it too quickly. Complete rest and quiet. That's the best thing for him. No excitement. |
| SANDRA: | That's what I'm trying to tell you doctor. He's no longer unconscious. |
| DOCTOR: | What? Why, I'd have said he'd remain unconscious for another eight hours. |
| SANDRA: | He's been talking to me for some time. |
| DOCTOR: | Oh, I'm sorry to hear that, Miss Martin. You should have called me. |
| SANDRA: | Is it apt to prove dangerous? |
| DOCTOR: | I can't tell about that yet, but certainly the best thing would have been complete rest for several hours after coming to. Certainly carrying on a discussion with you couldn't help him any. |

| | |
|---|---|
| MUSIC: | (TO CURTAIN) |
| | (CLOSING ANNOUNCEMENT) |
| CUTTING: | Did you know, ladies, that experts in nutrition believe that breakfast is perhaps the most important meal you serve your family each day—because on it depends what kind of a start they get on their day's work? How logical it is then that you make sure of your family's entire daily supply of vitamins at breakfast time by giving them a single One-A-Day Brand Multiple Vitamin Capsule each morning. That single One-A-Day Brand Multiple Vitamin Capsule (multiple because it contains eight different vitamins, all in one small capsule) supplies a person's full basic daily requirements of ALL the vitamins whose requirements are known. And you know how important the vitamins are for normal energy, digestion, nerves, and resistance to colds. But, you may ask, what about the cost? Well, in spite of the fact that One-A-Day Brand Multiple Vitamin Capsules are all laboratory tested, potency guaranteed, and of the highest possible quality, they are priced amazingly low. You can get a full sixty day supply of sixty capsules for only two dollars. So start your family's day off right by giving them each a single One-A-Day Brand Multiple Vitamin Capsule every day. Your druggist has them. Ask for the kind with the big "one" and the name Miles on the BLUE package. |
| MUSIC: | (THEME ESTABLISH AND FADE) |
| ANNCR: | Now that Sandra has been acquainted with Hacks true feeling and understands the cause of his bitterness, will she be able to overlook the great change in him and find that she can love him as much as before? Or will the new personality overshadow and overpower the man Hack once was? Listen tomorrow, as "Lady Of The Press" returns to see what effect her visit had on the injured Hack in episode twenty in "THE PICTURE OF DEATH." |
| MUSIC: | (UP AND UNDER) |

ANNCR: Lady Of The Press is written by Dwight Hauser, and produced by Gordon T. Hughes and is brought to you each day, Monday through Friday at this same time by the makers of ALKA SELTZER.

MUSIC: *(UP TO FILL)*

ANNCR: [Dick Cutting speaking] This is CBS. The COLUMBIA BROADCASTING SYSTEM

# EPISODE #20

# "PICTURE OF DEATH"

| | | |
|---|---|---|
| SPONSOR: | ALKA SELTZER | MAY 26, 1944 |
| AGENCY: | WADE 4:00—4:15 PM, PWT PN | |

---

ANNCR: The makers of Alka Seltzer present—"LADY OF THE PRESS"

*MUSIC:* *(STING. QUICK PUNCTUATION)*

ANNCR: The adventures of Sandra Martin, radio's newest romantic-mystery serial!

*MUSIC:* *(THEME-ESTABLISH AND FADE OUT:)*

CUTTING: If you mothers want to see some big smiles on the kiddie's faces when it's time for their so-called Cod Liver Oil vitamins—give them One-A-Day Brand Vitamin A and D Tablets. They taste like candy, you know, even though each One-A-Day Brand Vitamin A and D Tablet does contain the same amount of these vitamins as one and one-half teaspoonfuls of minimum USP cod liver oil—an amount which is actually twenty-five percent more than their minimum daily requirements. And don't forget, mother, that vitamins A and D are mighty important to you and dad, too. So give the whole family the protective benefits of ample amounts of vitamins A and D. The cost is so low—just slightly over a penny a day, when you buy the large family size package. Your druggist has them—One-A-Day Brand Vitamin A and D Tablets, in the YELLOW package with the big "one" and the name Miles. Be sure though you get the genuine One-A-Day Brand because no other is "just as good".

MUSIC: (THEME ESTABLISH AND FADE UNDER:)

ANNCR: And now, "Lady of the Press," and episode twenty—in—"THE PICTURE OF DEATH".

MUSIC: (STING AND QUICK FIGURATION FADES OUT UNDER:)

ANNCR: In a delirium, and believing himself still to be at a war front in Sicily, Hack Taggart has revealed his true feelings about Sandra to a nurse at the hospital, believing that she is Sandra and that she has come to his aid. Inadvertently, the nurse has told Sandra something of the way Hack feels, although she has been careful not to betray to completely the feeling he displayed to her. However, the information she does have gives Sandra a new mental lease on the love of this man who has apparently become so bitter against her. She does not yet know the exact cause for his bitterness but now believes that it must be based upon some illusion with which she can cope. She feels that it would have been impossible for Hack to express such thoughts about her unless he felt some of the same things when rational. This has given her new hope and courage. The picture before her is much brighter as she returns to her apartment after this latest visit to the hospital.

SOUND: DOOR CLOSE

DOVEY: Hello, Sandra. Where have you been?

SANDRA: At the hospital.

DOVEY: What are you doing? Rereading the magazines?

SANDRA: No, they let me see him today.

| | |
|---|---|
| DOVEY: | Hack? Well, then I guess he must be better, huh? |
| SANDRA: | He was, I think, but he got all mixed up in a delirium. He thought he was still in Sicily and that I had come to him there. |
| DOVEY: | Gee! That must have been sorta rough on you. |
| SANDRA: | Yes, but I'm thankful for one thing: seeing him that way made me realize I couldn't give up. |
| DOVEY: | It did? Well, what's the answer? |
| SANDRA: | I don't know the answer yet, Dovey, but now that I finally have a clear picture of the problem, maybe the answer won't be so hard to work out. |
| DOVEY: | You're really nuts about that guy, aren't you? |
| SANDRA: | I guess so. I've never really given up hope that things would be the same between us again. Now, I know they must be if I'm ever to find real love. |
| DOVEY: | Well, he threw you for a loop once. If you'll take my advice, you'll not leave yourself quite so wide open again. |
| SANDRA: | Now is the time when he really needs me, Dovey. |
| DOVEY: | Yeah, but do you need him? |
| SANDRA: | Yes, I do. I need him more than anything else in the world. |
| DOVEY: | Well, in that case, I guess you're just about as bad off as a gal can get. What are you going to do about it? |
| SANDRA: | Just try and let things ride along smoothly. Try to understand him and overlook the things I don't understand until he really gets back to being himself again. |
| DOVEY: | And when do you expect that happy state to occur? |

SANDRA: I don't know, Dovey. Maybe soon, and maybe never. All I know is that the only possible thing I can do now is to wait and hope, and do all in my power to help him and to make life as pleasant and easy for him as possible.

DOVEY: Well, you've got a lot more courage than I'd have. Of course, you've also got a case of romance on your hands, which I don't have, darn it.

SANDRA: You wouldn't understand this kind of love, Dovey. You only write about it.

DOVEY: That's right. No man yet has been able to get me that close to the five yard line. And why is that?

SANDRA: Maybe you aren't enough of a romanticist to let love mean so much to you.

DOVEY: I dunno, I've never had enough of it to tell what it does mean. Sure, plenty of guys take me out. They spend money on me, and I get around a lot, but, in the final analysis, it seems they just sorta keep me around for laughs. You've got the right system, honey, whatever it is. I'll keep on writing the sob stuff for my public, but, my advice to you is hang onto what you have like it was your life itself.

SANDRA: Don't worry, I intend to.

DOVEY: And what do you intend doing about this court scrape you're in?

SANDRA: There's nothing much I can do about it now.

DOVEY: Well, you're certainly not going to just sit here and take whatever they want to throw at you sitting down, are you?

SANDRA: No, but what I have in mind doing about it depends upon a lot of spade work which has to be done between now and the trial, spade work that's going to take a lot of help from both Hack and Skip.

DOVEY: Such as?

SANDRA: Well, Dovey, here's the whole picture in a nut shell. I'm convinced that Elbert Hoagan murdered Frances Evers at the behest of the Black Market Operators whom she was about to expose.

DOVEY: So?

SANDRA: I've got to prove that! I've got to get the same or stronger evidence than she had. Then, if I can prove she had it, there's their motive. Then, if we can get Hoagan and face him with the facts, he'll probably talk.

DOVEY: Seems to me that you're basing your defense on an awful lots of "ifs" and "Probablys."

SANDRA: I guess I am, but can you think of anything better.

DOVEY: Yes, I can.

SANDRA: What?

DOVEY: Forget the whole thing. Let the Black Market operators know that you're willing to drop the whole thing and they'll stop bothering you.

SANDRA: Oh, no, that's one thing I won't do. I didn't get to be the highest-paid reporter on the Courier by ducking issues. Fine one I'd be to let a thing like this go on just to save my own skin.

DOVEY: You'll be in an awful fix without it, baby.

SANDRA: Don't worry, I'm not going to lose it. It just looks bad for the present, but I'll come through alright, and I'll put those crooks out of business while I'm at it.

DOVEY: Okay, okay, so you don't need a soap box. I just asked a question. I didn't ask for a lecture. Now suppose we forget the whole thing and get some sleep? It's late.

| | |
|---|---|
| SANDRA: | Yes, and I'm tired. I hope I can sleep. |
| DOVEY: | Now that things are straightened out a little more, you ought to stand a better chance. |
| SANDRA: | Yes, except for one thing— |
| DOVEY: | And what's that? |
| SANDRA: | The man who took those shots at Skip and me. |
| DOVEY: | What about him? He missed you, didn't he? |
| SANDRA: | Sure, but that was the same man who stole the evidence file and kidnapped Hoagan and came here and threatened me. |
| DOVEY: | So what? |
| SANDRA: | Just this: he was the man Hack was chasing when he had the wreck . . . and he got away! |
| *MUSIC:* | *(BRIDGE)* |
| HACK: | *(ANGRY)* I don't care what the doctor's orders are. These are my orders and you better carry them out. |
| NURSE: | *(DUB)* But, please, Mr. Taggart. you're not supposed to upset yourself. |
| HACK: | I'm not upsetting myself. You're upsetting me! Now, do I get that telephone brought in here, or do I get up and go out to make the call? |
| NURSE: | Alright, I'll probably lose my job for going against orders, but you'll lose your life if I don't. Honestly, anyone would think you wanted to fall back into unconsciousness again. |
| HACK: | As against the intelligence of this hospital staff, there is a lot in its favor. Now get me that phone. |
| NURSE: | Alright. Just lie quietly, and I'll bring it in. *(FADE)* There's a plug next to your bed. The phone's just out here. |

| | |
|---|---|
| SOUND: | *DOOR OPEN AND CLOSE* |
| HACK: | *(MUTTERING TO HIMSELF)* Tell me I can't make a phone call. We'll see. I'll show them who's running my case around here. *(PAUSE) (THEN SKEPTICALLY)* NURSE? NURSE! *(SCREAMS)* NURSE!!! |
| SOUND: | *DOOR OPEN* |
| NURSE: | *(PATHETICALLY)* Mr. Taggart, please! I'm hurrying as fast as I can. If you must make me disobey orders, must you also arrange to have me caught at it? |
| HACK: | I just didn't want you to trick me, like going to call the Doc instead of bringing the phone. |
| NURSE: | You can see that I brought it. |
| HACK: | I can now. I couldn't while you were still outside. |
| NURSE: | Ohh! |
| SOUND: | *PLUGGING PHONE IN A SOCKET-LIFT RECEIVER* |
| NURSE: | Do you know the number you want to call? |
| HACK: | Certainly. |
| NURSE: | Alright. Now, you may have five minutes, no more. I'll be back then, and I'll expect complete cooperation from now on from you. |
| HACK: | You're just lucky you don't get anything worse from me. I'm a dangerous character. Now out! This is private. |
| NURSE: | I'm not in the least interested in your personal affairs. I'm only interested in seeing to it that you continue having them. |
| SOUND: | *FOOTSTEPS. DOOR OPEN. CLOSE* |

| | |
|---|---|
| HACK: | (CHUCKLES) |
| SOUND: | DIALING PHONE. PAUSE. PHONE RING (ON FILTER) (REPEAT) |
| HACK: | Alright. come on, come on. |
| SOUND: | REPEAT RING. RECEIVER OFF HOOK |
| SKIP: | (FILTER. SLEEPILY) Hello? |
| HACK: | Hello, Skip? |
| SKIP: | Yeah. |
| HACK: | This is Hack. |
| SKIP: | Who? |
| HACK: | Hack. Hack Taggart. |
| SKIP: | What? You mean you've come to? You're gonna live? |
| HACK: | That's the bad news for you. |
| SKIP: | You ain't kiddin'. Flicker me eyelids! I thought you was out of my hair for good. |
| HACK: | No such luck. |
| SKIP: | No, I guess not. I always was an unlucky character. Hey! What's the idea wakin' me up in the middle of the night? Couldn't you wait until morning to call an' say you was gonna live? |
| HACK: | I didn't call you for that. |
| SKIP: | No? Well, what's on your mind? Scout meetin'? |
| HACK: | No. Sandra. |

| | |
|---|---|
| SKIP: | Still delirious, are ya? |
| HACK: | No, I'm all right now. That's why I have her on my mind. Know where she is? |
| SKIP: | Sure. I guess she's home. |
| HACK: | You guess so? It wouldn't have occurred to you to make sure, would it? |
| SKIP: | I ain't in the habit of followin' her, if that's what you mean. |
| HACK: | Well, you better start forming that habit. At least until I get well enough to do it. |
| SKIP: | What's eatin' you, anyway? |
| HACK: | Look, you pin head, don't you realize that the guy I was after got away? |
| SKIP: | Sure. Look who was chasin' him. |
| HACK: | And you realize that he's the one who's been tryin' to get both you and Sandra for the last week? |
| SKIP: | Yeah. |
| HACK: | Then, why in the name of—look, you get over to Sandra's place and keep watch, and don't take your eyes off her for the next few days. She's going to need protection until I get out of here. |
| SKIP: | And after that? |
| HACK: | After that, I'll take care of it myself. Now get over there and don't waste anytime on the way. It's after midnight now. |
| SOUND: | *RECEIVER ON HOOK* |
| MUSIC: | *(BRIDGE)* |

| | |
|---|---|
| SOUND: | CLOCK TICKING CONTINUE TEN SECOND. FUMBLING WITH KEY IN LOCK |
| SANDRA: | *(FRIGHTENED..WHISPER)* D-D-Dovey? Dovey, are you asleep? Dovey? Are you asleep? |
| DOVEY: | *(YAWNING)* I was. Why? |
| SANDRA: | Shhh. Listen, do you hear anything? |
| DOVEY: | *(PAUSE)* Wait a minute. Yes, I do. Somebody fooling with the lock on our door. |
| SOUND: | LOCK CLICKS |
| SANDRA: | *(TERRIFIED)* It—it opened. |
| SOUND: | DOOR OPEN—CLICK OF SWITCH |
| VOICE: | Hello, Girls. Mind if I come in? |
| SOUND: | *(TO CURTAIN)* |
| CUTTING: | Tell me, friends—how are you coming along with your fight against annoying Springtime colds? Well, just remember that your resistance against colds can easily depend (among other things) upon the amount of vitamin A you have stored in your body. For that reason we suggest that you help keep up your normal resistance to colds twelve months a year by bolstering your diet with a single One-A-Day Brand Vitamin A and D Tablet every day. That's the easy, pleasant, low-cost way. Easy—because each One-A-Day Brand Vitamin A and D Tablet is so rich in vitamin content that a single tablet supplies you with your full normal daily requirements of both of these important vitamins. Pleasant—because even though each One-A-Day Brand A and D Tablet is as rich in these vitamins as a teaspoon and a half of minimum USP cod liver oil, it has no unpleasant taste. And low cost—just slightly more than a penny a day when you buy the large package—mighty |

little to pay for the protection they offer. Remember then, your druggist has One-A-Day Brand Vitamin A and D Tablets. Look for the big "one" on the bright YELLOW package—that's the "one" to buy to help you keep up normal resistance to colds.

MUSIC: (THEME ESTABLISH AND FADE DOWN UNDER)

ANNCR: Is it the same strange man who has once again taken the liberty of entering Sandra's apartment uninvited? Will Skip's carelessness in failing to provide protection for her result in Sandra's abduction? And, what of Hack? Now, that Sandra has decided to do all in her power to reawaken their lost love, will Hack allow himself to become the man he was before? Listen again Monday as our "Lady of the Press" faces new conflicts in episode twenty-one of "THE PICTURE OF DEATH".

MUSIC: (STING AND FADE DOWN UNDER:)

ANNCR: "Lady of the Press" is written by Dwight Hauser, and produced by Gordon T. Hughes, and is brought to you each day, Monday through Friday at this same time by the makers of ALKA SELTZER.

MUSIC: (UP TO FILL)

ANNCR: [Dick Cutting speaking] This is CBS. The COLUMBIA BROADCASTING SYSTEM.

# EPISODE #21

# "PICTURE OF DEATH"

| | | |
|---|---|---|
| SPONSOR: | ALKA SELTZER | MAY 29, 1944 |
| AGENCY: | WADE 4:00—4:15 PM, PWT, PN | |

---

| | |
|---|---|
| ANNCR: | The makers of Alka Seltzer present—"LADY OF THE PRESS" |
| MUSIC: | *(STING. QUICK PUNCTUATION)* |
| ANNCR: | The adventures of Sandra Martin, radio's newest romantic-mystery serial! |
| MUSIC: | *(THEME-ESTABLISH AND FADE OUT:)* |
| | *(OPENING COMMERCIAL)* |
| CUTTING: | If these are pretty busy, hectic days for you—as they are for most of us—here's something you'll find worth remembering. One of the handiest things you can keep around the house is a package of comfort-bringing Alka-Seltzer tablets. Then, when a headache or a touch of acid-indigestion comes along to slow you down, right when you're the busiest, or when you're trying to relax, Alka-Seltzer is ready to bring you the world of comfort you want, right when you want it. Is YOURS an Alka-Seltzer home? It SHOULD be! Why not make it one, by getting a sixty or thirty cent size package of these modern, comfort |

bringing tablets from your druggist the very next time you're out shopping? Many is the time you'll be glad you got acquainted with Alka-Seltzer!

MUSIC: (THEME UP AND FADE DOWN FOR)

ANNCR: And now, "Lady of the Press" and episode twenty-one—in "THE PICTURE OF DEATH".

MUSIC: (STING AND QUICK FIGURATION—FADE OUT UNDER)

ANNCR: Hack Taggart, still in the hospital convalescing from injuries sustained in the automobile wreck while chasing the strange man who fired shots at Sandra and Skip, seems to be the only one fully aware of the danger in which Sandra has been placed. While he seems to have done all in his power to present her case in an unfavorable light to the Grand Jury, he is none the less deeply concerned for her safety from the man who seems bent upon doing her harm. So far, her every effort to gather evidence against the Black Market operators has been frustrated by this strange man. Knowing the danger, Hack has asked Skip to watch over Sandra in his absence, but Sandra and Dovey are made aware of their danger when they are awakened in the middle of the night by the sound of someone fumbling with the lock on their door. Breathlessly, the two girls sit up in their beds as they hear the front door open and the light [switch] click.

SKIP: What's wrong with your door bell? I buzzed it a dozen times, but nothing happened.

SANDRA: Skip! Oh, you idiot, you nearly scared us to death!

SKIP: Oh? Sorry, but I wasn't sure you were here, and Hack told me to check up.

SANDRA: How did you get in?

SKIP: Sometimes, in the photographic business, a skeleton key comes in handy.

| | |
|---|---|
| SANDRA: | Well, don't ever use it again, unless you warn us beforehand. Why, we might have taken a shot at you. |
| SKIP: | Got a gun? |
| SANDRA: | No, but how could you know that? |
| SKIP: | In this case, what I don't know won't hurt me. |
| SANDRA: | Well, it certainly hurt us! Scared us out of any chance to sleep the rest of the night, didn't it, Dovey? *(PAUSE)* Dovey? Skip! Look at her! She's fainted. |
| SKIP: | *(FADING IN)* Yeah, yeah, I guess she has. Hey, I wondered what was keepin' her so quiet. |
| SANDRA: | Well do something, stupid. Don't just stand there. |
| SKIP: | What do you want me to do? Go out and come in again? |
| SANDRA: | No. Get a wet towel. Help me bring her to. Don't you know what to do when people faint? |
| SKIP: | Oh. All right. How do I get into these things? Spend the night playin' nursemaid to a sob sister. |
| SANDRA: | Stop beefing and hurry. |
| SKIP: | All right, but when she's settled, I'm taking over one of your davenports for the night. If I have to stay here and guard you, I'm going to do it as comfortably as possible. |
| *MUSIC:* | (BRIDGE) |
| CHIEF: | Well, Taggart, that was a narrow escape you had! |
| HACK: | You're right, Chief, it was. |
| CHIEF: | I just talked to the doctor, and he says you're coming along fine. |

| | |
|---|---|
| HACK: | I feel better this morning. |
| CHIEF: | When do you think you'll be out? |
| HACK: | I don't know. They haven't told me yet. |
| CHIEF: | Well, I imagine you'll be here a few days yet. The doc says you had a concussion. |
| HACK: | I don't doubt that. I wasn't losing any time when we hit. |
| CHIEF: | No. I guess not. |
| HACK: | How's Roake getting along? |
| CHIEF: | You mean, nobody told you about Roake? |
| HACK: | No. Why? |
| CHIEF: | He never knew what happened. He was killed instantly. |
| HACK: | Gee. That's too bad. He was a nice guy. Had a family, too, didn't he? |
| CHIEF: | Sure, and it's gonna be kinda tough for them. He was a relatively new man. The insurance won't be an awful lot. |
| HACK: | You know, Chief, as soon as I get out of here, I think I'll try and do something about that. Maybe I could promote some sort of a benefit among the boys for Roake's family. I sorta feel responsible. I ordered him to chase that car. |
| CHIEF: | Look Taggart, any officer knows when he takes the job that there will be risks. There's no way that Roake's misfortune can be construed as your fault. |
| HACK: | Not directly. I know. I just feel a sort of moral obligation. |
| CHIEF: | I'm glad to hear you say that, Taggart. That sounds more like the guy I used to know than anything I've heard since you got back. |

HACK: Yeah, well, there are some things that even war doesn't change.

CHIEF: Well, if this attitude regarding Roake's family is any indication, maybe the other things will be the same again before long.

HACK: Maybe. I can't tell about that yet.

CHIEF: I'm glad to see you getting along so well. We sorta miss you down at headquarters.

HACK: Thanks. I'd think a respite from my unorthodox methods would be a relief for you.

CHIEF: You've probably put more grey hairs on my head than any other man in the bureau, Taggart, but you've also brought in more guilty criminals. That's the important thing.

HACK: Thanks, Chief.

CHIEF: However, I've never quite learned to trust you completely.

HACK: No? That's too bad, Chief..

CHIEF: Take for instance this Evers Case. I swear I can't understand what you're up to, and if the D.A. ever finds out about that bullet in my desk, my goose is cooked. Why didn't you want that bullet introduced?

HACK: You mean . . . this bullet?

CHIEF: Where'd you get that?

HACK: I had the nurse get it out of my clothes. Wouldn't want this bullet to get into the wrong hands.

CHIEF: But—but—where did you get it before that? Is that the one that—

HACK: —was in your drawer? Yep, Chief, this is the one.

| | | |
|---|---|---|
| CHIEF: | Well of all the—what's the idea breakin' into my desk and stealin' the evidence? |
| HACK: | Oh, I was afraid you might get a little over zealous in offering evidence and forget our bargain. |
| CHIEF: | Does that give you the right to steal the evidence? |
| HACK: | To tell you the truth, Chief. this isn't evidence. |
| CHIEF: | What? |
| HACK: | Nope. It's a bullet I picked up out at the firing range. |
| CHIEF: | But it fell out of Sandra Martins' purse. |
| HACK: | Uh huh, because I took the liberty of putting it there. |
| CHIEF: | You what? Taggart! I swear you can pull some of the— |
| HACK: | Now just a minute, Chief. I had a good reason. |
| CHIEF: | You are going to need one. |
| HACK: | You know that Sandra and Skip have the negative of that picture of Hoagan firing the murder gun? |
| CHIEF: | Yes. |
| HACK: | Well, that picture would certainly go a long way toward clearing them. |
| CHIEF: | What's that got to do with you faking a bullet in Miss Martin's purse? |
| HACK: | Just this: if we didn't have some more incriminating evidence to hold against them, they'd have brought out the picture for evidence. I had to use it as a threat. |
| CHIEF: | Then, you don't actually believe that Sandra Martin and Skip Williams had anything to do with the murder? |

| | |
|---|---|
| HACK: | Certainly not. |
| CHIEF: | Then why in the name of all that's—why are you trying to pin it on them? |
| HACK: | I'm not. I'm simply trying to pin suspicion on them. |
| CHIEF: | And you're succeeding beautifully. |
| HACK: | Good, because the stronger the case looks against Skip and Sandra, the more apt the real guilty parties are to let their guard down. |
| CHIEF: | Now its guilty parties? A minute ago, the picture was conclusive proof that Hoagan did it. What's eating on you, Taggart? |
| HACK: | A desire to catch the people behind this thing . . . and I think I'm going about it in just about the right way to do it. |
| CHIEF: | I hope so, but couldn't you have let Miss Martin in on your plans? Did you have to let her think the case was as strong as it looks? |
| HACK: | Miss Martin isn't in what you might call a "frame of mind" suited to cooperation with me. |
| CHIEF: | That's beside the point. She's accused of aiding and abetting a murderer. ~~That's enough.~~ |
| HACK: | That's not all of it, unless the actual guilty parties are caught. She's apt to be convicted. Her acquittal depends upon their apprehension. |
| CHIEF: | So? |
| HACK: | And on top of that, maybe even her life depends upon it. The people Sandra Martin is out to get will stop at nothing to keep the truth from coming out… |
| CHIEF: | You mean even bumpin' her off? |

HACK: Exactly. That's why I can't let her know my plans. If she cuffed them, it would be her own neck—a neck, incidentally, of which I happen to be very fond.

CHIEF: Well, I'm certainly glad you're not overly fond of me. Seems to me your friendship is a rather dangerous thing.

HACK: Not as dangerous as my animosity, Chief.

CHIEF: Well, why don't you at least let her know how you feel about her? That might inspire some trust in you.

HACK: I'm not certain that I want that yet. If the time comes when I feel it's right for us to take up where we left off, I'll let her know. ~~But, not yet. For her sake, I can't do it, yet.~~

MUSIC: BRIDGE

SOUND: SOFT KNOCK

HACK: Yes? Who is it?

SANDRA: *(OFF)* It's Sandra, Hack. May I come in?

HACK: Oh. Oh, yes, Sandra. Come in.

SOUND: DOOR OPEN

SANDRA: Well, aren't we the convalescent? Sitting up in bed already.

SOUND: DOOR CLOSE

HACK: Sure, I wasn't hurt very bad; I got hit on the head.

SOUND: FOOTSTEPS FADE IN

SANDRA: *(CHUCKLES)* Silly. From what I've heard, you were very seriously injured.

HACK: Do I look seriously injured?

SANDRA: No, but you did night before last.

HACK: Yeah. I guess I was, at that. *(PAUSE)* What's on your mind, Sandra?

SANDRA: Nothing special. Just came to see you. Mind?

HACK: Why, no. It's very thoughtful of you. One of these places can get mighty boring unless your friends drop in.

SANDRA: Friends, Hack?

HACK: Sure. We are still friends, aren't we? You aren't really so sore at me, or you wouldn't be here!

SANDRA: It's not that, Hack. I don't pretend to know why you've done what you have. I must confess it's beyond my understanding why you should want to humiliate me so, but all that's rather unimportant now. Seeing you here, especially the last few days, and not knowing whether you were going to come through or not or what you'd be like if you did, [it] ~~has~~ made me realize that you can never make me hate you as much as you once made me love you. That's why I was hoping that you'd consider my coming here just a little bit more than a friendly call.

HACK: Sandra, I'd like to. Believe me. If I could have my choice of any wish in the world, it would be that you and I could go back to being more than friends.

SANDRA: Then, if that's what you want, and I'm willing, why can't we?

HACK: Because I don't want an uncertain future to put any ugly blots on a beautiful past.

SANDRA: Hack, people's futures can't always be blueprinted. You have to take chances on your future.

HACK: But, you have to look around and see that there aren't too many barriers.

SANDRA: And there are a lot before us?

HACK: Maybe and maybe not. I don't know for sure yet, but until I do know, we'll have to keep things on a friendly basis, Sandra.

SANDRA: Well, if that's the best I can do, I guess I'll have to accept it.

HACK: I hope you will. ~~Sandra~~...

SANDRA: At least a friendly basis will be better than the one we've been going on for the past few weeks.

HACK: I've not been unfriendly to you, Sandra.

SANDRA: No, no more than an executioner.

HACK: That's where you're wrong. One of these days you're going to find out that what I've done was the best thing that ever happened to you. You're going to thank me for getting you pinched.

SANDRA: *(MOCKINGLY)* And I suppose if they hang me I'll practically worship you?

HACK: They won't hang you. Just leave it to me.

SANDRA: I don't know about that. I came here to make up with you, but I'm not so sure about placing my whole legal future in your hands.

HACK: They're pretty good hands, Sandra.

~~SANDRA: All right...If you won't explain what you're up to...I'll just have to follow blindly, I guess...~~

~~HACK: You won't regret it.~~

~~SANDRA: I hope not.~~

HACK: After all, I got in here trying to catch the guy that took a pot shot at you. That should mean something.

| | |
|---|---|
| SANDRA: | That's right. By the way, what were you doing following me that day? |
| HACK: | Somebody has to stick around to protect your nosey little head. |
| SANDRA: | Oh, yes? Well, who do you think is going to do it with you in here? |
| HACK: | I told Skip to, and he better do a good job. That mobster and whoever is back of him aren't through with you yet. If you want my ~~advice~~ [opinion], I'd say they just barely had a good start. |
| MUSIC: | *(TO CURTAIN)* |
| | *CLOSING ANNOUNCEMENT:* |
| CUTTING: | Friends, have you ever had this experience? You put in a hard day's work and when night comes you eat—not because you're hungry, but because you feel you should. But you're so tired and out of sorts, your supper just won't digest, and the first thing you know, your stomach really starts to kick up a fuss. Well, when that occasionally happens, that's just the time to try Alka-Seltzer—for Alka-Seltzer can help you to REAL relief from much of your discomfort in short order! In fact, not until you've tried Alka-Seltzer, can you fully appreciate how fast it acts, how pleasant it is to take. Remember that, won't you? .and next time ask your druggist for Alka-Seltzer. He has it by the sixty and thirty cent size package for home use, and also serves it for your convenience by the glass at his soda-fountain. |
| MUSIC: | *THEME UP AND FADE DOWN UNDER* |
| ANNCR: | Will this new relationship, which Hack proposes—one of simple friendship—serve to bring Hack and Sandra back together? Can Sandra go on blindly trusting the motives of a man who has personally arranged her indictment by the Grand Jury, even though that man is the one with whom |

|         |                                                                                                                                                                                                     |
|---------|-----------------------------------------------------------------------------------------------------------------------------------------------------------------------------------------------------|
|         | she was once in love? Listen tomorrow as our "LADY OF THE PRESS" gets a new clue against the Black Market Ring in Episode twenty-two of—"THE PICTURE OF DEATH". |
| MUSIC:  | THEME UP AND FADE DOWN UNDER                                                                                                                                                                        |
| ANNCR:  | "LADY OF THE PRESS" is written by Dwight Hauser and produced by Gordon T. Hughes, and is brought to you each day, Monday through Friday at this time by the makers of—ALKA SELTZER.                 |
| MUSIC:  | UP TO FILL                                                                                                                                                                                          |
| ANNCR:  | [Dick Cutting speaking] This is CBS. THE COLUMBIA BROADCASTING SYSTEM.                                                                                                                              |

# EPISODE #22

# "PICTURE OF DEATH"

| | | |
|---|---|---|
| SPONSOR: | ALKA SELTZER | MAY 30, 1944 |
| AGENCY: | WADE 4:00—4:15 PM PWT, PN | |

---

ANNCR: The makers of Alka Seltzer present—"LADY OF THE PRESS"

MUSIC: *(STING. .QUICK PUNCTUATION)*

ANNCR: The adventures of Sandra Martin, radio's newest romantic-mystery serial!

MUSIC: *(THEME-ESTABLISH AND FADE OUT:)*

*(OPENING ANNOUNCEMENT)*

CUTTING: I'm sure all of you mothers realize that the so-called cod liver oil vitamins A and D are mighty essential for the aid they offer in keeping your children healthy. They need among other things Vitamin A to help keep us normal resistance to colds—and Vitamin D to help build and maintain strong bones and teeth. But maybe you're like so many mothers—you haven't found a PLEASANT way to give your children these important vitamins. If that's your problem, here's a mighty easy solution. Just give them a single pleasant-tasting One-A-Day Brand Vitamin A and D Tablet each day, and your worries are over. You see, each tablet contains the equivalent of one and one-half teaspoonfuls of minimum U.S.P. cod liver oil—an amount which is MORE than their basic daily requirements of these vitamins. The kiddies will enjoy the pleasant, candy-like taste of One-A-Day Brand Vitamin A and D Tablets. And of interest to you, Mother, is their low cost…as little as one and one-fifth cents a day! So ask your druggist for One-A-Day Brand Vitamin A and D Tablets NOW—remember, the YELLOW package with the big ONE, and the name Miles Laboratories.

MUSIC: (THEME, ESTABLISH AND FADE FOR)

ANNCR: And now, "Lady Of The Press" and episode twenty-two in "THE PICTURE OF DEATH".

MUSIC: (STING AND QUICK FIGURATION FADING OUT UNDER)

ANNCR: Through seeing Hack so close to death due to an accident suffered while trying to aid her, Sandra is brought to realize that nothing can take the place of her love for him. She has, therefore, determined to overlook the breach between them caused by Hack's seeming determination to assure her indictment by the Grand Jury. Hack has told her that he has acted in her own behalf, and although Sandra cannot understand this, she has agreed to accept the statement blindly in lieu of further proof. Even though Hack will only agree to a relation of friendship between them, Sandra feels she has won a small victory on the road back to the beautiful love they once knew.

SOUND: DIALING PHONE RING ON FILTER REVIEVER OFF HOOK

HACK: (FILTER) Hello?

SANDRA: Oh, Hack, this is Sandra.

HACK: Hello, Sandra.

| | |
|---|---|
| SANDRA: | So, they did leave the phone in your room? |
| HACK: | Certainly. I gave them orders to. |
| SANDRA: | Aren't you a little mixed up on who gives the orders in a hospital? |
| HACK: | Not a bit. When they concern me, I give them. |
| SANDRA: | You are convalescing. Why, you're practically yourself again. |
| HACK: | I'm as good as ever. It's silly keeping me here. |
| SANDRA: | How much longer do you think you'll be there? |
| HACK: | *(FLATLY)* About an hour. |
| SANDRA: | *(HAPPILY SURPRISED)* Oh? |
| HACK: | *(LET DOWN)* But, the doctor thinks a couple of days. |
| SANDRA: | Oh, then it better be a couple of days. |
| HACK: | I'm afraid it will be, regardless of what I want. They've got my clothes. |
| SANDRA: | That's one way of keeping you. *(CHUCKLES)* Hack, I called to tell you that I can't make it for visiting hours this afternoon. |
| HACK: | No? What's up? |
| SANDRA: | Have to go over the briefs of my defense with Bruce Elliot. |
| HACK: | Oh? |
| SANDRA: | But, I'll come tonight. |
| HACK: | *(BLASE)* All right. |

| | |
|---|---|
| SANDRA: | Well, you don't sound very enthused. |
| HACK: | Don't let me keep you from a boring afternoon with that mouthpiece. |
| SANDRA: | (DELIGHTED) Why Hack, you should jealous? |
| HACK: | I had a bad lunch. Don't let it fool you. |
| SANDRA: | Well, after all, it's your fault that I have to have an attorney. |
| HACK: | Well, go ahead and play law with him and will see whether or not he gets you out of it. |
| SANDRA: | I'm not so much interested in who gets me out as I am in making sure that I do. I'll see you tonight, then. |
| HACK: | All right, if you have time. |
| SANDRA: | You know I will have. |
| HACK: | Okay. |
| SANDRA: | Goodbye, and mind the nurses. |
| HACK: | How do you mean that? |
| SANDRA: | You guess. Goodbye. |
| HACK: | So long. |
| SOUND: | *RECEIVER ON HOOK* |
| SOUND: | *TELEPHONE BOOTH DOOR OPEN. .CAFE SOUNDS UP-FOOTSTEPS CAFE SOUND TO BACKGROUND.* |
| BRUCE: | Get your party? |
| SANDRA: | Uh huh. |
| BRUCE: | Sorry I have to bother you with these briefs, but it's really quite important. |

SANDRA: Don't I know it? Mr. Elliot, my time is yours—anytime.

BRUCE: I wish that could be true for more than just the briefing of this case.

SANDRA: Meaning?

BRUCE: How about going dancing with me tonight? And then, maybe supper afterwards?

SANDRA: *(IMPULSIVELY)* Why, I'd love to, Bruce. I haven't been dancing in oh I don't know how long. I guess during the last few weeks I've forgotten there was such a thing as entertainment.

BRUCE: Things shouldn't be that way with you, Sandra. You're too real, too lovely, and too vibrant a person to let life become drab and all business.

SANDRA: It's been such important business. So important that nothing else seemed to matter, but now that you mention it, I have missed the good times.

BRUCE: Facing a murder charge is no tea party. I know that. But, you simply must not let it get you down, Sandra.

SANDRA: That has been a very recent addition to my worries, Bruce.

BRUCE: Are there others?

SANDRA: Yes, of far more importance.

BRUCE: Can I help?

SANDRA: No, I don't think so, Bruce. This is something that's got to be pretty much a personal problem.

BRUCE: Well, maybe sometime I can become something beside a legal advisor. Perhaps sometime I can help with your personal problems. I'd like to, you know.

SANDRA: You're sweet, Bruce.

BRUCE: And, about tonight... will you come?

SANDRA: I'd love to, Bruce, only—

BRUCE: Only what?

SANDRA: Only I've already made other arrangements. Believe it or not, I'm going to sit up with a sick friend.

MUSIC: (BRIDGE)

HACK: I'm glad you came tonight, Sandra. I missed you this afternoon.

SANDRA: That's the best news I've heard in a long time, Hack.

HACK: What, that I missed you?

SANDRA: Uh huh.

HACK: Well, this place gets very tiresome after a few days.

SANDRA: You would have to spoil it, wouldn't you? Well, never mind. I want to talk to you.

HACK: Yeah? What about?

SANDRA: Things seem a little different between us lately, Hack, as though we were going in the right direction again. Do you think we are?

HACK: Maybe. I told you yesterday I couldn't be sure.

SANDRA: I know, Hack, I know. You can't be certain yet about us, but about yourself. Don't you think you can try to forget and shut out the bitterness now?

HACK: It's not so much bitterness anymore, Sandra, it's more disappointment now and frustration over not doing a job I set out to do.

SANDRA: But, you did your part. You shouldn't feel that way now. You're back home. You're part of the fight is over. You've helped prepare for the kill. Now it's up to others to deliver the knock out punch.

HACK: That's the punch that counts. That's the one I was holding.

SANDRA: But, you've got to realize that things are important here at home, too, and that you can play a big part in their importance.

HACK: Look, Sandra, each man sets his own limitations and defines his own boundaries. Some of us live in <u>houses,</u> others in <u>cities,</u> and <u>some</u> of us choose to realize that we live in the <u>world</u>. Somehow I can't get very much excited about the front lawn, or the city limits as long as freedom is in chains.

SANDRA: No matter how that idea affects you personally, Hack, no one can ever condemn you for believing it. I'll not say anything about it again. After all, the fact that you're capable of thoughts such as that is one of the reasons I care so much. I shouldn't want to talk you out of them.

HACK: Good girl.

SANDRA: Hack!

HACK: Just give me time, Sandra. There must be some way in which I can fit into the pattern of civilian life. It's just going to take time. Time for some adjusting and some thinking . . . and to bring a few of the ends to together.

SANDRA: Sure, Hack. I understand.

HACK: And maybe when the ends do come together we can tie a knot in them and keep them that way.

SANDRA: I love you, Hack. I'm through trying to tell myself that I don't. If you don't become again the person you were, then I guess I'll just have to go on being in love with a memory. Now, it's late. You need some rest. Sleep well, my darling, and don't ever let the flame go out.

MUSIC:            (BRIDGE)

SOUND:            NEWSPAPER OFFICE UP AND TO BACKGROUND

SANDRA:           Good morning, Skip.

SKIP:             Hi' baby. What's up?

SANDRA:           You busy this morning?

SKIP:             Not too busy. Why?

SANDRA:           I have a little job for you, if you have time.

SKIP:             Sure. What is it?

SANDRA:           Come into re-write and we'll talk about it.

SKIP:             Okay.

SOUND:            FOOTSTEPS DOOR OPEN-CLOSE-SOUND OUT

SKIP:             Now, what's on your mind, Sandra?

SANDRA:           Skip, we're going to set out in earnest to catch and expose the Black Market Operators of this city.

SKIP:             What have we been doin' up to know?

SANDRA:           We've been trying, I know. ~~But, there have been so many obstacles…Our mistaken impression of Hacks attitude and—~~

~~SKIP:~~           ~~Mistaken…? And you are sure it's not just because he's been but—that you believe him—~~

~~SANDRA:~~         ~~No…He just made me understand some things…Things which cause me to believe in him…So now that I'm convinced he's fundamentally on our side…Our work will be much easier…Also the Grand Jury hearing is out of the way.~~

SKIP: ~~To our disadvantage…~~

SANDRA: ~~Yes…But, It's not going to take up our time…~~ We can devote every minute to gathering evidence against the Black Market.

SKIP: Okay. Where do we start?

SANDRA: Right back where we were when those shots were fired at us.

SKIP: You mean you want to go back to that house? Have you lost your marbles? The mugs followed us there once. What's to stop them from doing it again?

SANDRA: We aren't going back to that house. We're going to try a different one this time, and we're not going to let them trail us.

SKIP: What are we gonna do, write a letter askin' them not to?

SANDRA: No, we're going to throw them off our track.

SKIP: That may be easier said than done.

SANDRA: I don't think so. How good are you at composite photography?

SKIP: Oh that's my meat, baby.

SANDRA: Good. Could you make a picture showing me at some desert resort.

SKIP: I guess so. If I could get a background of the resort, I could superimpose your picture on it. That's a cinch.

SANDRA: Swell. Now look, I brought this sun suit and I want you to take a picture of me in this. Then superimpose it against a desert resort background, will you?

SKIP: Sure. Wait until I get my camera.

| | |
|---|---|
| SANDRA: | Right. I'll change while your out. |
| SKIP: | Okay, but make it snappy. |
| SOUND: | FOOTSTEPS TO DOOR-DOOR OPEN-OFFICE SOUNDS UP |
| SKIP: | I warn you, I'll only be a jiffy. |
| SOUND: | DOOR CLOSE-OFFICE SOUND OUT—A FEW STEPS—RECEIVER OFF HOOK DIAL PHONE (THREE) |
| SANDRA: | Hello? Managing editor? Give me, Mr. Wilson, will you? Sandra Martin. Thank you. Hello, Mr. Wilson? I want to ask a favor of you. That's right. I feel the need of a rest after that trial. I'd like a week off. I'm going out to the desert for some sun. That's nice of you, Mr. Wilson. Thanks a lot. I'll be back in a week, and I'll be a lot better able to handle my job. Thanks a lot. Goodbye. |
| MUSIC: | (BRIDGE) |
| SKIP: | Okay . . . now hold still. |
| SOUND: | CLICK OF CAMERA |
| SKIP: | That's a beaut! One more now. |
| SANDRA: | Same pose? |
| SKIP: | Yeah. Gee you sure look pretty in that sun suit. These pictures sure ought to catch the eyes of the public. |
| SANDRA: | I hope they catch the eyes of that mug and whoever else is interested in following me. |
| SKIP: | Still now. Hold it. Hold it. |
| SOUND: | CLICK |
| SKIP: | That does it. Swell, baby. |

SANDRA: Thanks, Skip. *(FADE IN)* Think you got some good ones?

SKIP: Sweethearts. Now, what do you want me to do with 'em?

SANDRA: Pick out the best one and superimpose it against a desert background.

SKIP: When do you want it?

SANDRA: How soon can you do it?

SKIP: Well, do you want it good or do you want it Thursday?

SANDRA: I want it Thursday and good. You can do it.

SKIP: Okay, I'll try it. ~~But, a job like this takes several printings and developings and plenty of retouching.~~

~~SANDRA: I know…But, even it costs you some sleep…We've got to have that picture by the five star tomorrow.~~

SKIP: ~~And~~ Just what do you intend doing with it then?

SANDRA: I'm going to have it run on the front page . . . under the head….Sandra Martin relaxes at desert hideaway.

SKIP: Then what?

SANDRA: We run a story with it telling that in order to ward off a nervous breakdown caused by the nervous tension of the trial, I've run away to the desert for a rest. Then we give the name of the nearest town to my fictitious haven, and then [we can] sit back while our enemies go out of town looking for us. Then, once they've gone, we go to work. [That's the neatest trick of the week.]

MUSIC: *TO CURTAIN*

*(CLOSING ANNOUNCEMENT)*

CUTTING: Ladies, now that winter colds are a thing of the past, how about looking out for your family's summer colds—

and away beyond that, for NEXT winter's colds? It's a known fact that if your intake of Vitamin A is low, your resistance to colds may be lowered, so why not ASSURE yourself, at least, ample Vitamin A right straight through the whole year, to help guard against a deficiency and to help maintain your normal resistance to cold infections? That sounds sensible to me—and a sensible way to GET additional Vitamin A—plus Vitamin D—is with One-A-Day Brand Vitamin A and D Tablets. It takes only a single tablet each day to assure your minimum daily requirements of Vitamins A and D. And One-A-Day Brand Vitamin A and D Tablets cost but slightly over a penny a day, at all drug stores. So, for the vitamins that can help you maintain normal resistance to colds, ask your druggist for One-A-Day Brand Vitamin A and D Tablets. They come in the YELLOW package with the big ONE, and are made by Miles laboratories.

MUSIC: *(THEME ESTABLISH AND FADE UNDER)*

ANNCR: Will Sandra's plan to run faked pictures of herself on the desert succeed in throwing her enemies off the track? Or, will the plan of hers give her a sense of over confidence which of itself may trap her? Listen tomorrow as our "Lady Of The Press" sets out to evade her enemies in episode twenty-three of "THE PICTURE OF DEATH."

MUSIC: *(PUNCTUATION AND UNDER)*

ANNCR: "LADY OF THE PRESS" is written by Dwight Hauser and produced by Gordon T. Hughes, and is brought to you each day, Monday through Friday, at this same time by the makers of ALKA SELTZER.

MUSIC: *(UP TO FILL)*

ANNCR: [Dick Cutting speaking] This is CBS. THE COLUMBIA BROADCASTING SYSTEM.

# EPISODE #23

# "PICTURE OF DEATH"

| | | |
|---|---|---|
| SPONSOR: | ALKA SELTZER | MAY 31, 1944 |
| AGENCY: | WADE  4:00—4:15 PM, PWT, PN | |

---

ANNCR: The makers of Alka Seltzer present—"LADY OF THE PRESS"

MUSIC: *(STING) (QUICK PUNCTUATION)*

ANNCR: The adventures of Sandra Martin, radio's newest romantic-mystery serial!

MUSIC: *(THEME ESTABLISH AND FADE OUT:)*

*(OPENING COMMERCIAL)*

CUTTING: You know in these days when you hear so much about the wisdom of giving additional vitamins to the whole family, I know many of you budget-wise mothers wonder about cost, and, of course, quality. Well, in One-A-Day Brand Multiple Vitamin Capsules you have the complete answer. Miles Laboratories guarantee the potency and the high quality of their laboratory-perfected multiple vitamin capsules. And, just think, you get EIGHT different vitamins in one One-A-Day Brand Multiple Capsule—the vitamins which help keep up normal energy, nerves and digestion, normal resistance to colds—help maintain strong bones and teeth. And because only a single One-A-Day Brand Multiple Vitamin Capsule each day does the job, the cost is very low. Why say, the sixty-day size package of sixty capsules costs only two dollars! So guard your family against a possible vitamin deficiency and its consequences by asking your druggist for One-A-Day Brand Multiple Vitamin Capsules . . . the ones in the Blue package with the big ONE, developed by Miles Laboratories.

MUSIC: (THEME UP AND FADE DOWN UNDER)

ANNCR: And now, "Lady Of The Press", and episode twenty-three in "THE PICTURE OF DEATH"!

MUSIC: (STING AND QUICK FIGURATION INTO THEME FADE OUT UNDER)

ANNCR: Realizing, from past experience that her every move is being closely watched and checked by her enemies, Sandra has laid a plan whereby she hopes to throw them off her trail. In this way, she hopes to proceed with the gathering of evidence for an expose of the Black Market without further interference from the strange gun man who has caused her so much trouble up to now. Hack is well on the road to recovery, and knowing that he will be released from the hospital shortly, Sandra feels there is no longer any need for her to remain so closely by his side. We find her now preparing Hack for her absence.

HACK: Just what are you going to do, Sandra?

SANDRA: I'd rather not say, if you don't mind.

HACK: What's the matter? Still don't trust me?

SANDRA: It's not that so much as it is that I want my moves for the next few days to remain a complete secret to everyone.

HACK: Why?

SANDRA: Because I believe that in that way I stand a better chance of getting the evidence I want.

| | |
|---|---|
| HACK: | Well, if you'll follow my advice, you'll wait until I'm out of here and up and able to help you. This is a dangerous assignment, no job for you to tackle alone. |
| SANDRA: | On the contrary, I believe that's the only way for me to go about it. |
| HACK: | But don't you realize the danger connected with you going off by yourself and not letting anyone know where you are? |
| SANDRA: | People will know where I am, that is . . . the right people, and that's what I'm relying on. |
| HACK: | Well, I must confess you have me completely confused. I shan't rest easy until I hear from you again. |
| SANDRA: | I'll let you know the minute I feel I've accomplished what I'm setting out after. |
| HACK: | I still wish you'd take my advice. Of course, I'm in no position to prevent you from doing what you wish. |
| SANDRA: | That's a break for me. Now, you get well just as fast as you can, and don't worry about me. The more peace of mind you have the quicker you'll be able to help. |
| HACK: | All right, Sandra. They're sending me home tomorrow. It shouldn't be more than a couple of days before I'm back at the old grind again. |
| SANDRA: | Will you be glad to get back. |
| HACK: | There's another place I'd a lot rather go back to. |
| SANDRA: | I know. We decided to keep our minds off your discharge from the Army, didn't we? |
| HACK: | Yeah, but it leaves a pretty big hole in my life. |
| SANDRA: | Ah ah. Remember, you're going to try. |

| | |
|---|---|
| HACK: | Okay. Well, Goodbye, Sandra, and the best of luck. |
| SANDRA: | Thanks, Hack. I'll need it, but I'm just fool enough to think I'll have it this time. Goodbye. And, I'll see you soon. |
| HACK: | Goodbye, Sandra. I'll be thinking of you. |
| MUSIC: | (BRIDGE) |
| SOUND: | TRAFFIC |
| NEWSBOY: | Extra! Extra! Five Star Courier! Read all about it. Girl reporter near breakdown following indictment. Hides away in desert. Extra! Extra! Sandra Martin can't face it. Leaves for Crystal Springs. Extra! Extra! *(FADE OUT)* |
| MUSIC: | (BRIDGE) |
| SOUND: | NEWSPAPER OFFICE FOOTSTEPS FADING IN |
| BETTY: | Good afternoon, Courier. Yes'm, that would be classified. What? Oh, I don't think so. Yes'm. No'm. No'm, if there were any houses for rent they'd be in the classified. Huh? How can they fix the price on a commodity there isn't any of? Well, Gee. I don't know. Goodbye *(TO SKIP)* Oh, Hello, Skip. |
| SKIP: | Hi'ya, gorgeous. |
| BETTY: | Don't you ever do anything except kid? |
| SKIP: | Sure, sure. Lot's of times, baby. Hey, you get a five star yet. |
| BETTY: | Sure. There's one right there, and say, there's a picture of Miss Martin right on the front page. |
| SKIP: | Yeah. I wonder how that got there. |
| BETTY: | I dunno. Gee, I didn't even know she'd gone to Crystal Springs. |

| | |
|---|---|
| SOUND: | *RATTLE OF PAPER* |
| BETTY: | Gee, she sure looks pretty out there in the middle of all that sunshine, doesn't she? |
| SKIP: | Yeah. *(TO HIMSELF)* Yep. It's a good job. Just like the real thing. |
| BETTY: | Huh? |
| SKIP: | Oh nothin', baby. I was just sayin', looks like the picture had been made with the real pre-war film. |
| BETTY: | Did you take it? |
| SKIP: | Now, how would I take a picture at Crystal Springs? You know I ain't been away from this paper in weeks. |
| BETTY: | Yeah. That's right. |
| SKIP: | *(CONFIDENTIALLY)* Hey Betty, all kiddin' aside, you're a good friend of mine, aren't you? |
| BETTY: | Well, I like to think so, Skip. |
| SKIP: | And, you know that I fool just like a brother to you. And if there was something I knew that I thought you oughta know, you know I'd tell you, don't you? |
| BETTY: | Well, gosh, I guess so, Skip. |
| SKIP: | Well there is somethin'. Probably even your best friend wouldn't tell you, if that friend didn't happen to be me. But, there's something you ought to know for your own good, I mean. |
| BETTY: | Of course I want to know if there's something wrong with me. |
| SKIP: | It's gonna be kinda embarrassin', but I feel I just gotta do it. Promise you won't get sore? |

| | |
|---|---|
| BETTY: | Oh, no, Skip. I won't get sore. Tell me, what is it? |
| SKIP: | *(PEAK) YOU'RE LIGHTS ARE SHOWIN! (UPROARIOUS LAUGHTER)* |
| BETTY: | Oh, darn you, Skip Williams. Why do you keep pullin' that stale ole joke on me? |
| SKIP: | *(KILLING HIMSELF)* I dunno, baby. I guess it's cause you keep on fallin' for it. |
| SOUND: | *BUZZER* |
| BETTY: | *(IN PHONE)* Good afternoon, Courier. I will connect you. [Darn you Skip Williams] Good afternoon, Courier. One moment please. |
| SKIP: | Look, baby, I'm takin' the rest of the day off. If anybody wants me, I'm out cold until tomorrow morning. Keep your lines straight. I gotta date with a fraud. |
| BETTY: | *(FADING)* Good afternoon, Courier. Mr. Wilson is out now! |
| SOUND: | *PLUGS* |
| BETTY: | One moment. I will connect you. Good afternoon, Courier. Yes'm, we have a Sunday edition. What? Why, it comes out on Saturday, of course. |
| MUSIC: | *(BRIDGE)* |
| SOUND: | *KNOCK ON DOOR* |
| SKIP: | *(WHISTLING)* |
| SOUND: | *REPEAT KNOCK—DOOR OPEN* |
| SANDRA: | *(SOTTO VOCE)* Hello, Skip. Come in quickly. I don't want anybody to know I'm still here. |

| | |
|---|---|
| SOUND: | DOOR CLOSE |
| SKIP: | Flicker me eyelids! The way things are turnin' out I'm beginning to feel like we are guilty. All this hidin' and undercover stuff. |
| SANDRA: | This is the best way for us to prove we're not guilty. That is if everything goes all right. Tell me, did the photo come out all right? |
| SKIP: | Yep. Here it is right smack on the front page. |
| SANDRA: | Good old, Wilson. Let me see it. |
| SKIP: | Here you are. |
| SOUND: | RATTLE OF NEWSPAPER |
| SANDRA: | *(SCANING)* Sandra Martin goes—Crystal Springs—can't face public. Near nervous breakdown over indictment. *(MUMBLES)* Well, they certainly didn't spare the horses, did they? |
| SKIP: | If that doesn't make people think you're out of town nothin' will . . . unless you really go. |
| SANDRA: | With all this publicity, Crystal Springs is the last place I want to be for the next few days. That's a good job of composite photography, Skip. |
| SKIP: | Good job? It's pure art, that's what it is. |
| SANDRA: | All right, so it's art. I just hope our good friend, the mug, appreciates fine art long enough to take a look at it. |
| SKIP: | Any guy that's as interested in you as I seem to be is pretty apt to take a gander at a spread like that about you. |
| SANDRA: | Gee, I'd give a lot to see his face when he reads it. I wonder just what he'll do about it. |

| | |
|---|---|
| TECH: | *BEGIN BOARD FADE* |
| SANDRA: | You know, Skip, this looks to me like the perfect set u. If I were in his place, I'd be on the next bus for Crystal Springs so fast it would make your head swim. |
| TECH: | *BOARD FADE TO ZERO FADE IN ON* |
| SOUND: | *PHONE DIALING* |
| MAN: | Hello, Boss? This is your right hand boy. Yeah, that's right. Say, I know you don't like to have me callin' you too much, but have you seen the Five Star Courier? You have huh? Then, I guess you know why I'm callin'. ~~Yeah, that's what I thought....~~ The minute I piped her map on that front page I sez to myself, "You know, son, you're getting kind a pallid. Seems to me a few days in the sun would do you a lot of good. Might be Crystal Springs. It would be just the spot to take on a few a them violet rays. Yeah, Boss. That's just what I figured. What a nice swell spot for it. It'll be nice and quiet. Plenty of room. Not many people up there this time of the year. And, gee, think of all the possibilities for getting rid of any evidence. Yeah. Okay, Boss. I'll be on my way in side of an hour. Oh, sure, Boss. You can count on it this time....~~She~~ [That Dame] don't know it but she only got a one way ticket. Goodbye, boss. |
| SOUND: | *RECEIVER ON HOOK* |
| MAN: | *(MENACING CHUCKLE)* |
| MUSIC: | *(PUNCTUATE AND INTO BRIDGE)* |
| DOVEY: | Hey, am I dreamin'? |
| SANDRA: | What do you mean? |
| DOVEY: | Are you sittin' there, or aren't you? |
| SANDRA: | Of course. |

DOVEY: And you've been in town for the last few weeks, haven't you?

SANDRA: Of course.

DOVEY: And, this is today's paper, isn't it?

SANDRA: Better tell her, Sandra, that such mental effort might be dangerous to one with such meager equipment.

DOVEY: (BLOWING UP) Will you button your lip, menace? I'm just tryin' to tell Sandra that there's a mighty libelous looking article on her in the Courier.

SANDRA: I know all about it, Dovey. As a matter of fact, I wrote it.

DOVEY: You what?

~~SANDRA: I wrote it and got Wilson to print it....I've got a little plan on the fire...One which might bring about some rather startling results.~~

~~DOVEY: But...the picture...It shows you, sittin' under a palm tree... And those hills in the background are Crystal Hills....I been there...I know...~~

SANDRA: That's right.

DOVEY: But, you haven't been there. How on earth did you get a picture of yourself like this?

SKIP: Rembrandt painted it for her. What did you think?

DOVEY: Someday, I'm going to do humanity the service of silencing that mouth of yours forever.

SOUND: *TELEPHONE RINGS*

SANDRA: Answer it, will you, Dovey? And remember that under no circumstances am I here.

| | |
|---|---|
| DOVEY: | Okay. |
| SOUND: | FOOTSTEPS-RECEIVER OFF HOOK |
| DOVEY: | Hello? |
| HACK: | *(FILTER)* Hello, Dovey? |
| DOVEY: | Yes. |
| HACK: | This is Hack Taggart. I'm callin' about Sandra. |
| DOVEY: | Yes. What about her? |
| HACK: | What about her? Have you seen the latest Courier? |
| DOVEY: | Sure. Why? |
| HACK: | Well, it says she's gone off to Crystal Springs for a rest. |
| DOVEY: | That's right. Don't you think she had one coming? |
| HACK: | That's not the point. ~~The point is that she'll be in the most extreme danger up there alone.~~ |
| ~~DOVEY:~~ | ~~What makes you think that?~~ |
| ~~HACK:~~ | ~~With a spread like that, the people who are out to get her will be up there in no time…If she had to go why couldn't she have done it quietly..~~ |
| ~~DOVEY:~~ | ~~I don't know..? Why don't you ask her?~~ |
| HACK: | ~~That's exactly what I intend doing.…~~I've made arrangements for my release from here right away. I'm going up there and bring her back. |
| DOVEY: | Oh, are you? |
| HACK: | Yes, and here's what I want you to do: get in touch with Skip Williams and tell him to stop printing pictures of her, and to have the Courier stop running stories on her whereabouts. |

| | |
|---|---|
| DOVEY: | ~~Why don't you tell him yourself?~~ [Alright, I'll try to find him.] |
| HACK: | ~~I've been calling all over town for him…Can't locate him… And, I haven't the time to wait around…~~ I'm concerned about Sandra, and I don't intend leaving her up there alone any longer than I can possibly help. |
| ~~DOVEY:~~ | ~~All right… I'll try to find him.~~ |
| HACK: | ~~Thanks….~~ Goodbye. |
| SOUND: | RECEIVER ON HOOK |
| DOVEY: | Well, you're boyfriend has fallen for your gag along with everyone else. You know, Sandra, you may be sorry you pulled this. He's getting up out of bed before he's supposed to in order to go off up to Crystal Springs on a wild goose chase looking for you. |
| MUSIC: | (TO CURTAIN) |
| | (CLOSING COMMERCIAL) |
| CUTTING: | I wonder, ladies, when you are planning a meal, do you think of your family's "likes and dislikes" rather than what they should eat? Well, of course, you probably try to serve them a well-balanced diet which will supply them with essential food elements, including ample vitamins which they must have for good health. But since this is far easier said than done, we suggest that you relieve yourself of one food worry by giving each member of your family a single One-A-Day Brand Multiple Vitamin Capsule each day. That way you can be sure that they get their basic daily requirements of the vitamins whose requirements are known—the vitamins they need to help maintain normal energy, nerves, digestion, resistance to colds, and strong bones and teeth. So avoid the undermining influence of a possible vitamin deficiency in your family now. The cost is so low you can hardly afford NOT to ask your druggist for One-A-Day Brand Multiple Vitamin Capsules right away. THEY'RE the ones, you know, that come in the |

|         |                                                                                                                                                                                                                                                                                                                                                                            |
|---------|----------------------------------------------------------------------------------------------------------------------------------------------------------------------------------------------------------------------------------------------------------------------------------------------------------------------------------------------------------------------------|
|         | BLUE package with the big ONE and the name Miles Laboratories . . . your assurance of the highest quality vitamins that money can buy!                                                                                                                                                                                                                                     |
| MUSIC:  | (THEME. ESTABLISH AND FADE UNDER FOR)                                                                                                                                                                                                                                                                                                                                      |
| ANNCR:  | And so, two men depart for Crystal Springs in search of Sandra Martin. One, her enemy and cohort of the Black Market; the other, her friend and former lover, Hack Taggart. Will their rendezvous bring their conflict to a conclusion? And if so, which will win out over the other? Listen tomorrow as the disappearance of our "LADY OF THE PRES", makes the headlines in episode twenty-four of THE PICTURE OF DEATH! |
| MUSIC:  | (PUNCTUATION AND FADE UNDER)                                                                                                                                                                                                                                                                                                                                               |
| ANNCR:  | "Lady Of The Press" is written by Dwight Hauser and produced by Gordon T. Hughes and is brought to you each day Monday through Friday at this same time by the makers of—ALKA SELTZER.                                                                                                                                                                                      |
| MUSIC:  | (UP TO FILL)                                                                                                                                                                                                                                                                                                                                                               |
| ANNCR:  | [Dick Cutting speaking] This is CBS. THE COLUMBIA BROADCASTING SYSTEM.                                                                                                                                                                                                                                                                                                     |

# EPILOGUE

What happened next?
Here's a clue from an ad that ran in the *Fresno Bee* in mid June:

And beyond that?
Jack French and Barry Weiss, in the book, *Private Eyelashes,* reviewed the series scripts at the Thousand Oaks Library in California, and found that although the early episodes focused on wartime issues, such as counterfeit ration cards, *Lady of the Press* eventually strayed into a standard soap opera territory. Before too many months, Sandra Martin married a playboy, later divorced him, and continued to be chased by Hack Taggart. By the final episode of the series April 27, 1945, just days before VE Day, Sandra Martin rejected both suitors, planning instead to chart her own course first and foremost as a "Lady of the Press."

www.ingramcontent.com/pod-product-compliance
Lightning Source LLC
Chambersburg PA
CBHW071957220426
**43662CB00009B/1166**